THE DYNAMICS OF MODERN ASIAN DESIGN

THE DYNAMICS OF MODERN ASIAN DESIGN

MATERIAL CULTURE AND SOCIAL AGENCY

Edited by Sandy Ng and Megha Rajguru

BLOOMSBURY VISUAL ARTS
LONDON · NEW YORK · OXFORD · NEW DELHI · SYDNEY

BLOOMSBURY VISUAL ARTS
Bloomsbury Publishing Plc, 50 Bedford Square, London, WC1B 3DP, UK
Bloomsbury Publishing Inc, 1385 Broadway, New York, NY 10018, USA
Bloomsbury Publishing Ireland, 29 Earlsfort Terrace, Dublin 2, D02 AY28, Ireland

BLOOMSBURY, BLOOMSBURY VISUAL ARTS and the Diana logo are trademarks of Bloomsbury Publishing Plc

First published in Great Britain 2026

© Editorial content and introductions, Sandy Ng and Megha Rajguru, 2026
© Individual chapters, their authors, 2026

Sandy Ng and Megha Rajguru have asserted their right under the Copyright, Designs and Patents Act, 1988, to be identified as Editors of this work.

Cover design by Louise Dugdale
Cover image: Lacloche Frères, *Compact*, 1923–24, gold, enamel, diamond, and pearl, Liang Yi Museum, Hong Kong

All rights reserved. No part of this publication may be: i) reproduced or transmitted in any form, electronic or mechanical, including photocopying, recording or by means of any information storage or retrieval system without prior permission in writing from the publishers; or ii) used or reproduced in any way for the training, development or operation of artificial intelligence (AI) technologies, including generative AI technologies. The rights holders expressly reserve this publication from the text and data mining exception as per Article 4(3) of the Digital Single Market Directive (EU) 2019/790.

Bloomsbury Publishing Plc does not have any control over, or responsibility for, any third-party websites referred to or in this book. All internet addresses given in this book were correct at the time of going to press. The author and publisher regret any inconvenience caused if addresses have changed or sites have ceased to exist, but can accept no responsibility for any such changes.

A catalogue record for this book is available from the British Library.

A catalog record for this book is available from the Library of Congress.

ISBN: HB: 978-1-3504-2782-2
PB: 978-1-3504-2781-5
ePDF: 978-1-3504-2784-6
eBook: 978-1-3504-2783-9

Typeset by RefineCatch Limited, Bungay, Suffolk
Printed and bound in India

For product safety related questions contact productsafety@bloomsbury.com.

To find out more about our authors and books visit www.bloomsbury.com and sign up for our newsletters.

CONTENTS

List of figures   vi

Introduction   *Sandy Ng and Megha Rajguru*   1

Part I: The Nature and Experience of Materiality

1. Trash or Treasure? The East Asian Sherd as Material and Medium   *Stacey Pierson*   17
2. Found Objects in Hong Kong Jewellery Design: Social Connections and Material Agency in Southern China   *Anna Grasskamp*   35
3. Maintaining Material Culture: An Essay on Meanings and Values of Things and Technology in Central Seoul   *Anneke Coppoolse*   57

Part II: Design, Material Culture, and Mediation

4. Health Booms and Bubbly Bodies: *Hanako* Magazine, Women, and Beauty in the 1980s Japanese Bubble Economy   *Hui-Ying Kerr*   83
5. Adornment and the Self: Ornamental Design and the Modern Woman in China   *Sandy Ng*   107
6. Religious Aesthetics: Collecting Chinese Gods   *Valentina Gamberi*   127

Part III: The Biography of Design

7. The Aesthetics of Concrete Watchtowers: The Hybrid and Contextual Architecture of Kaiping   *Kwok-wah Tung*   149
8. The Home and the Street: Poverty, Development, and Heritage in Housing Design in India in the 1980s   *Megha Rajguru*   171
9. The Weft of Nations: Circulating Imagery of Chinese Textile Technology on the Eve of Britain's Industrial Revolution   *Roslyn Lee Hammers*   191

List of contributors   211
Index   215

FIGURES

1.1	Lacoste porcelain polo shirt by Li Xiaofeng.	17
1.2	Qing dynasty blue and white porcelain sherds.	20
1.3	Casa do Fresco entrance detail, Fronteira Palace, Lisbon.	23
1.4	China House, Tianjin.	24
1.5	The "Lowther Casket", an ormolu-mounted Chinese porcelain casket.	25
1.6	"Translated Vase_Nine Dragons in Wonderland" by Yeesookyung.	26
1.7	Bouke de Vries, "Dead Nature no. 4", 2009.	27
1.8	Stoneware tea bowl with gold lacquer repairs.	29
2.1	liina klauss, "River of Rubbish", 2014.	39
2.2	Chan Wing-sze, Cissy, "Far Sea Ring", 2020.	42
2.3	Chung Ka-pang, Adrian, "Living", 2016–21.	42
2.4	Ching Sze-yin, Cicy, "Made in Hong Kong Series", 2000–21.	44
2.5	Chan Po-fung, "I would still find you", 2013.	47
3.1	Outline of Seoul today.	59
3.2	A printed circuit board at a repair business in Sewoon Sangga.	62
3.3	Close-up of a wall in the long-running repair shop in Sewoon Sangga.	64
3.4	Used tailoring scissors of a sewing master with decades of experience in Seoul's garment industry.	66
3.5	A side view of a mechanical pocket watch under repair at a shop in Sewoon Square.	69
4.1	*Hanako* magazine, issue 125, 6 December 1990.	86
4.2	Kutashi "Crazy Telephone" advertisement, *Hanako* magazine, issue 32, 19 January 1989.	87
4.3	*OL Shinkaron*, Risu Akizuki.	88
4.4	*Hanako* magazine, issue 45, 20 April 1989.	91
4.5	*Hanako* magazine, issue 92, 5 April 1990.	92
4.6	*Hanako* magazine, issue 46, 27 April 1989.	93
4.7	*Hanako* magazine, issue 92, 5 April 1990.	94
4.8	*Hanako* magazine, issue 58, 27 July 1989.	96
4.9	*Torabāyu* advertisement, *Hanako* magazine, issue 66, 28 September 1989.	98
5.1	Cosmetics case, mirror stand, and screen, late sixteenth to early seventeenth century.	111
5.2	Cosmetics chest with a folding mirror stand, seventeenth century.	112
5.3	Dressing table, *c.* 1900.	113
5.4	Lacloche Frères, *Compact*, *c.* 1925.	115

Figures

5.5	Advertisement for the Central Automobile Company, 20 April 1924.	116
5.6	*Necessaire*, c. 1925.	117
5.7	Photo taken in a studio, early twentieth century, China.	118
6.1	De Groot's water official (水官), one of the three emperor-officials subordinated to the Jade Emperor.	136
6.2	De Groot's annotation on the base of the god of water.	136
7.1	Yinglong Tower.	151
7.2	The typical composition of a concrete watchtower, as exemplified by Ruishi Tower.	153
7.3	Shengfeng Tower (left), Jinjiang Tower (middle), and Ruishi Tower (right).	156
7.4	The living room on the fourth floor of Ruishi Tower.	157
7.5	The fifth-floor cantilevered colonnade of Ruishi Tower.	158
7.6	The main core of Ruishi Tower.	159
7.7	The colonnades of the hall on the sixth floor of Ruishi Tower.	160
7.8	Composite columns on the fourth floor of Shengfeng Tower.	160
8.1	Cluster housing, Aranya Township.	176
8.2	Homes in close proximity to one another.	176
8.3	Urbanization and self-building, Artists' Village.	177
8.4	Street layouts.	178
8.5	Design for sociability.	179
8.6	Outdoor spaces for domestic activities.	181
8.7	External architectural features.	182
8.8	Pedestrianized streets, Artists' Village.	183
8.9	Pedestrianized streets, Aranya Township.	183
8.10	Women carrying water containers.	186
9.1	"Chekiang" (Zhejiang). From *Novus atlas Sinensis* (New Atlas of China), 1655.	192
9.2	Detail from "Chekiang" (Zhejiang).	193
9.3	Plate of "Textile Manufacturing". From *Description géographique*, 1736.	194
9.4	Plate of "Silk Manufacture". From *Description of the Empire of China*, 1738.	195
9.5	"A Twisting Mill", from the plate "Silk Manufacture".	198
9.6	"Fang che" (Spinning wheel). From the *Complete Book of the Administration of Agriculture*, 1636.	199
9.7	"Da fang che" (Large spinning wheel). From the *Book of Agriculture*, 1530.	199
9.8	Model reconstruction of "Da fang che" (Large spinning wheel).	200
9.9	"Winding from the Clews to the Bobbins". From *Description of the Empire of China*, 1738.	203
9.10	"The Spinning Jenny". From *History of the Cotton Manufacture*, 1835.	203

INTRODUCTION
Sandy Ng and Megha Rajguru

This edited volume examines design from a material culture perspective, with a view to understand the material culture of everyday life and study the production, consumption, disposal, and upcycling of objects in the context of cultural and social changes in Asia. It does this by examining the ways that designed objects embody or initialize these changes, examining the biographies of designs and materials, as well as the experiences of the makers and users witness to those changes. While this book focuses on modern Asia, spanning the eighteenth century until the present day, the twentieth century features most extensively, studying the revisiting and preserving of pasts through processes of material reconstruction, restoration, or revival. Several authors focus on China, considering the transnational movement of objects, such as printed images of machinery and technological production of textiles from China to Britain, postcards portraying European architecture accessible in Kaiping and used by local builders, and cosmetic cases produced in France and imported into China. They examine modern networks of production, use, and circulation, as well as commercial, ecological, and social interests.

Across the book, the authors undertake object-centred approaches, foregrounding the material object, artefact, or building in their analyses. While they employ a tried-and-tested method that Jules Prown has proposed – the three-stage method, engaging in precise description, focusing on the internal evidence of the object, followed by an exploration of the possible connections between object and people based on intellectual and emotional responses[1] – the authors develop these further to articulate the ways in which material objects help re-examine histories of modernities across Asian contexts. In particular, they are interested in the materials that have been used to produce these objects, but also how these have survived and entered various cultural, economic, and social contexts. Through this process, the book engages with critical material histories, addressing the modalities of power wherein material circulates and is manipulated, challenging aesthetic frameworks that undermine local knowledge, and reframing gendered histories through studying the consumption of goods.

The authors undertake the construction of collective biographies of objects and sites through a process of "thick description", a method of reading culture and its contexts developed by Clifford Geertz (1926–2006).[2] Using written, visual, oral, as well as material sources, they investigate object meanings, and in doing so, uncover insights about the people who created, used, and lived with those objects in particular locations across Asia. This approach, while drawn from anthropology and ethnography, is particularly relevant here, as the authors understand these locations and contexts through visits during fieldwork, or living in these regions and studying primary research materials amassed through archival sources. Close readings of objects and places connect these chapters.

Material culture, design history, and object agency

Similar to the intellectual framework proposed by Arjun Appadurai and the authors in *The Social Life of Things*, in this book the authors' analyses of objects show how they function in relation to events and social shifts, to articulate identities and examine the place of objects and material goods in social relationships.[3] The chapters highlight the dynamic correlation between the designed objects, the makers, and users. As articulated by Judy Attfield, focusing on material culture has important implications in the study of design, as it opens up the possibilities of design history writing to include objects of the everyday, including those with "attitude". Designed with aesthetic intention but not necessarily classified as "good" design, these "undisciplined" objects form part of the mundane and of everyday clutter.[4] A dominant concern for a canonical approach to design history has been dismantled for at least two decades, and replaced by an interest in object histories belonging to this "everyday clutter", with a view to broaden understandings of social contexts and frameworks of value. As such, this volume brings into the fold histories of objects that can be found in the markets, on shelves, in cupboards, museum stores, and on beaches; or the buildings in towns, and their surrounding streets, thereby demonstrating the interaction between people and designs that redefine or shape cultural and social identity historically, and in particular, historical and geographical contexts.

This book covers a broad period, of at least a hundred years, from the twentieth century up to the contemporary. This coverage is intentional, as many of the chapters include references to multiple periods, where remnants of the past appear in the contemporary moment, or where design has particular historical contingency. The authors are concerned with the value of objects in relation to shifting histories and contexts, where value is embedded in the historical significance of objects, or in their material, their aesthetic, and use. For example, East Asian ceramic sherds of the "celadons" and "blue and white" porcelain on display in museums as well as market stalls that are examined by Stacey Pierson, hold value as "ruins" or "resonances" of the past and are intrinsically tied to the aesthetic, but also to their material histories, referencing a global trade driven by aesthetic demand in the past.

Material culture – and allied disciplines such as archaeology and museum studies – employ object study in historical research, and despite the primacy of historical texts for historians, the material turn from the 1970s has paved the way for significant research by scholars such as Igor Kopytoff, Daniel Miller, Christopher Tilley, and as discussed previously, Judy Attfield, and many others.[5] Numerous texts on material culture abound, with many examining histories of commodities and consumption, object biographies, and cultural identities, and include objects as well as buildings in their studies. These objects and buildings "act as vital conduits through which cultural values are transmitted and given material immortality", across temporalities and geographies.⁶ This quality of objects has been noticed and addressed by design historians and informed design historical research and its methodologies. The expansion of design historical methodologies has allowed for a study of objects whose designers are unknown, and generated an interest in the uses or consumption of everyday objects. These have somewhat blurred the boundaries between the two disciplines. Prown's 1982 essay is a reminder of an object-based focus for the study of cultures, which includes their production, an area of interest for design historians. Prown notes:

> Although the fundamental concern of material culture is with the artifact as the embodiment of mental structures, or patterns of belief, it is also of interest that the fabrication of the object is a manifestation of behavior, of human act.
>
> . . . in the discussion of culture and society, belief and behavior are inextricably intertwined. The material culturalist is, therefore, necessarily interested in the motive forces that condition behavior, specifically the making, the distribution, and the use of artifacts.
>
> . . . issues such as the availability of materials, the demands of patronage, channels of distribution, promotion, available technology, and means of exchange, which require the investigation of external evidence, are pertinent.⁷

Written over four decades ago, Prown's analytical frameworks focus on binarism, specifically "man-made" versus "nature" or "our" versus "their" culture. These binaries are increasingly being collapsed or challenged within material culture studies, and design history, as well as across disciplines such as cultural geography, archaeology, and history. Material culture research incorporates studies where objects are active, autonomous, and integral parts of human experience. They are not mere cultural receptacles that acquire meanings which can then be unearthed and interpreted by researchers. Instead, inanimate objects have agency, a concept employed by scholars of material culture for historical analysis. Simply put, agency here is related to how "things can act back"; action follows agency, which is the potential for animism emerging from the material object. Likened with people's capability to act, in material culture, however, agency is often used to infer that objects are bestowed with this potential and "the power of agency lies within their materiality itself".⁸ Tim Ingold critiques this position and suggests that materiality and agency, similar to fetishism, where the material object's presence is what drives its course of affairs, offers a limited understanding. He elaborates that agency resides not in its material form, but arises from the object's substance, the material itself (wood or stone are examples he uses), and its involvement in the processes and relations of the world, as it changes and transforms. Christopher Tilley responds to Ingold by describing the agency of objects as "providing affordances and constraints for thought and action", which acknowledges that "the material properties of things profoundly affect human conduct, both enabling and empowering people's lives and constraining them".⁹ Through their qualities, such as shape, function, and decoration, which are possible to produce as a result of their specific material composition, they become instrumental in creating and shaping experiences, identities, and relationships.

Aligning with the work of Ingold, in their essay "The Malice of Inanimate Objects: Material Agency", Andrew Jones and Nicole Boivin discuss the concept of agency attributed to inanimate objects, problematizing the presupposed dichotomy between the "material" and the "cultural", assumed in order to assign a form of animacy or fetishism to the material. They propose ways to rethink agency. Inspired by Bruno Latour's Actor-Network-Theory (ANT), they suggest that material agency prompts us not only to think about materiality, but also the concept of society, as mutually related. In ANT, Latour's intentions were to recalibrate the meanings of the social, to consider the concept of a collective within which a range of actors (human or non-human) act.[10] Latour's work most crucially shifts attention to how power operates within the social, and within this, agency cannot be seen as an attribute belonging to subjects or objects, as neither are pre-fixed entities. It is through the performance and intra-action between people and things that agencies occur. Jones and Boivin, therefore, conclude:

> Agency is not then simply subject-centred ability to act, but instead defines the way in which courses of action are mediated and articulated over time, whether the action is physically carried out by people or by things.[11]

Granting objects agency and power invites a different view of the roles that people play and how lives are shaped. Frank Dikötter's case study of modern China underlines the ways in which Chinese people shaped the uses and meanings of foreign objects which were themselves shaped by the materials being used. He reconsiders historical understandings of the correlation between globalization and modernity. Western modernity did not dominate Chinese people and replace local tradition; instead, the people actively appropriated modern designed objects to suit their beliefs and lifestyle.[12]

In their work on writing material culture history, Anne Gerritsen and Giorgio Riello refer to the way objects interact with the world as the "material interconnectedness" between people and things, emphasizing "it is in the human-object relationship that history is written".[13] In this context, objects are materials as well as interpretive concepts. This is particularly evident in the chapters that look at the ways in which makers or users respond to materials (organic or inorganic), such as Grasskamp's analysis of the uses of trash in the production of jewellery, described as "vital materiality". Here, the materiality of waste, such as the plastic fish-shaped container for soya sauce accompanying takeaway *sushi bento* boxes, is reformulated as a decorative ring, and becomes a creative resource, but only through improvisation in the processes of making. Similarly, Ng's chapter examines the cosmetic case, its various designs, and the modern Chinese woman's relationship with it in the performance of modernity, as heuristic, and as one that offered social and material agency to the woman. Here, the uses of these cosmetic cases, and their aesthetic agencies for the modern woman in early twentieth-century China, were mutually related.

Expanding from material agency, the authors in this book are attentive to the aesthetic qualities of objects and their potential to produce affect. The making of objects, beyond good or bad design, or aesthetically pleasing or not, involves the potential to influence the biography of the object. The aesthetic possibilities of design, similar to art, can arouse specific responses from the viewers or those who interact with it, such as "fear, desire, admiration or confusion".[14] In this book, various authors examine the aesthetic qualities of objects, such as Valentina Gamberi, who looks at Chinese religious statuary at the Wereldmuseum Leiden and the Musée des Confluences in Lyon, arguing that their aesthetics were ascertained by the worshippers within the specific territory of Taiwan, framed by the worshippers belonging to the specific region and as part of a cultic interactive framework. Curatorial interactions with these in the museological sensoria within a colonial context abstracted their original aesthetic and spiritual meanings, that had been shaped by the communities living with the objects. Kwok-wah Tung's chapter is also concerned with visual aesthetics; here of the concrete watchtowers in China, arguing that the local craftsmen, despite being commissioned by wealthy patrons, imbued their aesthetic sensibilities in their designs. In material culture studies as well as design history, aesthetic choices are intertwined with social identities and taste. They operate within discursive frameworks where shared understandings of the indices or meanings of aesthetics operate across social groups. Wolfgang Fritz Haug has argued that within a capitalist context, in addition to fulfilling need, "commodities "court" their buyers', and that "the aesthetics of consumer objects are integral to their economic function of creating profit for the producer".[15] Jean Baudrillard has argued otherwise, that exchange produces utilities, and in design, aesthetic value is made to align with functionality. He suggests that the object operates within a sign system and signifies its functionality. These discussions are particularly crucial for the studies in this book, as the concept of aesthetics operates in polyvalent ways. Here, need is secondary to the social function of aesthetics, and is crucial to the ways in which objects operate across social class and gender lines.

Considering objects and humans as intra-actors when taking into account object agency prompts the revisiting of the methodological framework of tracing biographies, assigned to objects as to persons. Anthropologists, art historians, and scholars of material culture have studied the ways in which objects are linked with humans, and the narratives that formulate through their journeys and lifecycles, highlight social and material relationships. The work of Maureen MacKenzie, examining string bags used by the Telefol men and women in central New Guinea, traces gender relations.[16] Widely used across the region, from the remotest rural areas to the expanding towns, the string bag or the bilium is used to transport, store, and shelter personal belongings, including food and babies. It also functions as a garment, an ornament, and ritual adornment. The focus on a single artefact and examining the social life of bilium sheds light on the social, cultural, and economic significance of the object. More widely, it provides insights into an object that is deeply rooted in cultural practices and "owes nothing to western cultural forms".[17] In the 1986 volume *The Social Life of Things*, Igor Kopytoff raised a series of questions that one could ask of objects. Answers to these not only help understand object biographies and therefore the social meanings of objects, understanding commodities and their exchange also sheds light on economic processes and societal structures. As Kopytoff suggests, "what one glimpses through the biographies of both people and things in the societies is, above all, the social system and the collective understandings on which it rests".[18] Kopytoff's focus on commodities in "complex societies" underpins the attention to objects' exchange values in capitalist societies. In this book, object biographies are traced by the authors to study the material meanings of objects within capitalist modernities in China, South Korea, and India from the eighteenth century. Images of textile manufacturing from Early Modern China help Roslyn Lee Hammers trace its technological significance in China, and its copies circulating in Europe, crucial for technological innovation. A biographical approach in studying objects and buildings, produced with specific aesthetic sensibilities and technological advancement, supports the interrogation of consumption practices across Asian contexts. From the consumption of printed magazines to cosmetic cases in South Korea and China, respectively, scholars discuss the shaping of modern society. John Comaroff has argued that "culture is constructed through consumption", implying that material objects produce cultural order, structuring social fields and making visible abstract cultural categories. Pierre Bourdieu's work is notable here, demonstrating taste as indexical in relation to social identity and symbolic capital. Michael Dietler and others (David Howes, Daniel Miller) have traced the ways in which consumption processes become dynamic when they traverse cultural boundaries. Focusing on coloniality and exchange of material goods, Dietler surveys consumption as a process of "structured improvization that continually materializes cultural order by also dealing with alien objects and practices through either transformative appropriation, and assimilation or rejection".[19] Material economies and the lifespans of objects through transnational flows of materials and goods in colonial and postcolonial contexts construct social and cultural relationships. Their consumption, such as by the women of early twentieth-century China, was fundamental to their identity as modern women. Dressing tables became part of the daily routine, and the use of an imported Parisian *necessaire* forged feminine identity, and expressed social class as well as taste. These were part of a wide range of modern commodities consumed and desired through popular magazines, boutiques, and department stores.[20]

Throughout the book, the authors engage with technological histories of objects. From the images of textile manufacturing in Early Modern China, technological functional objects in Seoul's markets, such as the circuit board and a mechanical pocket watch, through to markers of development in India – plumbing for housing and a bicycle – the authors in this volume are concerned with the social shaping of technology: how these are made, consumed, and repaired. Through analyses of objects and their representation, their value, and circulation, they are concerned with the tasks that technologies undertake, as well as their modern value and relevance. They address their possibilities when they use the latest technological knowledge or material, but also when these become obsolete. In Material Culture studies, the material of science, technology, and society (STS) undertakes the framework of the social construction of technology or SCOT. This approach involves the study of the skills of production, as well as the tools, the science that underpins the production (John Law discusses this in relation to the laws of the natural world), and finally, in relation to safety and economic interests. Law argues that the study of SCOT is "embedded in patterns of working and living, and in the objects that are implicated in such patterns".[21] Anneke Coppoolse's chapter in this book encapsulates the material significance of technology. Gentrified and converted to a service economy, the markets and museums in Seoul continue to see the circulation of objects from past manufacturing trades: electronics, sewing, and watch repair. Coppoolse studies these within contemporary life, addressing their legacy as well as the skills of the people who continue to use and repair these objects. The social relevance of technologies in material and design history holds an important place, as they are crucial agents in modernization, and they shift and change meanings, becoming obsolete and replaced with newer forms of technology. This area of study in historical terms offers great potential and helps shift the attention from a binary framework of "traditional" or "modern" material forms, to considering technological modernities and material knowledge that historical examples can offer. This is evident in the chapter authored by Hammers, where the knowledge of textile production techniques and the designs of mechanical tools had long been published in China before adapted and edited for circulation in Britain on the cusp of the Industrial Revolution.

Asia and object-based studies

Design history in Asia has attracted increasing interest since the four articles written by Yuko Kikuchi, Wendy Siuyi Wong, and Yunah Lee were published in *Journal of Design History* and since the publication of *Encyclopaedia of East Asian Design* co-edited by Haruhiko Fujita and Christine Guth.[22] In these seminal texts, the authors attempt to de-centre design's histories, focusing on East Asia as a framework for study and as a site where modern nations between the early and the mid-twentieth century were historically intertwined in colonial contexts. This history, and the history of the Cold War, have layered onto art, design, and craft, transnational flows of ideas, people, and power, from Japan, the United States, and China. As Kikuchi and Lee suggest, design and craft as modern terms were translated into East Asian contexts, adapted for local use, as does Wendy Wong in her study of counterfeiting and cultural translation.[23] Since then several texts, including Daniel Huppatz's *Modern Asian Design* (2018) and Yunah Lee and Megha Rajguru's *Design and Modernity in Asia* (2022) have traced histories of design across Asia. Both these books have attempted to draw upon themes and examine particular examples or case studies, employing approaches that study transnational exchange, production of national identities, and the historical contexts that facilitated the production of design in Asia. These books do not claim to offer a comprehensive survey of each region. They address Asia as a site with interconnections (Kikuchi and Lee, for instance, consider the shared nature of Chinese characters against the backdrop of Confucianism and Buddhism). They seek to engage with methodologies and frameworks that have contributed towards the "global" project of design history. China, Hong Kong,

India, Japan, South Korea, and Singapore feature in many of these books, and almost all these consider design's histories across borders. *Asian Material Culture in Context*, edited by Marianne Hulbosch, Elizabeth Bedford, and Martha Chaiklin, is a collection of essays that focuses on case studies from China, Indonesia, Japan, Malaysia, and Singapore.[24] Acknowledging that the chapters are representative, rather than exhaustive, of Asian material culture, they focus predominantly on examples of objects, such as beadwork, jewellery, traditional dress, or performance, which are treated as cultural artefacts using ethnography as a research method. While most essays consider diaspora communities and material cultures in particular locations, the book is one of the texts that focuses on Asian material culture specifically.

These crucial works have created scope for further research. A need for design history and understandings of material culture that engage with urgent concerns related to post-industry – the dumping of industrial garbage in Southeast Asian countries, the remains of plastic packaging in river beds, the crisis in housing – are critical. Design history and material culture research continues to remain relevant to help understand cultural and social histories, as well as political economies that shape the material fabric of contemporary life. Marianne Hulbosch, Elizabeth Bedford, and Martha Chaiklin point out that material culture "not only defines a people or practice but brings them together, often operating on a number of levels that transform, create, signify a particular time, place, society, attitudes, beliefs and practices that draw from the past but at the same time adapt to the present".[25] In contexts such as Kaiping, China, or Mumbai, India, the built environment references heritage. Beyond fast modernization evident in the global cities of Asia, the production of buildings across classes, either built to showcase wealth or for basic shelter, continue to hold sway. Hulbosch et al. turn to historical case studies to understand how power operates in relation to design, how design can empower or control, and the ways in which design has helped shape individual or collective identities.

Similar to existing scholarship on Asian design, the research presented in this anthology also expands the scope within the fields of global design history, national and transnational histories of design, continuing to de-centre design history beyond the Euro-American canon, and employing a range of methodological strategies. The authors draw upon sources from allied disciplines (beyond design history and material culture) such as visual culture, art history, and heritage studies to discuss materiality and object histories. Through the three themes that organize the chapters in this book – the nature and experience of materiality, design and mediation, and the biography of a design – it articulates how design is instrumental in the intricate cultural and social changes that are distinctive to cultures within Asia in the modern age. Specific context and theoretical approaches, including the tensions between the local and global ("glocalisation"), materialization, hybridity, cultural authenticity, Asian modernity, gender identity, human-spatial interaction, and upcycling are particularly important, aiming to address particular characteristics of material culture in Asia while locating them in a broader global context.

In the context of Asia, where modernities and their experiences have had material ramifications, where colonial pasts, extractive power, and Orientalist perspectives have been layered onto objects, the work of writing histories of objects and their materialities is unfinished. As Peter van Dommelen has argued, material culture histories can unlock untold stories of social groups otherwise ignored.[26] He has suggested that material culture can move discussions beyond literary texts that postcolonial scholars have engaged with, to examine objects, expanding across different media (from everyday newspapers, to clothes, buildings, and spaces). Van Dommelan argues that while anthropologists have addressed colonial contexts in their quest to challenge Western authority, archaeology has been slower to adopt this methodological framework to engage with subaltern positionalities or alternative histories. He argues for material culture to be more engaged with postcolonial studies, with a view to expand the field and attend to the hybrid forms of materials and identities.

While postcoloniality is not the only approach this volume uses to examine power and materiality, considering colonial pasts, modernity, and global transnational exchanges enables the authors of the chapters in this book to examine material values of things. Across the book, the authors are concerned with the ways in which goods – from waste and sherds, to ornamental objects and heritage monuments – have been valued, consumed, and conserved. They interrogate the locales of these objects, their shifting cultural meanings locally with specific material resonance within Asian culture, and the relevance of these meanings that often move beyond the local, indicating tensions between the local and global such as glocalisation, hybridity, cultural authenticity, and Asian modernity. It is through the material qualities of the objects, as well as their production, design, and consumption in particular locations, that values are produced, and agencies are enacted. The agency of the materials themselves present them as "trash and treasure", a "subversive found item", or as heritage in their geographical locations.

Structure of the book

The structure of the book, three parts dedicated to three themes, is intended to articulate the complex and dynamic characteristics of design and material culture in modern Asia. Each chapter delves into the historiographies of objects, the roles things have played in human activities, and the historical evidence involved that elucidates the origin and changes in cultural history. The authors study a range of primary sources, such as written texts, images (of design, art photography, painting, magazine photos, and popular illustrations), and surviving material objects and structures (ceramics, jewellery, buildings, etc.) in various collections and localities.

Through exploring how ceramics, discarded and found objects are given innovative forms and meanings in their reincarnation, the chapters in Part 1, "The Nature and Experience of Materiality", demonstrate that the reinvention of material is critical in the ways design is produced and valued. The intricate correlation between materials, design practice, and social change becomes apparent through examining how the makers and the users find ways to generate new meanings and reaffirm identities through their interactions with designed objects. Foregrounding questions of authenticity, meaning, and value, the chapters look at the significance of the appreciation and incorporation of designed items into daily life. Stacey Pierson discusses various ways in which sherds of East Asian ceramics have been used and consumed in global contexts, and explores the consequent impact on the conceptualization of these fragments as both material and medium. Anna Grasskamp investigates creative practices of reusing organic and inorganic discarded materials by focusing on wearable and collectible objects made by artists and designers in Hong Kong. She argues that the power of waste materials in the hands of creative practitioners based in South China can be seen as undermining the material hierarchies of commercial trade, blurring distinctions between the "local" and the "global". Drawing from ethnographic encounters, site visits, and museum displays, Anneke Coppoolse's chapter presents three designed objects – a circuit board, a pair of scissors, and a pocket watch – that represent distinct cultural and social meanings and values in the industries around a historically significant stream called Cheonggyecheon in Seoul, South Korea.

The chapters in Part 2, "Design and Mediation", place mediation to the fore as a key component in gender and religious representation. Our authors interrogate the significance of visual appearance in material representations of modern women and religious artefacts in cultural understandings of material objects such as magazines, objects of adornment, and statues. Hui-Ying Kerr examines the popular lifestyle magazine *Hanako*, which targeted young, single, working "Office Ladies" through features that focused on the exciting opportunities for leisure opening up in the Bubble Economy in Japan in the 1980s. She uses visual analysis of articles and advertisements in the magazine taken from 1988 to 1990 to critically understand how women were portrayed in these images through dress, composition, environment, and accompanying copy, revealing not only what was expected of them as consumers of products and services, but also changing perceptions of acceptable feminine behaviour in the dynamic landscape of the Bubble Economy. Sandy Ng discusses how Chinese women in the early twentieth century used designs such as cosmetic cases and dressing tables to articulate self-awareness that affirmed their identities. She proposes that designs that were created for women were integral to the adaptation of changing lifestyles and mentality in the modern era. In her chapter, Valentina Gamberi applies the concept of transcultural objects to museum artefacts. Her research emphasizes how museum aesthetics have been forged by collectors' agency through focusing on Jan Jakob Maria de Groot's (1854–1921) Chinese folk religious statues at the Wereldmuseum Leiden, comparing how de Groot commissioned and used them within his publications and imagined the manners in which they should be exhibited with ethnographic accounts on the carving process of Chinese god statuary in Taiwan.

Part 3, "The Biography of Design", includes analyses of concrete, urban design, and textile production, specific to particular cultural and social contexts across Asian cultures. The diversity of topics, as well as methodological approaches, explore the complexity in the ways that designs are created, disseminated, maintained, and utilised by different demographics of people across Asia. Kwok-wah Tung investigates the Kaiping concrete watchtowers (*diaolou*), which were designated as World Heritage sites by UNESCO in 2007. Their unique aesthetics characterize the built and natural environments in Southern China that embodies a cultural process of glocalization, resulting in an alternative form of modernization, which not only reflects the locals' innovative endeavours and aesthetic sense, but also helps to mediate a harmonious and tranquil lifestyle in the region. Megha Rajguru's chapter analyses the ways in which postcolonial architects Charles Correa and Balkrishna Doshi imagined the minimal interior amid national and international development agendas of poverty eradication and housing provision in the early 1980s in India. Through a study of drawings, photographs, and texts produced by these architects, it examines the materialization of development concepts in the production of the home, such as participation, economic self-help, and alignment to needs. Her work critically examines how developmental ideas of self-help manifested in design, producing domestic spaces that were seen to be authentic to ways of living in India. Roslyn Lee Hammers reclaims the role of representations of Chinese textile technology in the formation of the British Industrial Revolution in her chapter through a close reading of texts and images that were published around 1740 in Europe of Chinese textile equipment. She maintains that the representations were consulted to develop the technology that inaugurated the Industrial Revolution and that prior to the 1750s Chinese technology was regarded as superior in Europe.

Notes

1. Jules D. Prown, *Art as Evidence: Writings on Art and Material Culture* (Yale University Press, 2002), 78–87.
2. Clifford Geertz, *The Interpretation of Cultures: Selected Essays* (Fontana Press, 1993).
3. Arjun Appadurai, *The Social Life of Things: Commodities in Cultural Perspective* (Cambridge University Press, 1986).
4. Judy Attfield, *Wild Things: The Material Culture of Everyday Life* (Bloomsbury Visual Arts, 2000), 12, 5.
5. Igor Kopytoff, "The Cultural Biography of Things: Commoditization as Process", in Arjun Appadurai (ed.), *The Social Life of Things: Commodities in Cultural Perspective* (Cambridge University Press, 1986).
6. Serena Dyer, "State of the Field: Material Culture", *History* (London) 106, no. 370 (2021): 286.
7. Jules D. Prown, "Mind in Matter: An Introduction to Material Culture Theory and Method", *Winterthur Portfolio* 17, no. 1 (1982): 7.
8. Tim Ingold, "Materials against Materiality", *Archaeological Dialogues* 14, no. 1 (2007): 12.
9. Christopher Tilley, "Materiality in Materials", *Archaeological Dialogues* 14, no. 1 (2007): 19.
10. Bruno Latour, *Reassembling the Social: An Introduction to Actor-Network-Theory* (Oxford University Press, 2005).
11. Andrew M. Jones and Nicole Boivin, "The Malice of Inanimate Objects: Material Agency", in Dan Hicks and Mary C. Beaudry (eds.), *The Oxford Handbook of Material Culture Studies* (Oxford University Press, Oxford, 2010), 351.

12. Frank Dikotter, *Exotic Commodities: Modern Objects and Everyday Life in China* (Columbia University Press, 2006).
13. Anne Gerritsen and Giorgio Riello (eds.), *Writing Material Culture History* (Bloomsbury, 2015), 7, 113.
14. Janet Hoskins, "Agency, Biography and Objects", in Christopher Tilley (ed.), *Handbook of Material Culture* (Sage, 2006), 76.
15. Jerry Palmer, "Introduction to Part 1", in Mo Dodson and Jerry Palmer (eds.), *Design and Aesthetics: A Reader* (Routledge, 1996), 11.
16. Maureen A. MacKenzie, *Androgynous Objects: String Bags and Gender in Central New Guinea* (Routledge, 2019).
17. MacKenzie, *Androgynous Objects*, 20.
18. Kopytoff, "The Cultural Biography of Things", 90.
19. Michael Dietler, "Consumption", in Dan Hicks and Mary C. Beaudry (eds.), *The Oxford Handbook of Material Culture Studies* (Oxford University Press, 2010), 218.
20. See Sandy Ng, "Adornment and the Self: Ornamental Design and the Modern Woman in China", chapter 5 in this volume.
21. John Law, "The Materials of STS", in Dan Hicks and Mary C. Beaudry (eds.), *The Oxford Handbook of Material Culture Studies* (Oxford University Press, 2010), 176.
22. Haruhiko Fujita and Christine Guth (eds.), *Encyclopedia of East Asian Design* (Bloomsbury Visual Arts, 2020).
23. Yuko Kikuchi and Yunah Lee, "Transnational Modern Design Histories in East Asia: An Introduction", *Journal of Design History* 27, no. 4 (2014): 323–34.
24. Marianne Hulbosch, Elizabeth Bedford and Martha Chaiklin, *Asian Material Culture* (Amsterdam University Press, 2009).
25. Hulbosch et al., *Asian Material Culture*, 15.
26. Peter van Dommelen, "Colonial Matters: Material Culture and Postcolonial Theory in Colonial Situations", in Christopher Tilley (ed.), *Handbook of Material Culture* (Sage, 2006), 104–24.

References

Appadurai, Arjun (ed.). *The Social Life of Things: Commodities in Cultural Perspective*, Cambridge University Press, 1986.
Attfield, Judy. *Wild Things: The Material Culture of Everyday Life*, Bloomsbury Visual Arts, 2020.
Dietler, Michael. "Consumption", in Dan Hicks and Mary C. Beaudry (eds.), *The Oxford Handbook of Material Culture Studies*, Oxford University Press, 2010, pp. 209–28.
Dikotter, Frank. *Exotic Commodities: Modern Objects and Everyday Life in China*, Columbia University Press, 2006.
Dyer, Serena. "State of the Field: Material Culture", *History* (London) 106, no. 370 (2021): 282–92.
Fujita, Haruhiko and Christine Guth (eds.). *Encyclopedia of East Asian Design*, Bloomsbury Visual Arts, 2020.
Geertz, Clifford. *The Interpretation of Cultures: Selected Essays*, Fontana Press, 1993.
Gerritsen, Anne and Giorgio Riello (eds.). *Writing Material Culture History*, Bloomsbury, 2015.

Hicks, Dan and Mary C. Beaudry (eds.). *The Oxford Handbook of Material Culture Studies*, Oxford University Press, 2010.

Hoskins, Janet. "Agency, Biography and Objects", in Christopher Tilley (ed.), *Handbook of Material Culture*, Sage, 2006, pp. 74–84.

Hulbosch, Marianne, Elizabeth Bedford and Martha Chaiklin. *Asian Material Culture*, Amsterdam University Press, 2009.

Huppatz, Dan. *Modern Asian Design*, Bloomsbury, 2018.

Ingold, Tim. "Materials against Materiality", *Archaeological Dialogues* 14, no. 1 (2007): 1–16.

Jones, Andrew M. and Nicole Boivin. "The Malice of Inanimate Objects: Material Agency", in Dan Hicks and Mary C. Beaudry (eds.), *The Oxford Handbook of Material Culture Studies*, Oxford University Press, 2010, pp. 333–51.

Kikuchi, Yuko and Yunah Lee. "Transnational Modern Design Histories in East Asia: An Introduction", *Journal of Design History* 27, no. 4 (2014): 323–34.

Kopytoff, Igor. "The Cultural Biography of Things: Commoditization as Process", in Arjun Appadurai (ed.), *The Social Life of Things: Commodities in Cultural Perspective*, Cambridge University Press, 1986, pp. 64–94.

Latour, Bruno. *Reassembling the Social: An Introduction to Actor-Network-Theory*, Oxford University Press, 2005.

Law, John. "The Materials of STS", in Dan Hicks and Mary C. Beaudry (eds.), *The Oxford Handbook of Material Culture Studies*, Oxford University Press, 2010, pp. 173–90.

Lee, Yunah and Megha Rajguru. *Design and Modernity in Asia: National Identity and Transnational Exchange 1945–1990*, Bloomsbury, 2022.

MacKenzie, Maureen A. *Androgynous Objects: String Bags and Gender in Central New Guinea*, Routledge, 2019.

Palmer, Jerry. "Introduction to Part 1", in Mo Dodson and Jerry Palmer (eds.), *Design and Aesthetics: A Reader*, Routledge, 1996, pp. 3–12.

Prown, Jules D. "Mind in Matter: An Introduction to Material Culture Theory and Method", *Winterthur Portfolio* 17, no. 1 (1982): 1–19.

Prown, Jules D. *Art as Evidence: Writings on Art and Material Culture*, Yale University Press, 2002.

Tilley, Christopher (ed.). *Handbook of Material Culture*, Sage, 2006.

Tilley, Christopher. "Materiality in Materials", *Archaeological Dialogues* 14, no. 1 (2007): 16–20.

Van Dommelen, Peter. "Colonial Matters: Material Culture and Postcolonial Theory in Colonial Situations", in Christopher Tilley (ed.), *Handbook of Material Culture*, Sage, 2006, 104–24.

PART I
THE NATURE AND EXPERIENCE OF MATERIALITY

CHAPTER 1
TRASH OR TREASURE? THE EAST ASIAN SHERD AS MATERIAL AND MEDIUM
Stacey Pierson

Introduction

In 2010, the artist Li Xiaofeng 李晓峰 (b. 1965) created a limited-edition polo shirt for Lacoste that was made from fragments of Chinese porcelain sewn together with metal wires in an approximation of the brand's iconic knit shirts (Figure 1.1).[1] This commission, which was titled "The Porcelain Polo", reflected not only Li's unique approach to sculptural work, but also what at first glance appears to be a new conception of ceramics. This new conception, in which the sherd – or broken ceramic fragment – is used as a medium or material in its own right, transcends the traditional classification of sherds as refuse or remains. Yet, as in Li's work, today ceramic sherds are being used in new ways as upcycled

Figure 1.1 Lacoste porcelain polo shirt by Li Xiaofeng, exhibition at Arts et Metiers Museum, Paris, 2010. Photo by Stephane Cardinale/Corbis via Getty Images.

materials in a range of different contexts, including museum displays, architecture, and contemporary art and craft. Ceramic sherds have even become collectible objects in their own right. For example, collectors can visit the extensive sherd market at the self-styled "home of porcelain" in Jingdezhen, China where sherds purporting to be newly excavated can be purchased by anyone and added to their collections. When sherds representing fragments of whole pieces are considered to be independent objects in this way, it is evident that the classification of sherds as collectibles is only the latest development in a wider phenomenon of redefining ceramics that spans the globe and different time periods that is also concentrated on ceramics from or referencing East Asia.

In the built environment, sherds of ceramics from East Asia have been used as decorating materials for architectural spaces in, for example, Europe, Britain, and East Africa since at least the fourteenth century.[2] In parallel to this, from the eighteenth century onward, works of art and jewellery have been made from East Asian sherds by a number of makers, such as the *marchands mercier* in eighteenth-century Paris, who used them as a medium for artistic production similar to the way they are used sculpturally by Li Xiaofeng. In addition, with the development of archaeology as a discipline and practice in the nineteenth century, ceramic sherds came to be considered a primary source of material evidence for human activity and for dating of sites, owing to their durability and widespread distribution. With archaeology entering the museum, this in turn has led to the display of sherds in exhibitions and galleries, often to support the dating of whole objects but increasingly as individual objects of evidence and presentation. Since at least the mid-twentieth century, museums have intentionally collected sherds, echoing the trend for collecting souvenirs of "ruins" during the eighteenth-century aristocratic travels known as the Grand Tour in Britain and Europe and the related travels to Asia by nineteenth-century travellers who collected architectural material.[3] Many of these "ruins" were buildings decorated with ceramic tiles, bricks, and decorative elements, the remains of which were easy to acquire and, therefore, collect. Considered through this wide lens, the ceramic sherd is, therefore, a category of material culture that has a defined presence, a broad utility, and an identity that is separate from, but associated with, their original integration within the fabric of whole ceramics or structures.

Yet, in spite of the widespread utilization of sherds in various media and contexts over a broad geographical and historical span, very little literature has focused on sherds generally or studies of sherds as a medium. Instead, within the vast literatures of archaeology, anthropology, and materials science, even art history and collecting, which for reference purposes will just be touched upon here and limited to the English language, ceramic sherds usually appear in the following types of studies: as data in studies of archaeological sites or of cultures, including shipwrecks; in manuals for archaeological methods; ceramic analysis, production, and characterization studies; archaeological evidence for cultural phenomena and practices such as "abundance" or "trash" (rubbish) and, more recently, in my own work in collecting studies examining the plunder of ruins.[4] Yet none of these has the sherd as its focus or its topic but the scope of the literature in which sherds appear, plus the evidence of their utility in multiple contexts, suggests that such a focus is now warranted.

Trash or Treasure? The East Asian Sherd as Material and Medium

With a view to characterizing what might be called "sherd culture" as a phenomenon with a history and specific modes of consumption, in this chapter I will therefore introduce various ways in which sherds of East Asian ceramics, as a primary example, have been used and consumed in global contexts, and explore the consequent impact on the conceptualization of these fragments as both material and medium. Structured around the question of how we experience the materiality of the sherd when it is used as a medium, the chapter will situate the sherd within four material contexts: archaeology, architecture, contemporary art and craft, and restoration. In archaeology, I will examine ceramic archaeological sites in China and the afterlives of sherds from these sites in several different contexts, including display and collecting. In architecture, I will show how East Asian ceramic sherds have been used to decorate buildings and structures in three selected locations: Europe, China, and East Africa, and how this rematerializes the surface of these structures and transforms them into sculptural spaces that are experienced in new ways by inhabitants, visitors, and viewers. Sherds as a sculptural medium can also be observed in contemporary art and craft as we have seen with Li Xiaofeng's work, from the construction of garments using sherds, to the creation of new vessels composed of sherds. A historical example from eighteenth-century Europe will also be discussed to propose a precedent. The works constructed from sherds mainly rely on wires or adhesives to join the component parts and similar adhesives are used in restoration processes where fragmented objects are made whole again, creatively rejoined and reconfigured. With its creative elements, restoration can therefore be seen as a form of craft, and one which uses ceramic sherds as a primary medium. A good example of this is the restoration technique developed in Japan that is known as *kintsugi*, which will be discussed in this chapter.

The types of ceramics from which sherds appear to be used most often are high-fired stonewares and porcelains manufactured in East Asia. Sherds of ceramics from producers around the world have been used in sherd culture but the re-use and upcycling of sherds (or their imitations) tends to concentrate on those from East Asia. This is due in part to their durability and sturdiness but also, I will argue, their aesthetics and visual associations with East Asia. The earliest high-fired ceramics were made in East Asia and they were therefore the most widely traded and most frequently encountered ceramics before the twentieth century. Such familiar types as "celadons" and "blue and white porcelain" were invented in East Asia and are therefore considered the benchmark aesthetic and style for such wares. As a result, fragments of East Asian high-fired ceramics dominate the sherd culture landscape.

Through the examples explored here, this chapter will aim to define sherd culture as a complex material culture phenomenon in which the sherd has a materiality that transcends its own composition and fragmentary state. I will show how a sherd is not just a representation of incompleteness; it is an independent object formed from the destruction of another. It can also be a medium for creation, such that sherds can be seen to challenge assumed notions of completeness and associated values. Sherds operate at the margins of dematerialization and rematerialization, demonstrating the fluidity of material and medium as expressed in their broad utility. This chapter will ultimately argue for their classification as both trash and treasure.

Archaeology

A good starting point for a study of the materiality and consumption of sherds is archaeology and the status of sherds as archaeological material. Surviving in this context as refuse, the remains of human habitation or burial, ceramic production and trade detritus, ceramic sherds are among the most useful archaeological evidence for the dating and characterization of sites.[5] They are durable, and therefore survive, but they also have formal qualities that can help explain human culture and history. As archaeological finds, sherds are evidence of human activity and are, therefore, characterized and classified as such in this discipline. Because of their global distribution, sherds of East Asian archaeological ceramics can further be considered as both inter- and cross-cultural evidence. For example, if we look at a recently excavated site in China, the Nandaku 南大库 or "southern storage area" of the former imperial palace in Beijing, we can see the remains of thousands of ceramic vessels used at court from the fourteenth to the nineteenth centuries (Figure 1.2).[6] All these vessels over time were thrown into a trash pit that was rediscovered during building works at what is now the Palace Museum. Since their discovery, they have been exhibited as the remains of "imperial porcelain" production and have illuminated the tableware landscape of the imperial family.[7] Through their exhibition and publication, especially in the Palace Museum, viewers can experience these broken porcelain fragments as both trash, or refuse, and as imperial objects.

Chinese porcelain and stoneware have also been found in trash heaps outside China where they are similarly considered to be evidence for dining and drinking habits in another time and place. For example, the remains of a coffeehouse in Cambridge, England were excavated between 2005 and 2012 and found to contain fragments of numerous eighteenth-century Chinese porcelain vessels.[8] These, along with the other finds, help to illuminate the materiality of coffeehouses but also the trade in, and availability of, Chinese porcelain in England at that time. Chinese porcelain and stoneware fragments found at other sites in England can be seen in museum collections such as that of the Museum of London, where displays of these sherds are used to explain London life. In the permanent display gallery

Figure 1.2 Qing dynasty blue and white porcelain sherds, excavated from the Nandaku in the Forbidden City, 2019. Photo by Stacey Pierson.

"Expanding City", a fragment of a tea bowl excavated from the site of Tom's Coffee House is displayed, where it helps to tell the story of London's rebuilding after the great fire.⁹

Such museum displays mirror the presentation of sherds in exhibitions, often those dedicated to periods of ceramic production, such as the recent series of shows in China and Hong Kong of "Interregnum porcelains": *Filling the Interregnum: Ming Mid-15th Century Ceramics from Jingdezhen*, Art Museum, The Chinese University of Hong Kong (2012) and *Lustre Revealed: Jingdezhen Porcelain Wares in Mid Fifteenth Century*, Shanghai Museum (2019), which both featured numerous excavated sherds of vessels from mid-fifteenth-century levels at Jingdezhen. Many of the pieces displayed were reconstructed but their fragmentary nature was much in evidence. With the aim of developing connoisseurship of Chinese porcelain of this period, the sherds function as artefacts in these exhibitions, rather than refuse. However, many sherds are collected by and retained in permanent museum collections, which in turn has fuelled the private collecting of sherds, enforcing their status as individual collected objects.¹⁰

The fragments in these collections and exhibitions function in additional ways beyond documentation or the authentication and dating of whole objects. They are also sold, like whole objects, in their own markets. One sherd market, that may be the original one, is the Taoci guwan shichang 陶瓷古玩市场 in Jingdezhen, China, which features in a recent history of the city by Professor Anne Gerritsen, *City of Blue and White: Chinese Porcelain and the Early Modern World* (2020). At Jingdezhen, the sherds are laid out on blankets early in the morning and collectors come to purchase examples of what purport to be authentic archaeological souvenirs. While many of the sherds are fake – that is, created from intentionally broken and aged modern copies – the buyers are not made aware of this, unless accompanied by an expert. If genuine, their sale would be evidence of archaeological plunder and this fact may actually enhance their appeal to collectors who may or may not be aware of cultural property laws. In addition, Jingdezhen, like many historic production sites in China, is promoted as an archaeological and manufacturing tourist attraction, thus shaping its identity, and that of the things one can buy and see there, around ceramic remains. What is notable is how differently the sherds one can see there in museums and purchases in the market are experienced by general visitors and more specialist collectors. Unusually, in Jingdezhen sherds are presented alongside whole pieces as collectibles and objects of display both in museums and in market stalls. Their context and meaning is thus conflated with that of whole objects, blurring the now elided boundaries between what usually are considered to be separate categories of material culture, archaeological material and refuse, or vessels. The city itself today provides a somewhat confounding visitor experience akin to a theme park, with its industrial remains transformed into sites for tourism, and a luxury hotel located on a newly invented "ceramic street".¹¹

Architecture

The history of porcelain production in and around Jingdezhen is also built into the city's design as a tourist destination, with lamp posts covered in blue and white tiles as well as fragments inlaid into roads and walls. This design practice mirrors one that surprisingly has a much longer history outside of China and which incorporates Chinese and other East Asian ceramic objects and fragments into architectural surfaces. Particularly in Europe and parts of the Middle East such as Iran and associated locations such as Mughal South Asia and the Swahili Coast, there is a tradition of using whole ceramics as tiles and sculptural elements, which are embedded in the architecture in various ways. Well-known examples of this would be the porcelain rooms in European palaces of the seventeenth and eighteenth centuries as well as the *chinikhaneh* installed in part of the shrine at Ardebil in Iran during early seventeenth-century refurbishment works.[12] Less well known, but increasingly the subject of study, are the tomb pillars of Malindi, which were inset with Ming Chinese celadons and blue and white porcelains.[13]

However, perhaps inspired by the use of whole pieces, there are a number of architectural spaces that are decorated with fragments, rather than whole objects. While the inspiration for this practice has yet to be determined, there are certainly parallels with both mosaic work and shell grottoes. Mosaic work began with the embedding of stones in mortar and broken amphorae in pavements, and then progressed to the use of prepared *tesserae* or small cubes of stone, ceramic, or glass.[14] This latter technique continued post-Antiquity into the Medieval world beyond Europe to the Islamic world where mosaics decorated floors, walls, and ceilings.[15] This practice of embedding small pieces or fragments into a substrate, such as a floor or a wall, was extended beyond the use of tesserae to include natural materials like shells which were used to decorate the fanciful grottoes of antiquity, that were revived in Renaissance Italy and then spread throughout elite Europe and Britain.[16] In the early seventeenth century, some of these grottoes were decorated with fragments of porcelain embedded alongside shells. A famous, and still intact example, can be seen at the Palacio Fronteira in Lisbon that was built *c.* 1670. Here, and in other Portuguese palace structures, garden rooms were decorated with what can be seen as an extension of the mosaic technique which includes sherds of porcelain vessels along with shells that are known as *embrechados* (lit. "entwined") (Figure 1.3).[17] An interesting parallel can be drawn with the early European conception of porcelain as made from shell, in the period when porcelain was an unknown substance.[18]

While associated with European architecture, this kind of architectural decoration with sherds is not confined to Europe. In Ming- and Qing-dynasty China, a tradition of producing detailed surface patterns on ancestral halls and religious buildings developed in the Lingnan region which blends the mosaic technique with shard decoration. Referred to as "porcelain inlay", the technique consists of recutting brightly coloured ceramic tiles or vessel wasters into small elements that are then rearranged mosaic-style with high-relief, intricate motifs on a low-relief background embedded into the surface of architectural spaces. The high-relief elements are sculptural, whereas the background designs have a shell-like appearance that recalls the overlapping layout of shells in shell grottoes such as that seen in the Palacio Fronteira. Surviving, though much restored, examples of this Lingnan sculptural "inlay" technique can be seen in two temple spaces:

Figure 1.3 Casa do Fresco entrance detail, Fronteira Palace, Lisbon. Sérgio Nogueira/Alamy Stock Photo.

the Kaiyuan Temple (開元寺) in Chaozhou City, Guangdong and the Wat Arun (Temple of Dawn) in Bangkok, Thailand where the technique is said to have spread with migrants from Southeast China.[19]

More recently, sherd decoration has begun to make an appearance in Chinese domestic architecture with a most exuberant adaptation that can be seen in the redecoration of a French-style house in Tianjin, which utilized thousands of sherds along with whole pieces, stone, and glass to reanimate and completely cover the façade of what is known as "The Porcelain House", Cifangzi 瓷房子 (Figure 1.4).[20] This former European-style home of a porcelain collector opened to the public in 2007 and is a testament to the continuing fashion for, and practice of, upcycling of fragments in a European architectural space. Like its referents and antecedents, the fragments are embedded into the architecture, thus changing the experience and reception not only of the fragments, but also their new architectural context. Similar to the earlier Palacio Fronteira, the broken, uneven character of the sherds has been retained and serves here to transform the traditionally smooth surfaces into textured, disrupted visual planes, lending an animation to the surface that is at once compelling and unsettling.

The Dynamics of Modern Asian Design

Figure 1.4 China House, Tianjin. Antony Baxter/Alamy Stock Photo.

Contemporary art and craft

The use of sherds in architecture demonstrates not only their ability to transform surfaces but also their substantive utility as materials for construction. This practice also has a long history but its widespread geographical and chronological application has limited its recognition as part of a wider trend. Constructing objects from ceramic sherds is usually therefore only referenced in contemporary craft and artistic production. However, in the seventeenth-century Ottoman court and eighteenth-century European palaces and French furniture studios, Chinese and – in the case of Europe – also Japanese porcelain pieces and fragments were used to create new luxury objects and vessels. For example, in the Bowes Museum in Barnard Castle, England, is the "Lowther Casket", constructed from panels made from broken and reshaped enamelled Chinese porcelain vases, dating to the Kangxi reign period (1662–1722).[21] Probably made in a French workshop (although attributed to Vienna), the casket's decorated porcelain panels are secured to a wooden base and framed by an ormolu armature, creating a rectangular box with warm gilt, intense cobalt blue and bright red, green, and blue enamel floral and monochrome panels, the clear and bright glazed porcelain contrasting with the shimmering gold framework (Figure 1.5). The result is a visual and textural feast for the eyes.

It is perhaps that textural potential combined with the contrast of solid material injured by fragmentation that made and makes East Asian ceramic sherds appealing as

Figure 1.5 The "Lowther Casket", an ormolu-mounted Chinese porcelain casket, with porcelain panels of the Kangxi period (1662–1722) and mounts *c.* 1720–25, possibly Vienna. Courtesy of the Bowes Museum, Barnard Castle, County Durham. Acquired with the help of the Art Fund.

materials for the making of art and craft objects. Yet, by virtue of their origins and date, such ceramics can also have other resonances. The porcelain used in the casket was imported from China, signalling access to and mastery over a material representation of place. For a contemporary maker, working with sherds of antique ceramics can provide a link to the past. As the sculptor Li Xiaofeng noted in an interview about his work for Lacoste mentioned at the beginning of this chapter, the use of antique ceramic sherds enables him to connect with the spirit of the people in ancient times, referencing the fact that he often works with sherds of ancient ceramics which he collects from building sites.[22] While he made new sherds for his Lacoste "shirts", Li has also created such items as a Mao jacket from sherds of Song and Yuan (twelfth- to fourteenth-century) celadon vessels.[23] These found antique sherds connect his work not only to the past but also to archaeological finds and the upcycling that is inherent in the practice of using sherds as materials for construction or decoration, as in the case of architecture examined earlier. His use of similarly sized (and therefore reshaped) sherds as almost paillettes to make the Mao suit also references the ancient jade suits *yuyi* 玉衣 that were made for burial in the Han dynasty in China (*c.* second century BCE).[24] These "suits" were constructed of multiple square jade plaques that were then sewn together with gold wire around the bodies they encased. Their purpose was preservative on the one hand, but also transformative on the other in that they enabled the deceased to enter into the next realm.[25] Li's work with antique sherds thus connects past and present, garments and vessels as well as materials, challenging our ideas of what constitutes not only ceramic materiality but also textiles and their function. His work with new sherds also reworks the textile-making process, creating a garment from newly manufactured porcelain vessel sherds, the making of which can be seen as a form of creative destruction and reconstruction.

Other artists use ceramic sherds in an even more conceptual way to construct new ceramic vessels from the broken fragments. Yeesookyung 이수경, whose work can be seen in many museum collections, created a series starting in 2002 known as "translated vases", which are constructed from discarded sherds of traditional-style (but not old) Korean porcelains and celadons held together with epoxy and gold, thus referencing the Japanese repair method known as *kintsugi* 金継ぎ (Figure 1.6). In these works, original

Figure 1.6 "Translated Vase_Nine Dragons in Wonderland" by Yeesookyung at the 57th International Art Exhibition, La Biennale di Venezia, Venice, Italy 14 May 2017. Felix Hörhager/dpa/Alamy Live News. Dpa picture alliance/Alamy Stock Photo.

complete but flawed objects have been broken by their makers as wasters, and discarded, but they have been restored by Yeesookyung to an unflawed completeness through their conjunction with other fragments in the formation of a new whole object. Looked at closely, the individual characteristics of the original vessels and figurines can be discerned – a dragon-head spout on part of a ewer, painted flowers on the base of a jar, or the carved border patterns on the rim of a bowl. But unlike Li's almost geometric lines framing a sartorial structure, Yeesookyung's composed vessels have an organic shape that is unrelated to any existing object and is therefore unique, without referent. We experience the materiality of the sherds used by both artists very differently, even though the original material is essentially the same. In an interview about her "translated vases" series, Yeesookyung said that her aim is to restore the broken vessels and "facilitat(e) the mutation of these fragments into a new state", which is one of strength. She also sees the fragments as being vulnerable and "stressed" because they are both damaged and reproductions. They are a metaphor for the destruction of "treasure during the turmoil of Korean tragic history", thus in her work she is translating the language of these ceramics and transforming their narratives through remaking.[26]

For artists such as Li Xiaofeng and Yeesookyung, the ceramic sherds are thus containers of historical, cultural, and material meaning translated into new forms. For artists working outside East Asia, but using East Asian sherds as materials, the cultural resonance is also that of their own background but made visible through East Asian ceramic fragments. The Dutch artist Bouke de Vries is inspired by the long history of the consumption of Chinese and Japanese porcelain in the Netherlands to make new objects from sherds that reference Dutch still life paintings (Figure 1.7). In his works such as

Figure 1.7 Bouke de Vries, "Dead Nature no. 4", 2009. © Bouke de Vries.

Dead Nature 4 (2009), fragments of Ming blue and white bowls are suspended in a Perspex box with gaps between the fragments and combined with other media such as dried fruits so as to appear to be a complete bowl filled with fruit that is in the process of breaking and spilling its contents. This suspended animation effect lends a cinematic quality to the material which the viewer experiences as motion rather than a static form or installation. The combination of Chinese blue and white porcelain and fruits references seventeenth-century Dutch still life painting, thus also lending a transmedial and temporal quality to the artwork and the sherds within it. His visually unstable works are historicized and metaphorical but the opposite of the strengthened, reconstructed whole pieces produced by Li Xiaofeng and Yeesookyung.

De Vries's work is informed by his training as a ceramic restorer, which is highlighted in other of his works which are sculptures composed of various whole and reconstructed ceramics in which fragments have been joined using the *kintsugi* technique discussed below, for example *Guan yin with a nimbus of saucers* (2019).[27] His preference for using this technique, and for Chinese ceramic fragments, even extends to broken earthenwares which are less commonly utilized in reconstructive ceramic art, where the preference is for high-fired fragments. The painted neolithic jar which forms the base of *Deconstructed Neolithic Machang Jar* (2019) has been reconstructed using *kintsugi* but only partially so that there are empty spaces between the fragments which nonetheless read as a whole piece.[28] The eye fills in the gaps but the view is also disturbed because the pieces could be fitted together more closely but the artist has chosen not to, thus emphasizing the instability of the new form.

Restoration

De Vries's repair work is, therefore, intentionally incomplete and uses the specific technique of *kintsugi* as a visual referent that activates the instability of the piece. Yeesookyung also used this technique to create remade but uneven vessels which are visually suggestive of instability. In normal usage, however, the aim of such restoration methods as *kintsugi* is to restore a completeness and stability, while at the same time emphasizing the damaged nature of the whole object and providing it with a new aesthetic. In this method, lacquer (or resin) join lines are gilt, as are areas of missing material, as can be seen in a repaired tea bowl, where the broken bowl has been restored to completeness but not fully restored to its original, unbroken state (Figure 1.8). This bowl, and others mended in a similar manner, are themselves translated, speaking a new language in which the brokenness is part of the new aesthetic of the bowl which now has a disrupted yet decorated surface. The repairs are a memory of the original flawless object. The new bowl further has been constructed from fragments which fit together, but now as pieces to be used within a craft medium. Unlike invisible repairs, which tell a false story of the object's integrity, *kintsugi* work integrates the object's damaged narrative into its new iteration. It is, therefore, both repair and artistic production.

Figure 1.8 Stoneware tea bowl with gold lacquer repairs, Japan, seventeenth century. National Museum of Asian Art, Smithsonian Institution, Freer Collection, gift of Charles Lang Freer', F1904.323.

Traditional *kintsugi* is composed of gilt lacquer and the earliest use of lacquer to repair ceramics can be seen in Jomon-period ceramics excavated in Japan.[29] As Bonnie Kemske notes in her history of *kintsugi*, an important development leading to the use of gold lacquer repairs was *yobitsugi* ("patchwork joins") where a fragment from another pot is used to fill a gap and make the repair. What is considered to be the oldest example utilizes a Chinese blue and white fragment to repair a Seto stoneware vessel.[30] The adhesive used here is the same colour as the clay of the piece being repaired but the first use of gold lacquer to repair a broken ceramic has been attributed to the artist Hon'ami Koetsu (1558–1637) and the cracked tea bowl made by him known as "Seppo" (snowy peak) in the collection of the Hatakeyama Memorial Museum of Fine Art.[31] It was unusual for an artist to repair a flawed piece he had made himself but by the Edo period (1603–1868), gold repairs were produced regularly by the artisans skilled in the lacquer decoration technique known as *maki-e* ("sprinkled picture").[32] Lacquer artisans used their specialist craft skills to work on ceramics, thus integrating the two materials through the remaking of one using another.

Traditional and modern *kintsugi* is therefore an intermedial practice utilizing lacquer plus gold plus ceramic, with the ceramic fragments being used as part of the collective media. It is a different conception of "repair" which might be (and often is) reduced to a certain Japanese sensibility associated with so-called *wabi-sabi* 侘寂 aesthetics. But it could more accurately be seen as one of several approaches to the use and re-use of ceramic fragments in artistic production, where the medium is ceramic in a certain form that can be at once trash and treasure, depending on how it is manipulated and presented.

Conclusion

In this chapter, I have explored different approaches to the use of East Asian ceramic fragments as medium and metaphor, participating in a range of transformations: archaeological waste to museum object; vessels to tiles; fragments to whole; vessels to sculpture/garments; broken to restored. The sherd, reduced in most contexts to evidence of damage and secondary to a greater primary context or object, has been shown to have been used intentionally as a material in its own right. When foregrounded by either makers or viewers, sherds can be seen to be a category of object with distinctive characteristics and an independent existence. They are a versatile medium that, as secondary products, contain several narratives. Their production and use is also connected to the region of East Asia, where the earliest high-fired ceramics were produced and the most widespread distribution of any ceramic type was instigated with the world's first porcelain. The ceramic sherd is therefore culturally and visually associated with East Asia as the originary locus for porcelains and celadons. Within East Asia, the sherd additionally represents the long-standing traditions of ceramic manufacture, production, and commerce. No other ceramic culture is as well-known or respected, nor is any tradition of ceramic consumption as continuously long-standing. Thus the multifaceted nature of the sherd from East Asia as the transcultural, transmediary, and transformed object of a wider sherd culture.

Notes

1. https://www.yatzer.com/porcelain-polo-shirt-li-xiaofeng (accessed 30 May 2022).
2. For example, Chinese ceramics set into funerary architecture on the Swahili Coast, in the walls of the shell grotto at Palacio Fronteira in Lisbon, and the porcelain rooms in Britain, such as at Tart Hall in London. See Bing Zhao, "Global Trade and Swahili Cosmopolitan Material Culture: Chinese-Style Ceramic Shards from Sanje ya Kati and Songo Mnara (Kilwa, Tanzania)", *Journal of World History* 23, no. 1 (2012): 66; Penelope Hobhouse and Patrick Taylor, *The Gardens of Europe* (Random House, 1990), 144; and Juliet Claxton, "The Countess of Arundel's Dutch Pranketing Room: 'An Inventory of all the Parcells or Purselin, glasses and other Goods now remayning in the Pranketing Roome at Tart Hall, 8th Sept 1641'", *Journal of the History of Collections* 22, no. 2 (2010): 187–96.
3. Stacey Pierson, "Fragments of China: Destruction, Location and the Collecting of Chinese Architectural Remains in 19th century Britain", *Transactions of the Oriental Ceramic Society* 84 (October 2021): 37–50.
4. Zhao, "Global Trade and Swahili Cosmopolitan Material Culture", 41–85; the classic Prudence Rice, *Pottery Analysis: A Sourcebook*, 2nd edition (University of Chicago Press, 2015); Jian

Zhu, Hongjiao Ma, Naisheng Li, Julian Henderson and Michael D. Glascock, "The Provenance of Export Porcelain from the Nan'ao One Shipwreck in the South China Sea", *Antiquity* 90, no. 351 (2016): 798–808; Stacey Pierson, "Production, Distribution, and Aesthetics: Abundance and Chinese Porcelain from Jingdezhen, 1350–1800 AD", in Monica L. Smith (ed.), *Abundance: The Archaeology of Plenitude* (University Press of Colorado, 2017), 229–50; Craig Cessford, "Moving in Mysterious Ways: The Use and Discard of Cambridge College Ceramics", *Antiquity* 92, no. 364 (2018): 1076–93; Pierson, "Fragments of China".

5. Clive Orton and Michael Hughes, *Pottery in Archaeology*, 2nd edition (Cambridge University Press, 2013), 11.

6. Palace Museum Archaeology Institute, "故宫南大库瓷片埋藏坑发掘简报" (Brief Report on the Excavation of the Burial Pit of Porcelain Pieces in the South Library of the Forbidden City), *Journal of the Palace Museum*, 4, no. 186 (2016): 6–25.

7. For example, Palace Museum and the Archaeological Research Institute of Ceramic in Jingdezhen. *The Porcelain of Imperial Kiln in Ming and Qing Dynasties* (Forbidden City Publishing House, 2016), figs. 144–152.

8. Craig Cessford, Andy Hall, Vicki Herring and Richard Newman, "'To Clapham's I go': A Mid to Late 18th-Century Cambridge Coffeehouse Assemblage", *Post-Medieval Archaeology* 51, no. 2 (2017): 372–426.

9. https://collections.museumoflondon.org.uk/online/object/73557.html (accessed 30 May 2022).

10. The display and sale of sherds of East Asian ceramics recovered from shipwrecks has also contributed to the collecting of ceramic fragments as objects, with their status as remains contributing to their allure. Shipwreck ceramics, most of which are Chinese due to the scale of the trade from China, are now a category for both private and museum collecting with entire galleries dedicated to their display. A recent example is the Tang Treasures gallery in the Asian Civilisations Museum, Singapore, which exhibits much of the remains of what is known as the Belitung shipwreck, which sank in Indonesian waters in the late ninth century.

11. This is known as 陶溪川 Tao Xichuan and the hotel is the Tao Xichuan Hotel, run by Hyatt. https://www.hyatt.com/en-US/hotel/china/taoxichuan-hotel/jdzub (accessed December 2023). Arita in Saga prefecture, Japan has created a similar visitor experience that highlights the production history of local porcelain with dedicated museums presenting historical finds as well as sherds such as the Kyushu Ceramic Museum and tourist attractions such as the Arita Porcelain Park. https://saga-museum.jp/ceramic_en/ (accessed 24 October 2024).

12. On porcelain rooms, see Cordula Bischoff, "Women Collectors and the Rise of the Porcelain Cabinet", in Jan van Campen and Titus M. Eliëns (eds.), *Chinese and Japanese Porcelain for the Dutch Golden Age* (Rijksmuseum Amsterdam, 2014), 171–90. On the chinikhaneh at Ardebil, see Kishwar Rizvi, "Site of Pilgrimage and Objects of Devotion", in Sheila R. Canby (ed.), *Shah 'Abbas: the Remaking of Iran* (British Museum Press, 2009), 98–115.

13. Andrea Montella, "Chinese Porcelain as a Symbol of Power on the East African Coast from the 14th Century Onward", *Ming Qing Yanjiu* 20, no. 1 (2016): 74–93.

14. Katherine M.D. Dunbabin, *Mosaics of the Greek and Roman World* (Cambridge University Press, 1999), 30.

15. Liz James, *Mosaics in the Medieval World: From Late Antiquity to the Fifteenth Century* (Cambridge University Press, 2017).

16. Robin Watson, "Shells and Grottoes in Early Modern Germany", in Marisa Anne Bass, Anne Goldgar, Hanneke Grootenboer and Claudia Swan, *Conchophilia: Shells, Art and Curiosity in Early Modern Europe* (Princeton University Press, 2021), 127–54.

17. Cinta Krahe, "The Reception and Value of Chinese Porcelain in Habsburg Spain", in Anna Grasskamp and Monica Juneja (eds.), *EurAsian Matters: China, Europe and the Transcultural Object, 1600–1800* (Springer, 2018), 222.
18. Rose Kerr and Nigel Wood, *Science and Civilisation in China*, vol. V, part 12: *Ceramic Technology* (Cambridge University Press, 2004), 711.
19. Yanyu Li, Mingyi Zhao, Jingyi Mao, Yile Chen, Liang Zheng and Lina Yan, "Detection and Recognition of Chinese Porcelain Inlay Images of Traditional Lingnan Architectural Decoration Based on YOLOv4 Technology", *Heritage Science* 12, no. 137 (2024).
20. See feature on CCTV, 2011: http://english.cntv.cn/program/cultureexpress/20110525/103729.shtml (accessed 5 December 2022).
21. 2013.5. Currently on display in the metalwork gallery, the museum's acquisition was supported by the ArtFund: https://www.artfund.org/supporting-museums/art-weve-helped-buy/artwork/12402/regence-ormolu-mounted-chinese-porcelain-casket.
22. https://www.yatzer.com/porcelain-polo-shirt-li-xiaofeng (accessed 6 June 2022).
23. Li Xiaofeng, Parade No. 2, 2010, Song Period Shards, 123 × 48 × 29 cm, Red Gate Gallery, 2019.
24. Allison R. Miller, *Kingly Splendour: Court Art and Materiality in Han China* (Columbia University Press, 2020).
25. One fine example recovered from a tomb at Shizishan, Xuzhou was sewn together with gold threads. See James C.S. Lin (ed.), *The Search for Immortality: Tomb Treasures of Han China* (Fitzwilliam Museum, University of Cambridge, 2012), 46 and cat. 87.
26. "Yeesookyung – Why I Create", interview with the artist in association with the publication of *Vitamin C: Clay and Ceramic in Contemporary Art* (Phaidon). https://www.phaidon.com/agenda/art/articles/2018/january/24/yeesookyung-why-i-create/ (accessed 7 December 2022).
27. Private collection. Sold by Adrian Sassoon: https://www.adriansassoon.com/contemporary/guan-yin-with-a-nimbus-of-saucers-2019/ (accessed 7 December 2022).
28. https://boukedevries.com/works-2/nggallery/page/2/image/deconstructed-neolithic-machang-jar-a (accessed 7 December 2022).
29. Bonnie Kemske, *Kintsugi: The Poetic Mend* (Bloomsbury, 2021), 66 and fig. 53.
30. Kemske, *Kintsugi: The Poetic Mend*, 74 and fig. 59.
31. Kemske, *Kintsugi: The Poetic Mend*, 75.
32. Kemske, *Kintsugi: The Poetic Mend*, 79.

References

Bischoff, Cordula. "Women Collectors and the Rise of the Porcelain Cabinet", in Jan van Campen and Titus M. Eliëns (eds.), *Chinese and Japanese Porcelain for the Dutch Golden Age*, Rijksmuseum Amsterdam, 2014, pp. 171–90.

Cessford, Craig. "Moving in Mysterious Ways: The Use and Discard of Cambridge College Ceramics", *Antiquity* 92, no. 364 (2018): 1076–93. https://doi.org/10.15184/aqy.2018.115.

Cessford, Craig, Andy Hall, Vicki Herring and Richard Newman, "'To Clapham's I go': A Mid to Late 18th-Century Cambridge Coffeehouse Assemblage", *Post-Medieval Archaeology* 51, no. 2 (2017): 372–426. https://doi.org/10.1080/00794236.2017.1363146.

Claxton, Juliet. "The Countess of Arundel's Dutch Pranketing Room: 'An Inventory of all the Parcells or Purselin, glasses and other Goods now remayning in the Pranketing Roome at Tart Hall, 8th Sept 1641'", *Journal of the History of Collections* 22, no. 2 (2010): 187–96. https://doi.org/10.1093/jhc/fhp035.

Dunbabin, Katherine M.D. *Mosaics of the Greek and Roman World*, Cambridge University Press, 1999.

Gerritsen, Anne. *City of Blue and White: Chinese Porcelain and the Early Modern World*, Cambridge University Press, 2020.

Hobhouse, Penelope and Patrick Taylor. *The Gardens of Europe*, Random House, 1990.

James, Liz. *Mosaics in the Medieval World: From Late Antiquity to the Fifteenth Century*, Cambridge University Press, 2017.

Kemske, Bonnie. *Kintsugi: The Poetic Mend*, Bloomsbury, 2021.

Kerr, Rose and Nigel Wood. *Science and Civilisation in China, vol. V, part 12: Ceramic Technology*, Cambridge University Press, 2004.

Krahe, Cinta. "The Reception and Value of Chinese Porcelain in Habsburg Spain", in Anna Grasskamp and Monica Juneja (eds.), *EurAsian Matters: China, Europe and the Transcultural Object, 1600–1800*, Springer, 2018, pp. 221–38.

Li, Yanyu, Mingyi Zhao, Jingyi Mao, Yile Chen, Liang Zheng and Lina Yan. "Detection and Recognition of Chinese Porcelain Inlay Images of Traditional Lingnan Architectural Decoration Based on YOLOv4 Technology", *Heritage Science* 12, no. 137 (2024). https://doi.org/10.1186/s40494-024-01227-z.

Lin, James C.S. ed. *The Search for Immortality: Tomb Treasures of Han China*, Fitzwilliam Museum, University of Cambridge, 2012.

Miller, Allison R. *Kingly Splendour: Court Art and Materiality in Han China*, Columbia University Press, 2020.

Montella, Andrea. "Chinese Porcelain as a Symbol of Power on the East African Coast from the 14th Century Onward", *Ming Qing Yanjiu* 20, no. 1 (2016): 74–93. https://doi.org/10.1163/24684791-12340004.

Orton, Clive and Michael Hughes. *Pottery in Archaeology*, 2nd edition, Cambridge University Press, 2013.

Palace Museum Archaeology Institute. "故宫南大库瓷片埋藏坑发掘简报" (Brief Report on the Excavation of the Burial Pit of Porcelain Pieces in the South Library of the Forbidden City), *Journal of the Palace Museum*, 4, no. 186 (2016): 6–25. https://doi.org/10.16319/j.cnki.0452-7402.2016.04.001.

Palace Museum and the Archaeological Research Institute of Ceramic in Jingdezhen. *The Porcelain of Imperial Kiln in Ming and Qing Dynasties*, Forbidden City Publishing House, 2016.

Pierson, Stacey. "Production, Distribution, and Aesthetics: Abundance and Chinese Porcelain from Jingdezhen, 1350–1800 AD", in Monica L. Smith (ed.), *Abundance: The Archaeology of Plenitude*, University Press of Colorado, 2017, pp. 229–50.

Pierson, Stacey. "Fragments of China: Destruction, Location and the Collecting of Chinese Architectural Remains in 19th Century Britain", *Transactions of the Oriental Ceramic Society* 84 (October 2021): 37–50.

Rice, Prudence. *Pottery Analysis: A Sourcebook*, 2nd edition, University of Chicago Press, 2015.

Rizvi, Kishwar. "Site of Pilgrimage and Objects of Devotion", in Sheila R. Canby (ed.), *Shah 'Abbas: the Remaking of Iran*, British Museum Press, 2009, 98–115.

Watson, Robin. "Shells and Grottoes in Early Modern Germany", in Marisa Anne Bass, Anne Goldgar, Hanneke Grootenboer and Claudia Swan, *Conchophilia: Shells, Art and Curiosity in Early Modern Europe*, Princeton University Press, 2021, 127–54.

"Yeesookyung – Why I Create", interview with the artist in association with the publication of *Vitamin C: Clay and Ceramic in Contemporary Art* (Phaidon). https://www.phaidon.com/agenda/art/articles/2018/january/24/yeesookyung-why-i-create/.

Zhao, Bing. "Global Trade and Swahili Cosmopolitan Material Culture: Chinese-Style Ceramic Shards from Sanje ya Kati and Songo Mnara (Kilwa, Tanzania)", *Journal of World History* 23, no. 1 (2012): 41–85. http://www.jstor.org/stable/41508051.

Zhu, Jian, Hongjiao Ma, Naisheng Li, Julian Henderson and Michael D. Glascock. "The Provenance of Export Porcelain from the Nan'ao One Shipwreck in the South China Sea", *Antiquity* 90, no. 351 (2016): 798–808. https://doi.org/10.15184/aqy.2016.67.

CHAPTER 2
FOUND OBJECTS IN HONG KONG JEWELLERY DESIGN: SOCIAL CONNECTIONS AND MATERIAL AGENCY IN SOUTHERN CHINA[1]
Anna Grasskamp

While *objets trouvés* from the ocean's shores, for example shells, have played an important role in Chinese craftsmanship for centuries, modern types of found objects, such as items of plastic garbage picked up from polluted beaches, have recently been integrated into design as part of a response to growing concerns about sustainability. Focusing on southern China, in particular Hong Kong, this essay highlights aspects of global and local connectivity in art, design, and material culture by investigating several examples of the reuse of organic and inorganic (waste) materials in creative practices. Analysing items of wearable and collectible jewellery, the chapter investigates the "social lives" of found objects and discarded items that have been integrated into artefacts, with a special focus on ideas on "material agency" and ecologies of matter. Rooted in art history, the chapter's approach to craftsmanship, design, and material culture is informed by a number of interdisciplinary positions in the field, including the writings of the political scientist Jane Bennett, the philosopher Gaston Bachelard, and the chemist, biotechnologist, and engineer Chetput Venkatasubban Seshradi, as well as sources from the early modern period that address aspects of matter, materiality, and ecology. The chapter argues that through the lens of what Bennett calls "vital materiality",[2] the ways trash and discarded materials have been used by creative practitioners based in Hong Kong can be seen as subversive on several levels. First, as subverting the material hierarchies of commercial trade by using trash in place of precious materials; second as subverting the "local" and the "global" by using materials commonly perceived to be "local" as part of a global movement of material reuse; and third as subversive in terms of agency as the found items in these artefacts prompt and to a certain extent guide the maker's hands, rather than the other way round.

Jewellery design has been chosen as the case study because, within the wider field of creative practices that engage with recycling, it lends itself particularly well to in-depth research due to long-standing traditions of repurposing materials for decorative use. Goldsmiths and makers of wearables have not only integrated and reused organic materials and animal products for centuries, but have also developed manifold strategies to melt and reshape precious metal objects. They have remounted and reset valuable gemstones and other objects that were originally found in nature or passed down from one generation to the next. In addition to reuse and recycling, the practice of upcycling – the reuse of materials and objects to create new objects of greater value – has been crucial to recent jewellery design practices. In contemporary art markets and white cube museum settings, jewellery design from Asia plays a less visible and significant role than ink painting, sculpture, or installation art. Yet, jewellery making is a creative practice that is important for Hong Kong people in special ways, because most of them possess and inherit crafted objects for personal adornment and, due to cramped living spaces, it is mainly small decorative or artistic objects, rather than large sculptures or paintings that play significant roles in people's immediate living environments.

Found objects and material hierarchies

Recycling – the reuse of processed materials in the creation of new objects – has a short history in the daily practices of Hong Kong's middle-class households, but a long history in global art and design. For many centuries, Chinese material culture has played a special role in the recycling of objects and materials across cultural boundaries. This is illustrated by the reuse of Chinese porcelain vessels in early modern Europe, such as in the integration of Ming and Qing dynasty porcelain vessels as a ceiling decoration in Lisbon's former Santos Palace. While transcultural examples such as this illustrate how the values and uses attributed to artefacts from China can change in different cultural settings, in China itself objects would also be repurposed and recycled, for example across chronological divides. Examples include the reuse of ancient jade objects through the carving of Neolithic *cong* jades into new shapes, the attachment of Yuan dynasty hat knobs to the lids of Ming-dynasty incense burners, and the implementation of ancient jade plaques into the designs of wooden Qing dynasty jewellery boxes. While jade was considered the superior matter in Ming-dynasty material hierarchies of northern China, period sources describe pearls from the Guangdong prefectures as its southern equivalent.

Song Yingxing's treatise *The Work of Heaven and the Inception of Things* of 1637 refers to the northwestern province of Xinjiang where jade is "the glory of China's mountains" and to the southwestern prefecture of Liangzhou in Guangdong where "pearls reign supreme".[3] As with pearls, the moon and the forces of water are involved in the creation of jade and, like "jade that is still encased in its rock crust, the value of a pearl inside a mussel [or oyster] is unknown, and becomes manifest only after it has been taken out and examined".[4] The treatise establishes the ocean treasury as a counterpart to mountainous and subterranean treasure troves, presenting the practices of diving and fishing for maritime riches as the terminological and conceptual equivalences of mining and excavating; it frames pearls and gemstones as materializations of the northern earth's and the southern ocean's powers to produce and transform matter.[5] As this illustrates, in the Ming dynasty and earlier, southern Chinese material culture is branded as oceanic. In terms of craftsmanship, this implies a reliance on maritime materials such as shells and pearls, but also an intense engagement with artefacts entering China through maritime trade, in particular objects from the "Western Ocean" (*xi yang*).[6]

During the Qing dynasty, the southern Chinese city of Guangzhou, a forward-looking harbour city in terms of global innovations in craftsmanship and technology, emerged as the globalized, open-door counterpart to the imperially monitored northern capital Beijing. It was in Guangzhou where merchants of all countries merged and mingled and where there was also space for pirates and other subversive agents who undermined the strict imperial rules and regulations designed in Beijing. Here a truly globalized Eurasian material culture emerged, which supplemented and blended into the symbolically loaded microcosm of collectibles compiled at the imperial court.[7] This global material culture went beyond artefacts exported to Europe or made on the command of the imperial court; Guangzhou craftsmanship, for example carpentry, informed the material culture of the region itself.[8] The phenomenon of transculturation was not limited to the craftsmanship of art, artefact, and utensil-making but also affected China's botanical diversity as European and American plants arrived through Guangzhou, first for elite gardens, later – as nature replicates in uncontrolled ways – in the wild.[9] In this context, craftsmanship and material exchange take on powerful and arguably subversive roles, as it is through the tacit knowledge and activities of people such as pearl fishers, gardeners, Guangzhou workshop craftsmen, and agents involved in (illegal) trade practices that the material culture of southern China evolved, supplementing and to some extent countering Beijing's material ecologies that were shaped by imperial aesthetics and the "Qing palace machine".[10]

The historical distinction between material cultures of the north and the south further intensified when, in the twentieth century south of Guangzhou, in the British colony of Hong Kong, craftsmanship and design started to flourish. Having become a haven for artisans who fled the communist regime in mainland China, in particular those involved in the production of luxury commodities, Hong Kong came to replace Guangzhou and Shanghai as gold trade and jewellery centres after the Second World War,[11] emerging as a vibrant commercial hub. Today, global brand jewellery shops feature prominently in the city while the small-scale local practices of experimental jewellery craftsmanship are marginalized on the market and in scholarship. While commercial jewellery makers engage with a variety of cultivated materials (such as southern Chinese pearls and mother of pearl) as well as mined matter (including gold, silver, and gemstones), the materials that experimental jewellery artists in Hong Kong engage with include discarded plastic bottles and aluminium cans. In strong contrast to the established gold-fetishizing jewellery brands that Hong Kong is famous for, these trash-using makers pay attention to materials that are mined from the urban jungle of Hong Kong's streets and beaches.

Eco art, DIY, and activism

A creative engagement with trash is not Hong Kong-specific. Yet, it is important to note that Asia is currently the world's number one garbage dumping destination despite recent waste import bans to China.[12] Accordingly, the inhabitants of some Asian cities that contain more garbage than other metropolises have more intense relationships to discarded materials than people in places like Berlin, Tokyo, and New York. While contemporary artists' engagement with garbage has been analysed and conceptualized,[13] most recently as "constitutive of an ecological consciousness",[14] China-specific studies have come to alternative conclusions. Margaret Hillenbrand argues that contemporary art from China that employs garbage renders the figure of the ragpicker invisible and enables works that profess a "politically correct sympathy" for the myriads of people in China who live with and from waste while at the same time keeping them "out of the picture" in socially sanitized objects of art.[15] In contrast, Meiqin Wang argues that some of the very same trash-using artworks that Hillenbrand criticizes, "contribute to the growth of bottom-up civic consciousness and public space".[16] Wang's argument is in line with scholars of environmental activism in China who consider ecological art as a political statement and a critique by artists and activists of the communist regime's concept of "ecological civilization" (*shengtai wenming*) that presents the environmental crisis as a "non-Chinese" problem by ruling out Chinese responsibility and blaming global circumstances.[17] In addition, the works of Chinese artists who reuse discarded materials have been interpreted in line with the concept of "Material Art" (*caizhi yishu*), which emerged in the 1980s in different genres like painting, sculpture, installation, and performance.[18] These somewhat contradictory insights derived from research on the People's Republic of China are of limited use for understanding Hong Kong's art and design worlds, which are deeply entangled with mainland Chinese practices but also closely embedded within global circuits of creation, curation, and sales.[19] This mix between global, mainland Chinese, and local points of reference also informs creative practices in Hong Kong that engage with ecology, for example under the label of eco art.

Born in Beijing, educated in the United States and based in Hong Kong for many years, artist and university-based educator Zheng Bo (b. 1974) exhibits work concerned with Hong Kong-related and Hong Kong-unrelated aspects of (queer) ecology and art internationally. Together with his co-editor Lee Sohl, Zheng Bo has enriched the English-language scholarly discourse on art and ecology, which they describe as being formerly based on "reservoirs of ideas" drawn from "scientific studies, theories by thinkers in the West, indigenous cosmologies, and climate change activism", through contributions to a 2015 issue of the *Journal of Contemporary Chinese Art* dedicated to contemporary art and ecology in East Asia.[20] Belonging to a younger generation of Hong Kong eco artists than Zheng Bo, some of the works by Guangdong-born Hong Kong-based eco artist Trevor Yeung (b. 1988) employ "flora, fish and other biota" that the artist "calls his readymades".[21] Other important positions in the field of Hong Kong eco art are taken by artist-activists. They include Natalie Lo Lai-lai (b. 1988), who refers to herself as a half-farmer and half-artist/journalist, Michael Leung, who identifies as an artist/designer, researcher, and urban farmer, and Tsang Tak-ping (b. 1959), who, after working at the School of Design at Hong Kong Polytechnic University for many years, co-founded the School of Everyday Life and committed to living a secluded life of farming, promoting mindfulness and sustainability.[22] Many of the works of Hong Kong artists who engage with ecology (including those mentioned above) also draw on practices of recycling and reuse.[23] In the Hong Kong pavilion of the 52nd Venice Biennale in 2007, for which its curator Norman Ford took "the very problematic of national representation itself as a point of departure",[24] Hong Kong-based artists/architects Laurent Gutierrez (b. 1966)

Figure 2.1 liina klauss, "River of Rubbish", 100 cubic metres of marine debris collected on Shui Hau Beach in Hong Kong within two days, 2014.

and Valérie Portefaix (b. 1969), known as MAP Office, used Hong Kong-specific organic waste, namely oyster shells associated with the city's signature product oyster sauce, to allude to the territory of Hong Kong itself.[25] Another prominent example is Bali- and Hong Kong-based artist-activist liina klauss (b. 1974), who reuses inorganic garbage found along Hong Kong's coasts. Presenting herself as a "beach curator"[26] and an "art awareness activist",[27] liina klauss's projects include community-based activities in which volunteers participate in beach clean-ups and the creation of land art installations made out of discarded objects (Figure 2.1).[28]

As in many other cities worldwide, Hong Kong holds green events.[29] Some of them are specifically dedicated to recycling involving artistic components, including an intervention on the reuse of textiles at *Green Summer Festival* in 2014 led by jewellery artist and university professor Cicy Sze-yin Ching titled "Alchemy: Green Fiber Jewelry – an Idea Exchange".[30] Works such as those created by liina klauss and Cicy Sze-yin Ching in collaboration with volunteers can be understood within the framework of Do-It-Yourself (DIY) movements. liina klauss's interventions in public space can more specifically be understood as DIY urbanism and considered as impermanent "micro-spatial practices that are reshaping urban spaces".[31]

In Europe and Great Britain, the destruction suffered during the Second World War and subsequent shortages of material goods and skilled craftsmen played an important role in the systematic development of DIY practices and their promotion through journals during the 1950s and 1960s. These first covered skills such as bricklaying or wallpaper hanging and moved on to such things as the crafting of Christmas decorations and children's toys, furniture-making, and interior design.[32] In the United States, the emergence of DIY urbanism is rooted in nineteenth-century civic engagement.[33] In terms of global movements, DIY is, however, more commonly associated with the 1970s. The American counterculture of the hippie movement went beyond the making of items for domestic use by claiming public space, recycling materials as a political statement against capitalism and creating dome-shaped shelters inspired by the pioneering designer, architect, and inventor Richard Buckminster Fuller (1895–1983). Buckminster Fuller wrote extensively on his philosophy of design and, aware of the Earth's finite resources, was an early environmental activist who anticipated global warming and advocated for the use of technological innovations on behalf of all people. By the 1970s, his architectural designs for dome buildings were distributed via counterculture publications and inspired the Zomes of Drop City, a Colorado artists' community that used recycled materials they referred to as "the garbage of America".[34] While Buckminster Fuller's visions and the anti-capitalist and anti-consumerist agenda of the hippie communities of the 1970s informed subsequent DIY movements in the Western world, in Asia thinkers like the chemist, biotechnologist, and engineer Chetput Venkatasubban Seshradi (1930–1995) took recycling practices in Indian slums as the basis for the development of the "aesthetics of a new science around the scavenger and forager as a hero".[35] In Seshradi's understanding, the recycling of waste as "the only resource of a wasted people"[36] makes the recycler a storyteller who does not only extend the material life of an object but adds another chapter to waste's inventiveness. Not merely reworking materiality, recyclers engage with the potential of ideas and creativity to interpret the "polyphony of waste" that goes beyond obsolescence, essentially "subverting the very definition of uselessness" through memory and craft.[37] In his study of debates on waste in modern and contemporary India, Shiv Visvanathan refers to "craft as a skill" that "pluralizes waste into a variety of dialects which can be lived out in different ways"[38] through the body as a sensorium. Visvanathan transfers Seshradi's insights derived from his experiences in slums to the art world. In a similar way to Seshradi, who did not differentiate between what he observed in the slums and what he wished to develop for science, Visvanathan does not differentiate between the aesthetics of untrained recyclers and professional designers. Looking through the lens of waste, he sees both as interpreters of polyphonous matter and masters of bricolage where tinkering and improvisation are united across sociocultural divides by their perception of waste as a resource.

In Hong Kong, a city with a remarkable wealth gap between its "crazy rich" and a growing number of impoverished inhabitants,[39] recycling as a strategy for survival (as experienced by Seshradi in the slums of Chennai) exists side by side with other recycling practices: the city centre features cardboard collectors who struggle to recycle for a living alongside shops with second-hand clothes frequented by hipsters wearing Veja sneakers;[40]

its streets present us with self-designed "bastard chairs"[41] made from garbage for daily use and exclusive spaces in which artists and designers exhibit highly prized works made from recycled matter. While creative practices of engaging with garbage as a structural outcome of the "slow violence" towards poor, disempowered, and involuntarily displaced people is visible in Hong Kong, the "environmentalism of the poor"[42] is structurally less pronounced, developed, or widespread due to demographic differences than it is in India and mainland China. Margaret Hillenbrand's argument, inspired by the creative practices of a girl growing up in a house built on a Chinese garbage dump, that contemporary art from China that employs garbage renders the figure of ragpickers like this girl invisible, is therefore of limited applicability for understanding garbage-collecting practices and their artistic appropriation in Hong Kong. As I will argue below, Hong Kong-made wearables that result from creative practices of reuse form evidence of a relationship between scavenging and design in which some of the makers act in solidarity with "the figure of the ragpicker", partially because the fabric of the city carries political meanings that unite people across social divides.

Extending the life of objects in a disappearing city

The traditional importance of maritime material culture in Hong Kong is reflected in the Ming-dynasty treatise cited above that refers to China's southern coastal regions as having been the country's main sites for pearl cultivation since antiquity.[43] Although oyster pearl farming has undergone a recent revival in Hong Kong,[44] an awareness of the increasingly limited capacity of the ocean to supply pearls, corals, and shells for use by jewellery designers has grown. In fact, the shores of Hong Kong and other parts of Asia are covered in plastic objects. Local artists have responded to these changes by placing pearls and other maritime materials that are deemed precious alongside plastic bottle caps, sea glass, and other found objects from Hong Kong's beaches to create small sculptures and objects for personal adornment. These practices can be seen in line with the century-old southern Chinese engagement with maritime material culture as a twenty-first-century update in an age of ocean pollution, but they can also be understood within global frameworks of reuse. Take Chan Wing-sze Cissy's *Far Sea Ring* as an example (Figure 2.2). It is both locally and globally informed in terms of materiality and aesthetics. The plastic fish-shaped container that once held soy sauce is a standard item in contemporary takeaway *sushi bento* boxes all over the globe. As it is difficult to clean, it is not very suitable for reuse and thus contributes to the considerable amount of waste left behind after enjoying a takeaway bento. Chan's ring combines a pearl cultured in Hong Kong, an organic object grown out of local ecologies, with a plastic representation of a fish that symbolizes global fast-food culture and pollution. It is filled with small plastic pearls reminiscent of the micro plastic particles that have become part of fish as well as human bodies. This piece of jewellery aestheticizes both items, the organic object of the pearl as crafted by nature and the plastic fish that would normally be considered garbage (while reappearing in works by artists and designers worldwide).[45] It is not the

The Dynamics of Modern Asian Design

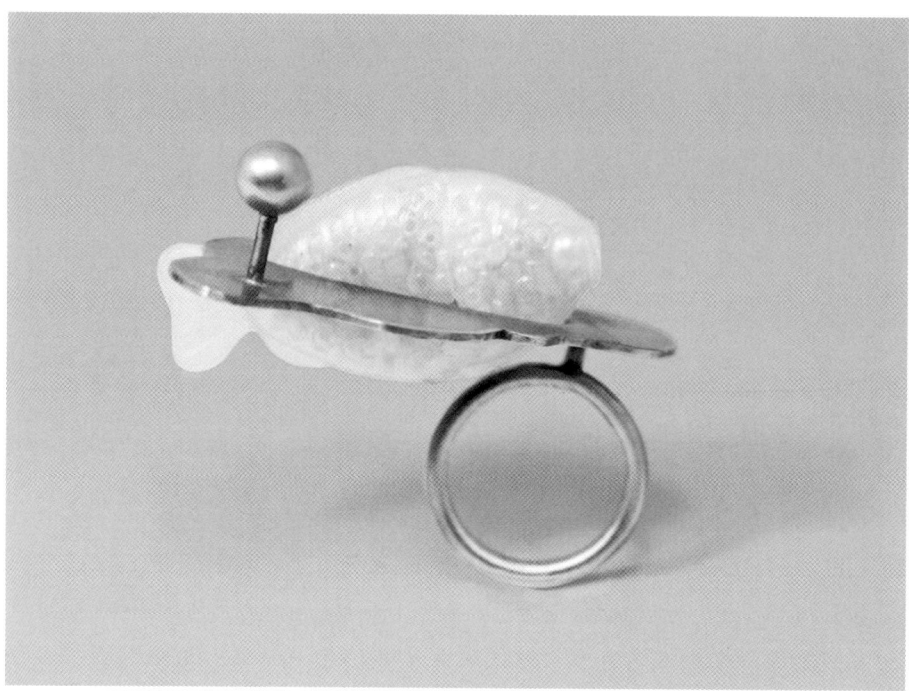

Figure 2.2 Chan Wing-sze, Cissy, "Far Sea Ring", plastic soy container, brass, pearl, 5.2 × 3.5 × 4.0 cm, 2020.

Figure 2.3a Chung Ka-pang, Adrian, "Living", construction work debris, etched brass, series of brooches of variable size, 2016–21. Free WalkIn.

Found Objects in Hong Kong Jewellery Design

Figure 2.3b (top), **2.3c** (bottom) Details of Figure 2.3a.

commonly perceived difference in material value that matters to Chan, whose design ennobles rubbish by lifting trash to the level of a pearl, but the carefully crafted frame of her ring makes us see another fundamental difference between the two items: while the industrially designed fish can be taken out of its metal frame and replaced by any other mass-produced soy sauce container, the pearl remains unique.

Fragments of the fabric of Hong Kong also play a key role in the work *Living* by Chung Ka-pang Adrian, a series of brooches created between 2016 and 2021 (Figure 2.3a). In contrast to Chan's pearl, these fragments are not locally cultivated and organically grown but manmade, as Chung presents us with brooches crafted from construction work debris and metal. Each brooch is provided with a date and the name of a place. Their display includes a frame of artfully etched brass plates that depict the floor plan of a building, denoting the specificities of the construction site origin of its component parts (Figures 2.3b, 2.3c). Chung's brooches ennoble debris and form evidence of the ever-changing urban fabric of Hong Kong, but they also document a city's destruction during the particular moment of the pieces' making between 2016 and 2021 when the city underwent fundamental instances of reorganization not only on a spatial and architectural level, but also socially and politically. In this sense, the brooches can be seen as holding on to places of the past and memories of a city in more than a material sense alone.

A similar approach is taken by another body of brooches, Ching Sze-yin Cicy's *Made in Hong Kong* series (Figure 2.4a). Like Chan and Chung, Ching ennobles everyday materials normally considered to be garbage by reusing and framing fragments of Hong

Figure 2.4a Ching Sze-yin, Cicy, "Made in Hong Kong Series", pressed glass from old screen, sea glass, gem stones, plastic, silver base metal stud, variable size, 2000–21. Free WalkIn.

Figure 2.4b (top), **2.4c** (bottom) Details of Figure 2.4a.

Kong sea glass found at the ocean's shore and shards from a type of pressed glass sheet traditionally used for so-called "Manchurian windows" or "Guangzhou-style stained glass windows" that are one of the defining characteristics of Lingnan architecture in the urban centres of Guangzhou, Foshan, Dongguan, and Hong Kong (Figure 2.4b). Upcycling pieces from pressed glass sheets that form part of the material heritage of southern China, Ching frames fragments of past craftsmanship in silver, treating them like jewels. Reusing lids of disposable plastic containers for takeaway food, she places them behind plastic sheets with the barely visible inscription "made in Hong Kong". This label became controversial in 2020, the same year that Ching's jewellery series began, when, in response to the political changes in Hong Kong, US president Donald Trump announced that goods imported from Hong Kong to the US should no longer carry the label "Made in Hong Kong" but instead be marked "Made in China", a proposal that was enforced by 29 July 2020.[46] For Hong Kong people, the abandonment of the "Made in Hong Kong" label did not only concern trade policies but directly touched identity issues, symbolically marking the erasure of features that make the city unique. All brooches in the series carry the semi-transparent "Made in Hong Kong" inscription, among them a large colourful one (Figure 2.4c). Made from gems, pate de verre glass, and sea glass found on Hong Kong's beaches, this brooch's colour scheme is the same as that of the famous Tutti Frutti jewellery by Cartier with its bold combination of bright pink, blue, green, and white jewels. While the Tutti Frutti pieces use diamonds, rubies, emeralds, and sapphires in leaf and berry shapes, the Hong Kong brooch treats pieces of sea glass like jewels, paying tribute to the colourful treasures found on Hong Kong beaches. Carrying the words "Made in Hong Kong", Ching's brooches proudly celebrate local materials.[47] Like Chung's ennoblement of construction site debris, at a crucial moment of sociopolitical transition Ching embraces discarded fragments of the fabric of a city that carry different symbolic meanings than comparable pieces of glass and plastic would in the material cultures of metropolises like Berlin, Tokyo, or New York. By immortalizing discarded things that were made in Hong Kong in her brooches, Ching holds on to fragments of urban material culture that existed before the introduction of the national security law in 2020 and before she relocated to Canada in 2021 as part of the exodus of thousands of inhabitants prompted by the handover of Hong Kong to China in 1997 and intensified by the introduction of the national security law in 2020. Belonging to the educated middle class of the city but performing like a waste collector, Ching arguably acts in solidarity with the figure of the ragpicker at a time when a politically divided city sees some of its poor and deprived unite with those committed to freedom of expression across social divides.

In addition to experimental jewellery artists like Chan, Chung, and Ching who exhibit and sell work directly or through the mediation of galleries specializing in crafts,[48] Hong Kong is also home to commercial brands whose serial production includes practices of reuse, such as the work of the prominent jewellery designer Kai-Yin Lo and the brand Playback Concept by Chan Po-fung. While the signature style of Lo's brand has been described as one that "integrates antique Chinese styles into contemporary designs",[49] for example through the reuse of ancient jade and bronze artefacts in some of her necklaces, two pieces of experimental jewellery by Chan Po-fung playfully recycle broken jade bangles in poetic ways. Under the title *I would still find you*, Chan presents a bracelet in a bracelet: an old traditional bangle carved from jade and broken into two pieces is combined with a new one crafted out of brass that forms its frame in a type of tab setting known as a turtle setting (Figure 2.5). The piece reflects on social interaction and relationships. Each half can be worn independently by different people but only when they unite can the bracelet become a complete circle. In *Reveal of Cracks* of 2019, Chan uses a cage-like silver casing to fixate and reunite three fragments of a broken jade bangle.

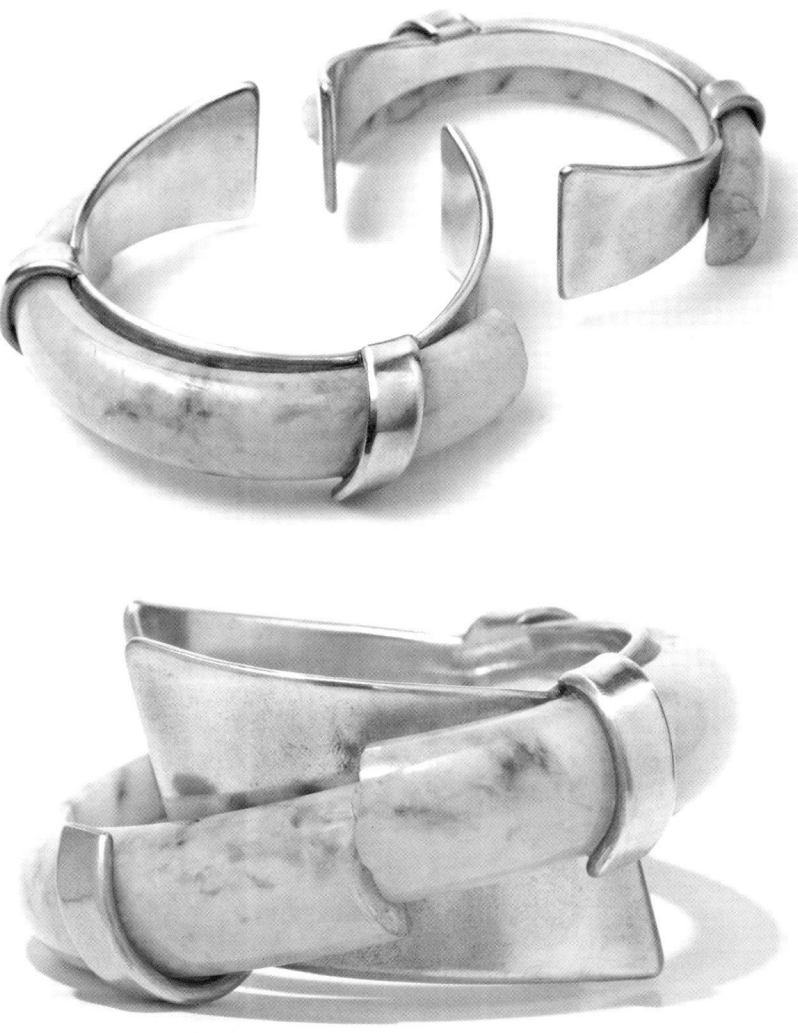

Figure 2.5 Chan Po-fung, "I would still find you", jade, brass, variable size, 2013.

It has movable hinges and almost looks like a scaffold built around a fragile core. Instead of hiding or covering up the cracks in the jade, the metal device highlights and proudly displays the bangle's brokenness. The octagon shaped frame in Chinese art evokes associations with the Book of Changes and a symbol called *bagua* consisting of eight shapes commonly known as "trigrams" that symbolize the fundamental principles of Daoist cosmology. Octagonal shapes are used in Chinese traditional architecture for entrances, window frames, and roof elements. They are not merely aesthetically pleasing, but also materialize a belief in certain spiritual principles and function as auspicious symbols. In Chan's work, an auspicious octagon frames a jade bangle traditionally believed to have talismanic powers.[50]

Furthermore, jewellery brands whose key marketing strategies highlight reuse are flourishing in Hong Kong. They include niin, which has been run for more than a decade by Hong Kong-based, UK-educated designer Jeanine Hsu who upcycles materials such as abalone shells collected from Hong Kong restaurants[51] and reuses brass, leather, and wood offcuts, and the slightly younger brand W;nk Atelier established by Maureen Hung and Connie Tang who transform pieces of plastic garbage into earrings, necklaces, and bracelets.[52] Hong Kong design brands such as Alchemist Creations and designers like Kevin Cheung have discovered and commercialized the potential of recycling by turning aluminium cans into watches, rings, and bracelets, wallpaper into cardholders, and plastic canisters into boom boxes.[53] Some of these makers have an explicit social agenda such as Alchemist Creations which is committed to employing people with disabilities.

All of these designers act on some level as scavengers, harvesting the city's garbage. There are two types of garbage, the trash that China and Hong Kong hold as a "giant bin for plastic waste"[54] filled by the United Kingdom and other nations, and locally discarded materials. The global and social lives of these two types of rubbish differ: while first-world trash forms part of Hong Kong's material culture being recycled or ending up as landfill without ever properly entering the lives of the city's inhabitants, locally discarded items temporarily form part of the fabric of Hong Kong in literal and symbolic ways. Accordingly, the previously mentioned designers are not only scavengers, but also archivists of Hong Kong who preserve fragments of the city that would otherwise be burned or end up in landfills by giving them a new life.

Conclusion: social connections and material agency

In the words of Song Yingxing, the author of the previously cited Ming dynasty treatise on craftsmanship and the use of natural resources, the extension of a material's life circle through the hands of craftsmen is an act of reincarnation, as evidenced by the term "reincarnated paper" (*huanhun zhi*) for recycled paper.[55] While in the Ming context of Song's treatise the term testifies to local scarcities of resources, in later periods it refers to the recycling of printed paper and entire libraries affected by censorship and political pressure.[56] Stripped of any religious connotations that the term reincarnation holds in English, *huanhun* can also be translated as "resurrected",[57] denoting a returning soul or spirit. The concept of *huanhun* therefore implies the existence of something like a soulfulness or spiritedness of matter. In this sense, it resonates with the contemporary approach of "vital materialism" and Jane Bennett's conceptualization of (trash) matter as active and vibrant,[58] both of which aim to overcome a "false dichotomy" that "separates the world into 'dull matter' (the *it* and the category of things), and 'vibrant life' (the *us*, the category of beings)".[59] Accordingly, the works discussed can be considered as enabling trash to *huanhun*, that is, enabling discarded matter to return in another guise. In addition, they illustrate Gaston Bachelard's understanding of "matter as an inherently captivating entity with the power to hold and shape human affect and imagination",[60] as they are not only made out of Hong Kong trash but literally built around it: taking garbage as inspiration, the works celebrate the power of matter to inspire creative imagination and creation while at the same time ensuring that the human affect held and shaped by the material culture of Hong Kong is sustained.

If we see the creative practices described above in line with the notion of *huanhun* and ideas on vibrant materiality and waste as "the humus of a reworked memory",[61] we can see the power of trash in the hands of Hong Kong designers as subversive on several levels: first, as subverting the material hierarchies of commercial jewellery by mining the streets of Hong Kong for discarded items instead of using precious materials such as gemstones, gold, and silver; second, as subverting the local and the global by using specifically local materials as part of a global movement of ecologically invested artists and designers; and, third, subversive in terms of agency as in all these examples it is the found item that prompts and to a certain extent guides the makers' imaginations and their hands, rather than the other way round.

Chan, Chung, and Ching extend the life of things and, by doing so, prevent the material culture and spirit of their city from vanishing, narrating a new story based on old fragments. As storytellers they reflect Seshradi's understanding of waste as "the only resource of a wasted people"[62] who add another chapter to waste's inventiveness. In the Hong Kong scenario, the "wasted people" are not living in slums like those Seshradi observed in Chennai, but are students and alumni like Chan, Chung, and Chan Po-fung (who were all taught by Ching at various points in their studies), who are part of a generation faced with massive sociopolitical changes and a mass exodus from Hong Kong. Against the background of a city in transition, where protesters have repurposed fragments of the urban environment as weapons, for example by throwing paving stones at police officers, Chung's construction debris pins and Ching's brooches employ the material language of jewellery to comment on social and political changes in the urban fabric of Hong Kong as a space, a city, and a community, preserving memory through the means of craft.

Notes

1. This chapter is part of a book project. Research and writing were supported by the General Research Fund Project 12609820 "Upcycling Hong Kong: The Circular Economy of

Recycling Material Culture in Pearl River Delta Jewelry Design" (2020–2022) from the Research Grants Council Hong Kong and a fellowship at Käte Hamburger Research Centre global dis:connect, Ludwig-Maximilians-Universität München (2022–2023).

2. Jane Bennett, *Vibrant Matter: A Political Ecology of Things* (Duke University Press, 2010).
3. Song Yingxing. *Tiangong Kaiwu*, 1637, in *T'ien-kung K'ai-wu: Chinese Technology in the Seventeenth Century*, trans. E-Tu Zen Sun and Shiou-Chuan S.C. Sun (Pennsylvania State University Press, 1966), 295. This translation of the treatise's title follows the one presented in Dagmar Schäfer, *The Crafting of the 10,000 Things: Knowledge and Technology in Seventeenth-Century China* (University of Chicago Press, 2011), 17–18; it is also known as *Tiangong Kaiwu* and *The Exploitation of the Works of Nature*. On different translations of the treatise's title, see Timothy Brooke, "Review of Dagmar Schäfer, The Crafting of the 10,000 Things", *Harvard Journal of Asiatic Studies* 73, no. 1 (2013): 158–59.
4. Song, *Tiangong Kaiwu*, 298.
5. Anna Grasskamp, *Art and Ocean Objects in Early Modern Eurasia: Shells, Bodies and Materiality* (Amsterdam University Press, 2021), 87–88.
6. For a discussion of this term, see Yangwen Zheng, *China on the Sea: How the Maritime World Shaped Modern China* (Brill, 2012), 210.
7. Shih Ching-fei, "Xiangya qiu suojian zhi gingyi jishu jiaoliu – Guandong, Qinggong yu shensheng luoma diguo" 象牙球所見之工藝技術交流 － 廣東、清宮與神聖羅馬帝國 (Concentric Ivory Spheres and the Exchange of Craft Techniques: Canton, the Qing Court and the Holy Roman Empire), *Gugong Xueshu Jikan* 25, no. 2 (2007): 87–138; Shih Ching-fei, *Riyue guanghua: Qinggong hua falang*, 日月光華：清宮畫琺瑯 (Radiant Luminance: The Painted Enamel Ware of the Qing Court) (National Palace Museum, Taipei, 2012).
8. As Kyoungjin Bae has shown through the example of round tables made in Guangzhou, traditional seating arrangements and social hierarchies were changed through transcultural designs appropriated in the region. Kyoungjin Bae, "Around the Globe: The Material Culture of Cantonese Round Tables in High-Qing China", in Anna Grasskamp and Monica Juneja (eds.), *EurAsian Matters: China, Europe and the Transcultural Object, 1600–1800* (Springer, 2018), 37–55
9. Yuen Lai Winnie Chan, "Nineteenth-Century Canton Gardens and the East-West Plant Trade", in Petra ten-Doesschate Chu and Ding Ning (eds.), *Qing Encounters: Artistic Exchanges between China and the West* (Getty Publications, 2015), 111–23.
10. Martina Siebert, Kai Jun Chen and Dorothy Ko (eds.), *Making the Palace Machine Work: Mobilizing People, Objects, and Nature in the Qing Empire* (Amsterdam University Press, 2021).
11. Wendy Siuyi Wong, "Contemporary Jewelry Design in Hong Kong", in Haruhiko Fujita and Christine Guth (eds.), *Encyclopedia of East Asian Design* (Bloomsbury, 2019), 155.
12. Ernest Kao, "China's Waste Ban Has Rocked the Recycling World and Revealed Hong Kong's Dire Record. What Next for the City's Rising Mountains of Trash?", *South China Morning Post*, 19 September 2018. Also see Lucy Siegle, *Turning the Tide on Plastic: How Humanity (And You) Can Make Our Globe Clean Again* (Trapeze, 2018), 63–67.
13. Lea Vergine, *Trash: From Junk to Art* (Electa, 1997); Vergine, *When Trash Becomes Art: TRASH Rubbish Mongo* (Skira, 2007); Gillian Whiteley, *Junk: Art and the Politics of Trash* (I.B. Tauris, 2011).
14. Amanda Boetzkes, *Plastic Capitalism: Contemporary Art and the Drive to Waste* (MIT Press, 2019).

15. Margaret Hillenbrand, "Ragpicking as Method", *Prism: Theory and Modern Chinese Literature* 16, no. 2 (2019): 291.
16. Meiqin Wang, "Waste in Contemporary Chinese Art", *IIAS Newsletter* 76 (2017): 33.
17. Wang, "Waste in Contemporary Chinese Art", footnote 17; Paolo Magagnoli, "The Civilized Artist Beautifies Pollution: Zhao Liang's Water and Beijing Green", *Journal of Contemporary Chinese Art* 3, no. 3 (2012): 367–76.
18. Wu Hung, "Material Art from China. An Introduction", in Wu Hung and Orianna Cacchione (eds.), *The Allure of Matter: Material Art of China*, exhibition catalogue (Smart Museum of Art, 2020), especially 32–33 and 37.
19. David Clarke, *Art and Place: Essays on Art from a Hong Kong Perspective* (Hong Kong University Press, 1996), and Clarke, *Chinese Art and its Encounter with the World* (Hong Kong University Press, 2011).
20. Zheng Bo and Lee Sohl (eds.), "Contemporary Art and Ecology in East Asia", *Journal of Contemporary Chinese Art* 3, no. 3 (2015).
21. Ysabelle Cheung, "Where I Work: Trevor Yeung", *Asia Art Pacific* 101 (2016): 155–58.
22. https://thingsthattalk.net/en/t/ttt:ThWzEN/stories/light-in-the-stinking-rose/the-lamp-and-its-maker (accessed 29 July 2022).
23. For recent media coverage of ecological artists in Hong Kong, see Enid Tsui, "Artists Make Their Art Sustainable, and Their Art About Sustainability as They Catch Up to 'Ecological Crisis'", *South China Morning Post*, 24 July 2019.
24. Wenny Teo, "52nd Venice Biennale", *Yishu* 6, no. 3 (2007): 30.
25. See MAP Office and Robin Peckham (eds.). *Where the Map is the Territory* (Hong Kong Office for Discourse Engineering, 2011).
26. https://www.instagram.com/liinaklauss/?hl=en (accessed 29 July 2022).
27. http://liinaklauss.blogspot.com/ (accessed 29 July 2022).
28. http://liinaklauss.com/index.php/portfolio-item/river-of-rubbish/ (accessed 29 July 2022).
29. For an overview, see https://www.wastereduction.gov.hk/en/green_event.htm (accessed 29 July 2022).
30. See http://www.cicy.net/curated-projects/alchemy-green-fibre-jewellery-an-idea-exchange-at-green-summer-festival2014/ (accessed 14 October 2019).
31. Kurt Iveson, "Cities Within the City: Do-It-Yourself Urbanism and the Right to the City", *International Journal of Urban and Regional Research* 37 (2013): 941.
32. https://www.sciencemuseum.org.uk/objects-and-stories/everyday-wonders/brief-history-diy (accessed 29 July 2022).
33. Emily Talen, "Do-it-Yourself Urbanism: A History", *Journal of Planning History* 14, no. 2 (2015): 135–48.
34. Simon Sadler, "Drop City Revisited", *Journal of Architectural Education* 59, no. 3 (2006): 12, citing Bill Voyd, "Funk Architecture", in Paul Oliver (ed.), *Shelter and Society: New Studies in Vernacular Architecture* (Barrie & Jenkins, 1978), 159. Also see Andrew G. Kirk, *Counterculture Green: The Whole Earth Catalog and American Environmentalism* (University Press of Kansas, 2007).
35. Shiv Visvanathan, "Rethinking Waste: Time, Obsolescence, Diversity and Democracy", in Raminder Kaur and Parul Dave-Mukherji (eds.), *Arts and Aesthetics in a Globalizing World* (Bloomsbury, 2014), 114.

36. Visvanathan, "Rethinking Waste", 114, citing Seshradi, Interview, 1995.
37. Visvanathan, "Rethinking Waste", 114.
38. Visvanathan, "Rethinking Waste", 117.
39. Fiona Sun, "Wealth Gap Between Hong Kong's Crazy Rich, Miserably Poor Widens since Handover", *South China Morning Post*, 20 June 2022; Yingqi Guo, Shu-Sen Chang, Feng Sha and Paul S.F. Yip. "Poverty Concentration in an Affluent City: Geographic Variation and Correlates of Neighborhood Poverty Rates in Hong Kong", *PLoS ONE* 13, no. 2 (2018); Thomas Piketty and Li Yang, "Income and Wealth Inequality in Hong Kong, 1981–2020: The Rise of Pluto-Communism?", *SSRN*, 1 June 2021.
40. For a highly insightful ethnographic study based on interviews and visual records focusing on one particular Hong Kong-based trash collector's experiences and views that go against an understanding of the city centre as a "place of presumed tidiness", see Anneke Coppoolse, "Under the Spectacle: Viewing Trash in the Streets of Central, Hong Kong", in Christoph Lindner and Miriam Meissner (eds.), *Global Garbage: Urban Imaginaries of Waste, Excess and Abandonment* (Routledge, 2015), 148–62.
41. Michael Wolf, "Bastard Chairs", *Works That Work* 1 (2013).
42. Rob Nixon, *Slow Violence and the Environmentalism of the Poor* (Harvard University Press, 2013).
43. Song, *Tiangong Kaiwu*, 295
44. Sarah Lazarus, "Pearl Farming in Hong Kong: Enthusiasts Restock Oyster Beds in City Waters to Revive a 1,000-Year-Old Industry", *South China Morning Post*, 18 February 2018.
45. For example, in works by the Japanese artist unit three and the design brand Heliograf from Sydney, this paragraph borrows from a discussion of the work published by Anna Grasskamp in collaboration with Ching Sze-Yin Cicy assisted by Chong Yan Xuan Kimberly, Hoi Kan Kong Thomas, and Kwok Pui Yi Esther under: https://thingsthattalk.net/en/t/ttt:TMCjtQ (accessed 31 July 2022).
46. AFP/Bloomberg, "WTO to Rule on US Ban on 'Made in Hong Kong' Label", 23 February 2021.
47. This paragraph is based on a discussion of the work published by Anna Grasskamp in collaboration with Ching Sze-Yin Cicy assisted by Chong Yan Xuan Kimberly, Hoi Kan Kong Thomas, and Kwok Pui Yi Esther under: https://thingsthattalk.net/en/zone/UpCyclingHongKong/t/ttt:TtKiEq (accessed 31 July 2022).
48. See, for example, the exhibiting and sale of works by Ching Sze-yin Cicy at Contemporary Crafts Centre in collaboration with Giant Year Gallery and SOIL; see https://www.craftbysoil.com/post/unpacking-a-solo-exhibition-of-ching-sze-yin-cicy-9-1-7-2-2021 (accessed 31 July 2022).
49. Wong, "Contemporary Jewelry Design in Hong Kong", 157.
50. This paragraph cites verbatim from a discussion of the works published by Anna Grasskamp in collaboration with Ching Sze-Yin Cicy assisted by Chong Yan Xuan Kimberly, Hoi Kan Kong Thomas, and Kwok Pui Yi Esther under: https://thingsthattalk.net/en/zone/UpCyclingHongKong/t/ttt:TXSKDn/details (accessed 31 July 2022).
51. Kelis Wong, "Natural Treasures", *The Standard*, 1 September 2017. Also see https://niinstyle.com/ (accessed 31 July 2022).
52. For a discussion of works by w;nk atelier published by Anna Grasskamp in collaboration with Ching Sze-Yin Cicy assisted by Chong Yan Xuan Kimberly, Hoi Kan Kong Thomas, and Kwok Pui Yi Esther, see https://www.thingsthattalk.net/en/t/ttt:TbEdib/stories (accessed 31 July 2022).

53. For a discussion of works by Alchemist Creations published by Anna Grasskamp in collaboration with Ching Sze-Yin Cicy assisted by Chong Yan Xuan Kimberly, Hoi Kan Kong Thomas, and Kwok Pui Yi Esther, see https://thingsthattalk.net/en/zone/UpCyclingHongKong/t/ttt:THSqdK (accessed 31 July 2022). Kevin Cheung presents his work under: http://kevin-cheung.com/about (accessed 31 July 2022).
54. Siegle, *Turning the Tide on Plastic*, 64.
55. "Reincarnated paper" is the translation chosen in Schäfer, *The Crafting of the 10,000 Things*, 243. Alternatively, it can also be translated as "resurrected paper"; see Song, *Tiangong Kaiwu*, 229.
56. Lucien X. Polastron, *Books on Fire: The Destruction of Libraries throughout History* (Inner Traditions International, 2007), 208.
57. Song, *Tiangong Kaiwu*, 229.
58. Bennett, *Vibrant Matter*.
59. James L. Smith, "New Bachelards? Reveries, Elements and Twenty-First Century Materialism", *Altre Modernità / Otras modernidades/ Autres modernités/ Other Modernities* 16, no. 10 (2012): 159.
60. Smith, "New Bachelards?", 163.
61. Visvanathan, "Rethinking Waste", 115.
62. Visvanathan, "Rethinking Waste", 114, citing Seshradi, Interview, 1995.

References

AFP/Bloomberg. "WTO to Rule on US Ban on 'Made in Hong Kong' Label", 23 February 2021. https://www.thestandard.com.hk/breaking-news/section/4/166052/WTO-to-rule-on-US-ban-on-%22Made-in-Hong-Kong%E2%80%9D-label%20;%20https://www.federalregister.gov/documents/2020/08/11/2020-17599/country-of-origin-marking-of-products-of-hong-kong (accessed 31 July 2022).

Bae, Kyoungjin. "Around the Globe: The Material Culture of Cantonese Round Tables in High-Qing China", in Anna Grasskamp and Monica Juneja (eds.), *EurAsian Matters: China, Europe and the Transcultural Object, 1600–1800*, Springer, 2018, pp. 37–55.

Bennett, Jane. *Vibrant Matter: A Political Ecology of Things*, Duke University Press, 2010.

Boetzkes, Amanda. *Plastic Capitalism: Contemporary Art and the Drive to Waste*, MIT Press, 2019.

Brooke, Timothy. "Review of Dagmar Schäfer, The Crafting of the 10,000 Things", *Harvard Journal of Asiatic Studies* 73, no. 1 (2013): 156–63.

Chan, Yuen Lai Winnie. "Nineteenth-Century Canton Gardens and the East-West Plant Trade", in Petra ten-Doesschate Chu and Ding Ning (eds.), *Qing Encounters: Artistic Exchanges between China and the West*, Getty Publications, 2015, pp. 111–23.

Cheung, Ysabelle. "Where I Work: Trevor Yeung", *Asia Art Pacific* 101 (2016): 155–58.

Clarke, David. *Art and Place: Essays on Art from a Hong Kong Perspective*, Hong Kong University Press, 1996.

Clarke, David. *Chinese Art and its Encounter with the World*, Hong Kong University Press, 2011.

Coppoolse, Anneke. "Under the Spectacle: Viewing Trash in the Streets of Central, Hong Kong", in Christoph Lindner and Miriam Meissner (eds.), *Global Garbage: Urban Imaginaries of Waste, Excess and Abandonment*, Routledge, 2015, pp. 148–62.

Grasskamp, Anna. *Art and Ocean Objects in Early Modern Eurasia: Shells, Bodies and Materiality*, Amsterdam University Press, 2021.

Guo, Yingqi, Shu-Sen Chang, Feng Sha and Paul S.F. Yip. "Poverty Concentration in an Affluent City: Geographic Variation and Correlates of Neighborhood Poverty Rates in Hong Kong", *PLoS ONE* 13, no. 2 (2018). https://doi.org/10.1371/journal.pone.0190566.

Hillenbrand, Margaret. "Ragpicking as Method", *Prism: Theory and Modern Chinese Literature* 16, no. 2 (2019): 260–97.

Iveson, Kurt. "Cities Within the City: Do-It-Yourself Urbanism and the Right to the City", *International Journal of Urban and Regional Research* 37 (2013): 941–56.

Kao, Ernest. "China's Waste Ban has Rocked the Recycling World and Revealed Hong Kong's Dire Record. What Next for the City's Rising Mountains of Trash?", *South China Morning Post*, 19 September 2018.

Kirk, Andrew G. *Counterculture Green: The Whole Earth Catalog and American Environmentalism*, University Press of Kansas, 2007.

Lazarus, Sarah. "Pearl Farming in Hong Kong: Enthusiasts Restock Oyster Beds in City Waters to Revive a 1,000-Year-Old Industry", *South China Morning Post*, 18 February 2018.

Magagnoli, Paolo. "The Civilized Artist Beautifies Pollution: Zhao Liang's Water and Beijing Green", *Journal of Contemporary Chinese Art* 3, no. 3 (2012): 367–76.

MAP Office and Robin Peckham (eds.). *Where the Map is the Territory*, Hong Kong Office for Discourse Engineering, 2011.

Nixon, Rob. *Slow Violence and the Environmentalism of the Poor*, Harvard University Press, 2013.

Piketty, Thomas and Li Yang. "Income and Wealth Inequality in Hong Kong, 1981–2020: The Rise of Pluto-Communism?", *SSRN*, 1 June 2021. https://doi.org/10.2139/ssrn.3888118 (accessed 31 July 2022).

Polastron, Lucien X. *Books on Fire: The Destruction of Libraries throughout History*, Inner Traditions International, 2007.

Sadler, Simon. "Drop City Revisited", *Journal of Architectural Education* 59, no. 3 (2006): 5–14.

Schäfer, Dagmar. *The Crafting of the 10,000 Things: Knowledge and Technology in Seventeenth-Century China*, University of Chicago Press, 2011.

Shih Ching-fei. "Xiangya qiu suojian zhi gingyi jishu jiaoliu – Guandong, Qinggong yu shensheng luoma diguo" 象牙球所見之工藝技術交流 – 廣東、清宮與神聖羅馬帝國 (Concentric Ivory Spheres and the Exchange of Craft Techniques: Canton, the Qing Court and the Holy Roman Empire), *Gugong Xueshu Jikan* 25, no. 2 (2007): 87–138.

Shih Ching-fei. *Riyue guanghua: Qinggong hua falang*, 日月光華：清宮畫琺瑯 (Radiant Luminance: The Painted Enamel Ware of the Qing Court), National Palace Museum, Taipei, 2012.

Siebert, Martina, Kai Jun Chen and Dorothy Ko (eds.), *Making the Palace Machine Work: Mobilizing People, Objects, and Nature in the Qing Empire*, Amsterdam University Press, 2021.

Siegle, Lucy. *Turning the Tide on Plastic: How Humanity (And You) Can Make Our Globe Clean Again*, Trapeze, 2018.

Smith, James L. "New Bachelards? Reveries, Elements and Twenty-First Century Materialism", *Altre Modernità / Otras modernidades/ Autres modernités/ Other Modernities* 16, no. 10 (2012): 156–67.

Song Yingxing. *Tiangong Kaiwu*, 1637, in *T'ien-kung K'ai-wu: Chinese Technology in the Seventeenth Century*, trans. E-Tu Zen Sun and Shiou-Chuan S.C. Sun, Pennsylvania State University Press, 1966.

Sun, Fiona. "Wealth Gap Between Hong Kong's Crazy Rich, Miserably Poor Widens since Handover", *South China Morning Post*, 20 June 2022.

Talen, Emily. "Do-it-Yourself Urbanism: A History", *Journal of Planning History* 14, no. 2 (2015): 135–48.

Teo, Wenny. "52nd Venice Biennale", *Yishu* 6, no. 3 (2007): 25–32.

Tsui, Enid. "Artists Make Their Art Sustainable, and Their Art About Sustainability as They Catch Up to 'Ecological Crisis'", *South China Morning Post*, 24 July 2019. https://www.scmp.com/

lifestyle/arts-culture/article/3019718/sustainable-artists-taking-ecological-themes-all-new (accessed 14 October 2019).

Vergine, Lea. *Trash: From Junk to Art*, Electa, 1997.

Vergine, Lea. *When Trash Becomes Art: TRASH Rubbish Mongo*, Skira, 2007.

Visvanathan, Shiv. "Rethinking Waste: Time, Obsolescence, Diversity and Democracy", in Raminder Kaur and Parul Dave-Mukherji (eds.), *Arts and Aesthetics in a Globalizing World*, Bloomsbury, 2014, pp. 99–118.

Voyd, Bill. "Funk Architecture", in Paul Oliver (ed.), *Shelter and Society: New Studies in Vernacular Architecture*, Barrie & Jenkins, 1978, pp. 156–64.

Wang, Meiqin. "Waste in Contemporary Chinese Art", *IIAS Newsletter* 76 (2017): 32–33.

Whiteley, Gillian. *Junk: Art and the Politics of Trash*, I.B. Tauris, 2011.

Wolf, Michael. "Bastard Chairs", *Works That Work* 1 (2013). https://worksthatwork.com/1/bastard-chairs (accessed 29 July 2022).

Wong, Kelis. "Natural Treasures", *The Standard*, 1 September 2017. https://www.thestandard.com.hk/sections-news-print/186937/Natural-treasures (accessed 31 July 2022).

Wong, Wendy Siuyi. "Contemporary Jewelry Design in Hong Kong", in Haruhiko Fujita and Christine Guth (eds.), *Encyclopedia of East Asian Design*, Bloomsbury, 2019, pp. 155–58.

Wu Hung. "Material Art from China. An Introduction", in Wu Hung and Orianna Cacchione (eds.), *The Allure of Matter: Material Art of China*, exhibition catalogue, Smart Museum of Art, 2020, pp. 15–41.

Zheng Bo and Lee Sohl (eds.), "Contemporary Art and Ecology in East Asia", *Journal of Contemporary Chinese Art* 3, no. 3 (2015).

Zheng, Yangwen. *China on the Sea: How the Maritime World Shaped Modern China*, Brill, 2012.

CHAPTER 3
MAINTAINING MATERIAL CULTURE: AN ESSAY ON MEANINGS AND VALUES OF THINGS AND TECHNOLOGY IN CENTRAL SEOUL

Anneke Coppoolse

Introduction

The old centre of Seoul, South Korea, comprises a unique conglomerate of people, things, spaces, and times. In the area – a commercial district with both narrow alleyways and wide avenues, but most of all a locale undergoing significant redevelopment – decreasing small-scale manufacturing and related businesses (e.g. electronic part shops, repair services) are responding and in part adapting to a rapidly changing urban environment while institutions and researchers, the Metropolitan Government,[1] and the general public have begun to acknowledge their cultural significance. In light of this, and with an emphasis on the changing ways in which people relate to the things, tools, and technologies that surround them, this chapter probes meanings, values, sentiments, and memories attached to objects specific to central Seoul – and to the practices involving their usage and repair.

Central Seoul has been written about extensively by architects and urban researchers, who primarily focus on the development of the area's built environment and function, and on its impending gentrification.[2] Although located in this built environment and in particular in certain areas around a stream called Cheonggyecheon, this chapter revolves around "things" that have shaped this distinct place; things that continue to persist in this place but also find new significance in museums and exhibition spaces. Existing studies by scholars of culture and society consider these things at the centre of Seoul in terms of the culture and practice of their production,[3] and with regard to the networks (of people and things) that facilitate their production and trade.[4] This chapter centres on the things themselves, drawing out stories about them, about the people connected to them, and about the spaces they occupy and shape, to understand the "regimes of value" in which they circulate – an idea loosely adapted from Arjun Appadurai's edited volume *The Social Life of Things*.[5]

In *The Social Life of Things*, Appadurai considers commodities: highly socialized things (or services) with "commodity potential", subject to exchange at certain moments in their "trajectory from production, through exchange/distribution, to consumption".[6] This trajectory is, according to contributing author Igor Kopytoff, a biography that is "culturally regulated" and in part "open to individual manipulation", meaning that the value of things can be understood differently by different people (buyers, sellers, and other actors) in varied moments and contexts. Appadurai's "regimes of value" is founded on this notion as it implies that the degree of value attached to things is profoundly variable and specific.[7] Although the centre of Seoul and its history are to a significant degree determined by commodities, this chapter does not consider the things under investigation as commodities alone. It prefers to consider them as socialized, culturally regulated things that are imbued with diverse forms of value and meaning – economic, but also social, historical, and cultural – depending on who deals with them, and in what context they are dealt with.

Preceded by a brief (and incomplete) historical account of central Seoul, intended to "set the scene" for the three vignettes, the compilation of stories about a printed circuit board, a pair of scissors, and a mechanical pocket watch makes a case for a perspective on the centre of Seoul as a place determined by the values and meanings of objects. As Appadurai argued, "even though from a *theoretical* [sic] point of view human actors encode things with significance, from a *methodological* [sic] point of view it is the things-in-motion that illuminate their human and social context".[8] The chapter is, therefore, founded as much on ethnographic encounters and site visits as it probes into those contexts in which the area's material culture is presented as a form of heritage (i.e. the Cheonggyecheon Museum, Iumpium: Sewing History Museum and Sewoon Electronics Museum). When making sense of objects in these spaces, thinking through their shifting values, meanings, and contexts, it draws on the work of Svetlana Alpers,[9] specifically on the notion of "the museum effect", and on James Clifford's ideas about the fabrication of relations between objects in museum displays.[10]

Central Seoul

Central Seoul may be a curious descriptor seeing that Seoul has multiple centres. South of Hangang (the Han River) there are Gangnam, a modern business node, and Yeouido, the main financial district which also houses South Korea's National Assembly. North of the River there is Jung-gu (Central District), which is another significant business core, the geographical centre of Seoul, and home to buildings such as the Deoksu Palace. The networks of things, people, and practices that the objects of this chapter form(ed), extend and transcend two of Jung-gu's fifteen administrative *dongs*:[11] Euljiro-dong, the area around Eulji-ro, and Gwanghui-dong, east of Euljiro-dong and including the area around Pyounghwa Clothing Market (Figure 3.1). Besides these two dongs, the objects of this chapter have plotted a vital segment of Jongno-gu, the district to the immediate north of Jung-gu. More exactly, the objects featured in this chapter mark an area spanning both sides of Cheonggyecheon, the stream that divides Jung-gu and Jongno-gu. The area around this stream has undergone periods of destruction and development throughout the centuries, and has therefore a unique socio-material history. This section on "Central Seoul" introduces some twentieth-century events in the area to contextualize the following three vignettes and the stories of the objects they feature.

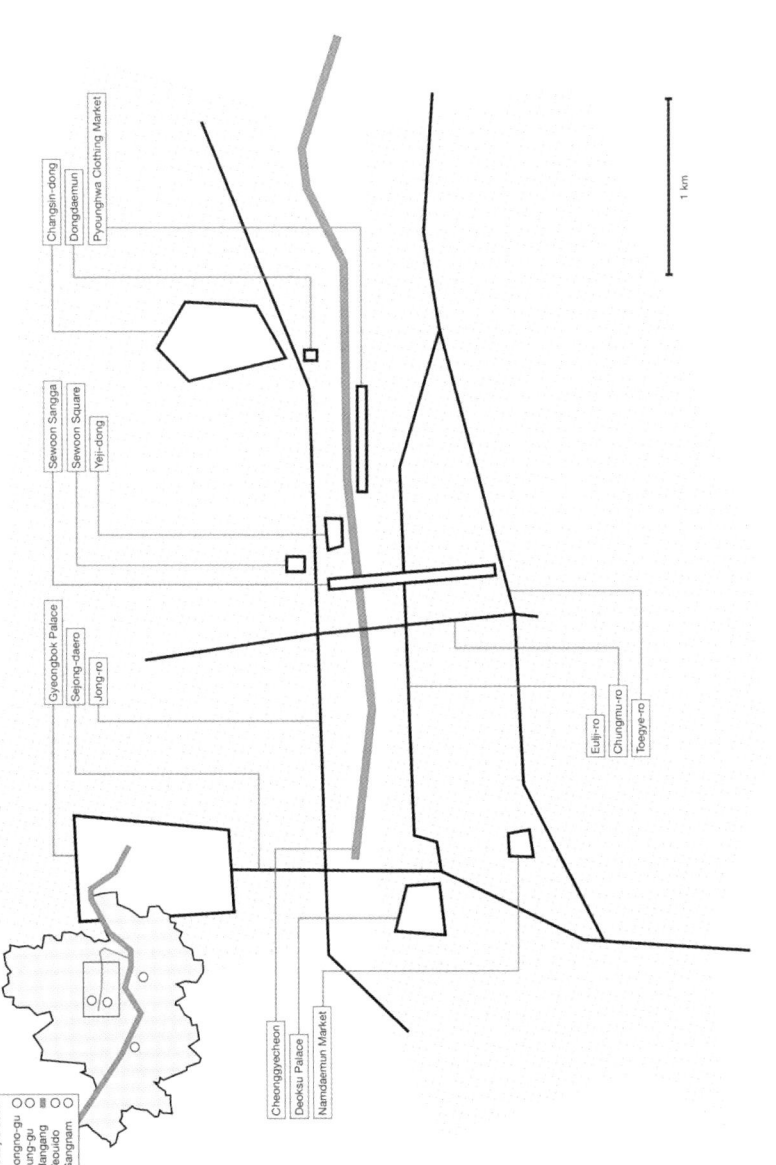

Figure 3.1 Outline of Seoul today with Hangang crossing through and centre points of commercial districts indicated. Magnified, the historical and geographical centre of Seoul with Cheonggyecheon. Map created by the author.

With the founding of the Joseon Dynasty (1392), Seoul (then Hanyang) was selected as the capital. Much smaller than contemporary Seoul, located north of Hangang, it had Cheonggyecheon crossing through from west to east. The location for Gyeongbok Palace and other buildings was determined through Confucian principles and feng shui.[12] Sejong-daero (or Sejongno)[13] connected the Palace to perpendicular Jong-ro (or Jongno),[14] which was the main business axis that ran parallel to Cheonggyecheon, from Sejong-daero to Dongdaemun (the eastern gate).[15] Today's Central Business District (CBD) and political centre[16] sit at the intersection of these two roads,[17] but following Cheonggyecheon (and Jong-ro) eastward, particular histories of things, and their trade, manufacture, and repair, shaped and continue to shape the urban fabric of the area. Despite – and due to – repeated damage following diverse conflicts until the Korean War (1950–53), a centre for trade and production developed along Cheonggyecheon. It was the home to tool and textile businesses since the Joseon Dynasty,[18] but a market for manufactured goods developed under Japanese occupation (1910–45), especially around Eulji-ro. Situated between Korean and Japanese residential areas, Euljiro served metal and wooden tool manufacturing businesses and the Japanese military.[19] The rise of movie theatres and increased demand for film posters in the 1910s[20] led to the establishment of printing houses around Chungmu-ro and Eulji-ro,[21] while business expanded also north of Cheonggyecheon. The area around Dongdaemun gained momentum as a commercial district. In an effort to compete with merchants south of Cheonggyecheon (and in Namdaemun Market), Korean merchants joined forces and developed Dongdaemun Market (in Yeji-dong) for wholesale-retail trade of domestic fabrics and daily necessities.[22] The commercial development of both sides of Cheonggyecheon since this time is key to the argument of this chapter and therefore requires some elaboration.

Seoul was badly damaged after Japanese rule (1945) and the ensuing Korean War (1950–53), and a period of considerable urban development followed, which resulted in the Cheonggyecheon area gaining greater economic significance. A population boom led to land shortages and property speculation. Migrants developed a squatter area on the banks of Cheonggyecheon, which evolved into a place for light manufacturing of textiles and clothing.[23] The textiles and clothing industry became South Korea's main economic sector.[24] Owing a great deal to the work of women[25] who had migrated to Seoul from the countryside,[26] textile and clothing manufacturing around Cheonggyecheon spurred further development of Dongdaemun Market as a key site for the clothing and textile trade.[27] Moreover, post-war relief aid generated abundant trade in American products – including clothing, but also food and medicine[28] – while Euljiro saw a market for (often smuggled) daily necessities and used items develop due to its proximity to the US army base.[29] The US military takeover of the Japanese army base propelled informal trade of daily necessities and second-hand tools and technology, in turn inducing variant repair of these second-hand items.[30] In the context of this informality, particular locality, unique productivity, and pre-existing history of tool manufacturing, what was later referred to as Cheonggyecheon Gigyegonggu Sangga (the Cheonggyecheon Machine Tool Arcade) began taking shape: a dense area of small factories and shops for the production, wholesale, and retail of metal, machine tools, electronics, etc. that covered several blocks on both sides of the stream.[31] The first of the three objects that drive this chapter, a printed circuit board, is from this area. In the next section, it helps narrate the area's current condition and the values and meanings of related objects within it. Yet, some final notes on how the Cheonggyecheon area developed in the decades succeeding the Korean War give this first story a stronger historical foundation.

In these decades, as business on the banks of Cheonggyecheon developed and fed South Korea's economy, economic and urban growth prompted the Metropolitan Government to drastically change its built environment. Big infrastructure projects were conceived[32] to tackle urban issues as a result of Seoul's rapid population growth (traffic congestion, dangerous living conditions in informal structures, etc.), but also to achieve a desired modern urban aesthetic that reflected South Korea's newly gained identity of a rapidly developing economy.[33] Despite the architectural and infrastructural haste with which the area around Cheonggyecheon was reconfigured, the goods, tools, and technology produced, repaired, and traded here – and the people involved in this trade – continued to leave their mark on the area. A telling example of this is the way in which the Pyounghwa[34] Clothing Market came about. In response to the Metropolitan Government's plans to build an overpass in the place of Cheonggyecheon, and under pressure from an organized group of people running their businesses there, the Pyounghwa Clothing Market was constructed on the stream's south bank, allowing these businesses to continue.[35] The market replaced the informal stilt structures of the squatter area and is now a key part of the Dongdaemun Fashion Cluster, the "mecca of K-fashion".[36]

Today, as South Korea has transitioned from a manufacturing to a service economy, shaping its knowledge-based society,[37] and as production around Cheonggyecheon has reduced[38] and the area has entered another moment of redevelopment,[39] the things and tools significant to the area persist. They continue to define central Seoul, which the following three vignettes will illustrate. Each vignette envelopes an object that is not only significant to the area but manifests unique ways of determining it. While the vignettes could have captured a multitude of objects, from arcade machines to spools of thread, and from pins and badges to pendant lights, the ones selected allow the chapter to highlight three distinct locales along Cheonggyecheon. Their trinity offers insight into different ways in which the objects are significant to their context. Following comparable yet unique trajectories, they shape their socio-spatial contexts as their meanings and values shift. The first is the printed circuit board.

Printed circuit board

In a small and electronics-filled repair shop at the end of a narrow corridor that is attached to a large, building-length indoor space with muted daylight entering through skylights several storeys up, we encounter an old, printed circuit board (Figure 3.2). The circuit board is one of countless electronics that have been repaired over many years by the master repair technician[40] who runs the shop. He has run his repair business, located inside the infamous mixed-use shopping plaza Sewoon Sangga, for decades. With an

Figure 3.2 A printed circuit board at a repair business in Sewoon Sangga. Photo by Haeun Kim.

interest in machines since he was a child and having gained experience working on repairs for Samsung prior to starting his own business, today his repair work has achieved nation-wide recognition. People visit his shop from all over the country.[41]

The circuit board contains an electric circuit with, on the right, a power supply board. Power supply boards connect with a power cord to a socket, ensuring that the incoming voltage of (in South Korea) 220 V is converted into safe supply voltages. The safe voltages are then passed on to other circuit boards via connectors, two of which feature towards the left (white parts). The circuit board presents a system of supply that, with the help of repairers, allows radios and televisions to continue to play and computers and machines continue to run. Such an object and its potential malfunction – a "socialized thing" inviting "social events" (i.e. visits to repair shops, subsequent sourcing of new parts in electronics shops) – connects the Sewoon Sangga-based repair technician's services to the needs of diverse people. Although, overall, demand for repair services is decreasing (electronics are increasingly affordable and replaceable, more irreparable products are being developed, and brands tend to run their own repair departments), this repair technician still has ample business. Yet, he believes that the reasons for people having items repaired have changed somewhat. Among his clientele are now cafe owners who have decorated their interiors with vintage audio equipment that requires repair, individuals who want to restore old electronics of personal value, and every now and then another repair technician needing a hand with a tricky repair.[42]

As a "socialized thing" inviting "social events", the circuit board and its many smaller parts working together is not only a wonderful "material analogy" for the shopping plaza

Maintaining Material Culture

in which it is being repaired, but also a representative part of this unique context. The context – Sewoon Sangga – is about connections, despite the original idea upon which it was founded. An emblem of authoritarian politics of the 1970s[43] and the preceding decade, it is a kilometre-long, mixed-use residential and commercial complex, built perpendicular to Cheonggyecheon, forming an elevated axis that runs from Jongno-gu, across the stream, to Toegye-ro in Jung-gu. It reflects the Metropolitan Government's ambition (and that of South Korea's military government that had assumed power in 1961[44]) to build symbols of progress and, following the introduction of a new city planning law in 1962 encouraging "improvement of degraded areas", served to further eradicate central Seoul's squatter area.[45] Considering the sociopolitical circumstances that gave rise to the megastructure, Sewoon Sangga epitomizes an epoch regardless of its short-lived success[46] as the upscale complex it was intended to be.[47] Notwithstanding its depreciation, it remained at the centre of the electronics ecosystem that had spontaneously developed some decades earlier; an ecosystem of electronics businesses and repair shops that had grown out of the informal market of second-hand technology which had formed in the squatter area after the Korean War.[48] Formed by "things-in-motion" – used goods entering the area – the electronics market, including the businesses inside Sewoon Sangga, evolved into a centre for anything electronic.[49]

Today, the lower floors of the first of the six remaining buildings of the megastructure in particular are filled with hundreds of small shops selling parts, prototyping, or repairing electronics. Broken electronics such as the circuit board still make their way to this place for repair – prompted by their economic or use value, or their sentimental or aesthetic value – upon which their social lives are extended through the skilful hands of people like the master repair technician. Yet, despite the continuation of electronics and repair businesses in this unique locale, the megastructure, its surroundings, and their socio-material contents are also changing. Having avoided complete demolition,[50] recent regeneration attempts at maintaining the industrial ecosystem have involved a drive towards tourism and the promotion of urban culture.[51] Under the re:Sewoon Project and a new name, Makercity Sewoon, various initiatives have been devised to connect new kinds of makers to the existing ecosystem[52] in the hope of "future-proofing" the area.[53] Following the renovation of Sewoon Sangga's full-length pedestrian walkway, cafes have opened in vacant shop spaces along it, and new kinds of visitors now frequent the site. On the same walkway, among other compact structures (so-called "Makers' Cubes"), a small museum has been erected: the Sewoon Electronics Museum, which, as per the Metropolitan Government's press release, presents "a collection of precious exhibits that allow us to look back on the past".[54] It features audio equipment and a plethora of other electronics that have been produced, traded, and repaired in the area over the decades. These "precious" items are former commodities that have been "revalued" – taken out of their original context and "replaced" within it; put on display in a specially constructed unit on the reinforced walkway.

In contrast to how Sewoon Sangga and the surrounding area are undergoing notable changes and incidentally in tune with the new museum that has been erected to capture the area's history of "things", the interior space of the repair technician's business with its many contents is a time capsule of sorts. It is a space for the restoration, preservation, and temporary storage of elements of time – old electronics and more. Besides carefully stacked radios (the repair of which is this technician's expertise), the little bit of wall space that is not covered with electronics preserves other markers of time: record covers (Figure 3.3). One is a record cover from 1976 of artist duo Two Ace, more familiar under their Korean name Geumgwa Eun ("Gold and Silver"). The singers went their separate ways in 1980 but persist on the wall of the repair shop, beside a hit album of trot-inspired[55] folk singer Serena Kim. These musical references form part of a large assortment of soundtracks to a particular moment in South Korea's history: the 1970s. This period of economic development, authoritarian politics, and rapid industrial modernization, in which "technological transformation facilitated reproduction and production of popular music", boosted the music industry and popularized music consumption as a "national pastime" while also influencing the sounds and themes of the music of the time.[56] The two record covers – objects on display – represent a moment in time, a memory, and yet another industry: a popular music industry that is tied to the (audio) electronics industry.[57] As objects representing the sound of a time and the development of a society, these record covers are things with particular meaning in a context such as Sewoon Sangga.

On the wall of the repair business, the record covers are juxtaposed with a third visual object: a flyer of Artclub Sewoon, from 2019. While the record covers represent a certain significant past in which the area around Sewoon Sangga as well as the industry within

Figure 3.3 Close-up of a wall in the long-running repair shop in Sewoon Sangga. Photo by Haeun Kim.

it developed massively, the flyer represents a significant present in which this same area and the industry within it are both maintained and considerably transformed. Artclub Sewoon, a series of two classical music concerts, was an initiative that developed out of Makercity Sewoon. The concerts were held in collaboration with the Suri Suri Coop,[58] a cooperative of craftspeople and technicians from Sewoon, and was delivered by means of a vacuum tube audio amplifier.[59] The object of the amplifier determined the concept for the two concerts. It was also the defining "thing" that forged a connection between the performing musicians, who used it to amplify their music, and the cooperative's technicians, who had been manufacturing and repairing such amplifiers for decades.[60] In the context of the two concerts, the amplifier had exceeded its use value: as an object with a long history ingrained in Sewoon Sangga, it had historical (possibly sentimental) value; as an object producing a unique sound, it had aesthetic value; as a thing forging new relationships, it had social value.

The Artclub Sewoon flyer on the wall of the repair shop presents a kind of mise en abyme in the combination of its depiction and its respective location. Featuring an indoor space with skylights and muted daylight, the image represents the exact place where the electronics shop is located: a place constructed based on ideas of modern existence yet determined by the objects within it; objects such as the amplifier or the circuit board. The circuit board – an object representative of the larger context of Sewoon Sangga and the electronics market – steers reflection on its meaning and on the meaning of the place in which it is found: temporarily tucked away in a shop at the end of a corridor off a space with skylights and muted daylight. It is a "thing-in-motion" illuminating its social context.

Scissors

Attached to a white background, protected by a glass cover, and accentuated with a neat, thin, wooden frame, we find a pair of tailoring scissors (Figure 3.4). There is fabric wrapped around the finger rings, which gives them their unique character without being any less recognizable as a Dragonfly – "Made in Korea", as engraved right above the pivot. Dragonfly tailoring scissors were first manufactured in 1945 by HEGA Corp., founded by Ahn Haeng-soon, whose trademark "Made by Haeng-soon" (行淳作) is also engraved, in Hanja (Chinese characters). Little information about the brand's history is available but as an exchange on Naver's knowledge sharing platform speculates, the founding of HEGA Corp. and the subsequent local manufacture of tailoring scissors may have been a response to a growing demand for better sewing facilities at the end of the Second World War and Japanese occupation.[61] There was an urgent need for daily necessities, including clothes, while in the ensuing decades the sewing industry rapidly expanded, making tailoring scissors a representative object of the time. Today, HEGA has manufactured this single product for three generations: Dragonfly tailoring scissors.[62] This particular pair of scissors is part of the collection of the Iumpium: Sewing History Museum, a museum that opened in 2018 but had to close its doors in early 2023, following

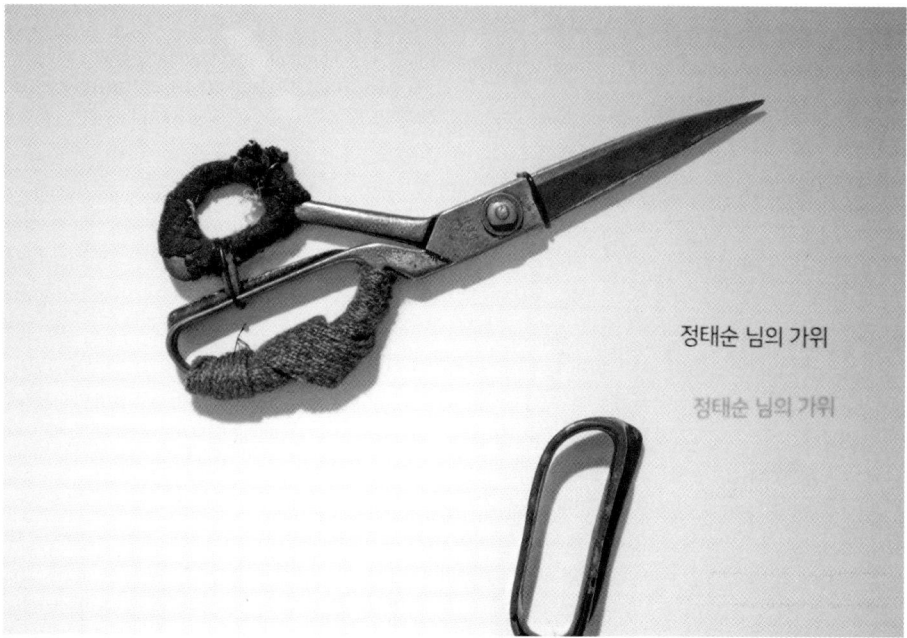

Figure 3.4 Used tailoring scissors of a sewing master with decades of experience in Seoul's garment industry. The scissors form part of the collection of the Iumpium: Sewing History Museum in Changsin-dong, Seoul, which has since closed. Photo by the author.

a change in Seoul's leadership.[63] Although the pair of scissors is now no longer on exhibition, its trajectory from commodity (locally manufactured quality scissors) to an object with particular use value (an essential tool in the sewing industry), to one with historical and cultural (also symbolic and visual) value (an exhibit), to an artefact awaiting future usage, offers insight into its meanings and values.

The Iumpium: Sewing History Museum, which was both a museum and cultural space, was developed as part of the regeneration project of the infamous yet declining "sewing village" of Changsin-dong in Jongno-gu, located adjacent to Dongdaemun and to Pyounghwa Clothing Market on the other side of equally nearby Cheonggyecheon (see Figure 3.1). Changsin-dong is a residential neighbourhood to which many garment factories moved in the 1970s, when stricter labour and safety regulations were enforced on factories in Pyounghwa Clothing Market[64] following unionization[65] and a fight for workers' rights.[66] Upon the development of the Dongdaemun area as a centre for K-fashion in the 2000s, the old sewing village of Changsin-dong gained fame as the place where K-fashion was produced, which contributed to its selection as Seoul's first regeneration project.[67] The apparel produced in Changsin-dong, and the meanings and values attached to these items, prompted the way in which the area would continue to exist. Among other undertakings, the Iumpium: Sewing History Museum was newly built in the 2010s and narrated the development and socio-economic significance of Changsin-dong in light of the larger history of Seoul's sewing industry and the contributions this industry made to South Korea's economic development.

The way in which the object of the scissors had been displayed in a frame on the museum wall, presented as a "thing" with a certain historical, cultural, and visual relevance, is comparable to how Sewoon Sangga's electronics had a small museum constructed around them on the renovated pedestrian walkway of the megastructure. In both cases, and in both places – sites of declining production – museums were built to present "precious" objects "that allow us to look back on the past".[68] In both cases, things from the (not so distant) past had been revalued and made part of regeneration schemes initiated by the Metropolitan Government and developed in conversation with the community (see note 1 for more information). These things, intended to represent a certain history and culture (but also identity, mastery, and authenticity), are what Appadurai refers to as *ex-commodities*: "things retrieved, either temporarily or permanently, from the commodity state and placed in some other state".[69] Sewing tools in Changsin-dong and electronics in Sewoon Sangga are things made "precious" as forms of heritage. Rather, these things – in their continuous service to their respective manufacturing industries and following the success they helped achieve along the way – "became" precious, socioculturally and historically.

The scissors, presented against the white background, look sturdy and well used. They feature among nine similar pairs of scissors, each uniquely customized with threads and fabrics around the finger rings or simply boasting traces of use as proof of authenticity and the mastery of their former owners, whose names feature beside them on top of a layer of protective glass. The ten pairs of scissors' shared composition is titled "Masters' Scissors". The original owner of the pair in Figure 3.4 is one of ten selected, present-day sewing masters with decades of experience working in Seoul's garment industry and with connections to Changsin-dong (she had participated in a temporary exhibition in 2018 after which the frame with scissors remained). Having long transcended their commodity phase, her scissors have spent much of their life serving their intended purpose. Yet, in the museum, they are as much out of place as they are in place. Hung on a white wall behind protective glass, they have been taken out of their original context: the sewing master's workplace. They also no longer serve their original purpose of cutting fabric. They appear "out of place", disconnected from the place they used to occupy and the function they used to have. Yet, together with the nine other pairs of scissors, they are part of a larger collection of tools, equipment, and stories about Seoul's sewing industry, all displayed (until early 2023) in the small, multi-storey museum in the sloped neighbourhood of Changsin-dong. This "new" yet "old" context implies a different kind of belonging. The scissors' new "social arena" (the museum) highlights a shift in their trajectory, while at the same time this trajectory is what determined the conditions of the museum: The scissors appear "in place".

Only recently have the scissors been identified as a notable cultural object – as an exhibitable artefact – for their emblematic quality as an object from Seoul's sewing industry, elevated by their former owner's merits. They have entered another regime of value. Over time, they have transitioned from being a simple manufactured object and tool, to being an object relevant enough to be looked at attentively. The act of isolating a crafted object "from its world" and displaying it in a museum for "attentive looking" is what art historian Svetlana Alpers calls "the museum effect".[70] Displayed behind a layer of protective glass in the museum context, the scissors possess a certain authenticity as a master's tool with traces of use found in the fabric wrapped around the finger rings signalling this too. Denied their original use and turned into artefacts, they have not only become precious things with cultural and historical meaning, they have become precious artefacts the displays of which exercise our eyes. Through the museum effect, the scissors have acquired a new kind of value – visual(-cultural) value prompted by the visual interest that is invested in their display.

Through curatorial processes of display, museums construct the contexts in which visitors are presented with objects and the stories connected to these objects. James Clifford argues in this regard that "in the assemblage of the material 'world'" (the gathering of cultural objects in museums), a subjective space is created which implies that it is impossible to represent any object within the assemblage accurately."[71] Things in museums are assembled based on ordering systems that say more about those establishing the order than about the realities of the objects within them: illusions of relations between objects on display – "mystified ... adequate *representations*" – override the actual social relations of the objects.[72] Alpers suggests that crafting the visibility of cultural objects formerly not looked at in this way and allowing visitors to freely explore these objects "without ... intimidating mediation between viewer and object" is therefore a desired approach for museums.[73] In the case of the display of ten used pairs of tailoring scissors, this may hold true to some degree. A spotlight and white background invite attentive looking at the isolated objects, bringing out the traces of use, allowing the visitor to imagine these scissors' and their owners' trajectories. Yet, the guiding caption beneath the display – a kind of "mediation between viewer and object"[74] – also offers a useful perspective, not just of the objects but of the ways in which they are perceived by those who curated their story. The caption describes the objects on display: "Scissors are an essential tool in the entire sewing process, including patterning, cutting, and sewing ..." (translated from Korean). However, it also reveals how the objects have been interpreted by the museum: "they are like a symbol of sewing. Although they are old and worn, the old tools that have been used for decades retain the beauty of their past" (translated from Korean). This is a mystification of sorts, however highlighting the new regime of value that the scissors have entered, illustrating a new kind of reality.

The sewing master's scissors were commodities until their initial purchase and only became part of the collection of tools-turned-artefacts following a lifetime of garment manufacture. As Alpers specifies, this kind of adaptation of cultural objects in museum collections, made to represent certain cultures, is understood as giving "recognition to a culture" – despite the limitations and problems[75] such representation implicates.[76] The historical and cultural value of the scissors is asserted by their visual display, by their mediation, and by the construction of their new context (the since-closed Iumpium: Sewing History Museum) but determined by the labour and mastery inscribed in, and symbolized by, them.

Mechanical pocket watch

On top of the glass counter of a timepiece repair shop in Sewoon Square, not far from Sewoon Sangga, we are presented with an exposed mechanical pocket watch (Figure 3.5). Its case has been opened and the watch has been placed face down, so that the movement with its different wheels and parts is on show. The owner of the repair shop, an engineer by training, specializes in movement – in clock mechanism repair – hence the exposed presentation.

Just like central Seoul's (declining) garment industry is found around Changsin-dong and Dongdaemun, and the lasting but changing electronics ecosystem around Sewoon Sangga, timepiece repair businesses are clustered around Sewoon Square (and the surrounding Jongno 3-ga). Historically, watch repair and even some production has taken place in nearby Yeji-dong – around so-called "Clock Alley".[77] Yeji-dong, in Jongno-1.2.3.4 ga-dong, was an old neighbourhood directly bordering Sewoon Sangga to the west and squeezed between Jong-ro to the north and Cheonggyecheon to the south. It also conveniently bordered the area referred to as the Cheonggyecheon Machine Tool Arcade.[78] However, different from Sewoon Sangga, which still exists as it escaped full redevelopment and has instead been regenerated, the part of Yeji-dong that enveloped Clock Alley met a different fate: complete demolition and redevelopment under the name Sewoon District #4. Interestingly, upon the site's demolition, redevelopment encountered delays caused by (among other reasons) objects from another time. Relics

Figure 3.5 A side view of a mechanical pocket watch under repair at a shop in Sewoon Square, not far from Sewoon Sangga, on the other side of Jong-ro. Photo by Haeun Kim.

and ruins – "buried cultural heritage", as it is officially called – from the Joseon Dynasty prompted excavation before new structures were built.[79] Many of the remaining watch repair people from the Yeji-dong cluster (which, like other central industries had reduced in size but not disappeared) moved to nearby Sewoon Square only recently, in the early 2020s (as well as to other nearby areas). Among the three industrial infrastructures touched on in this chapter, the one in Sewoon Square and in the surrounding Jongno 3-ga is the smallest but also particularly social. Similar to other infrastructures, the watch repair cluster originating in Yeji-dong involves distinct cooperation among its members. Technicians have their unique expertise, due to which repair is often a collective effort: for example, the engineer concerns him or herself with mechanics, a nearby colleague with polishing, and yet another with glasswork or plating.[80]

Returning to the pocket watch flipped open with exposed movement, its mechanics are complex yet relatively simple compared with some other timepieces the engineer has repaired over the years. Timepieces such as, for instance, cuckoo clocks with dancing dolls and other unique ornaments, are a lot more challenging. In terms of demand, requests for the repair of such complex clocks are, despite a fun challenge, relatively rare. Requests for the repair of mechanical watches, including pocket watches, are more common. These kinds of watches are less affected by trends and, as objects with a considerable lifespan (the engineer estimates around 100 years), business surrounding their repair is expected to continue despite the booming markets of digital and smart watches. Moreover, mechanical watches still have an appeal. Or, as the engineer described it, mechanical watches have their own "sentiment"; a sentiment that seems to be increasingly desirable in the digital age, following a drive towards "analogue moods".[81] Besides the commodity value of mechanical watches and their relative lifespan as objects telling time, it is their sentimental value that leads clients to Sewoon Square to request repairs.

Another development related to the repair of timepieces has been pointed out by the director of a "watch curation platform" that has been in operation for several years. The director was originally a researcher of Yeji-dong's Clock Alley and its ecosystem, but set up the platform to drive an interest in, and a sense of responsibility towards, "watch restoration" – an active attempt by someone from a younger generation to maintain a part of central Seoul's material culture. The deliberate use of the word "restoration" instead of "repair" reflects this as well. As she explains, "repair is included in restoration". It involves the functional recovery of an object while restoration goes beyond that. Restoration involves a form of preservation, based on a different kind of value that is attached to the object. She further explains that the largely tacit knowledge of watch repair is disappearing with the declining business and retirement of repair technicians, while there are also very few opportunities to train or do an apprenticeship – and neither is there much interest among the younger generation to engage in such training or apprenticeship.[82] With the decline of the industry, repair knowledge is disappearing to the point that in the near future it may be hard to find an engineer or technician who is familiar with the complex mechanics of specific timepieces,[83] or with other facets of watch repair. This makes the timepiece repair cluster around Sewoon Square as well as the watch curation platform's mission to restore timepieces notable – not just in light of the work towards the practical repair of timepieces, or the restoration of memories that are attached to them, but in light of an overall preservation of technology-specific knowledge.

In terms of the object of the mechanical watch and possible sentiments attached to it, the platform's director goes beyond appreciating its analogue mood or unique sentiment. She describes timepieces as "the smallest heritage in the world", in that they do not just reflect memories of time but also the personal memories of their owners[84] – an observation also made about some of the repairs that the engineer in Sewoon Square performs. Some people evaluate watches by their price, desiring luxury brands such as Rolex or Cartier; however, the director believes that individual watch enthusiasts can attribute their own values to these objects: personal values, shared memories. Restoration or repair of the object of the mechanical watch does not only extend its life. Mechanical watches (often second-hand) are obvious commodities, yet their social lives are diverse and multiple, as are the values that drive their "movement". With their restoration, these "things-in-motion" preserve in the words of the director, "a kind of legacy": that of an individual, a family, or even a community. This legacy, valorized through shared or individual memory, goes beyond pure economic value or even sentimental value. It is historical and preciously social. Moreover, as these timepieces enter into a different regime of value, they affect the socio-spatial contexts in which their lives are extended, restored, or preserved. Different from the stories about electronics or tailoring scissors, in which certain objects had museums built around them as their "original contexts" are both maintained and changed, the timepieces – equally "social things" inviting "social events" – prompted the repair cluster's move to Sewoon Square and nearby locations, as well as inspired the establishment of the watch curation platform. The objects and their economic, sentimental, historical, and social value "moved" people and determined spaces.

Things, values, places

The centre of Seoul has not only been shaped by "things-in-motion" – it has been coloured and enlivened by them. Throughout Seoul's eventful modern history, commodities, tools, and their values and meanings have contributed to the organization of this distinct place, while today, as the city's central areas are subject to redevelopment, the "things" in them both persist and shift, following distinct trajectories. Imbued with new meaning and new value, these things contribute to the transformation of their socio-spatial contexts as they enter new regimes of value: systems of exchange shaped by particular cultures and histories. The printed circuit board, the pair of scissors, and the mechanical pocket watch are telling examples of used goods that shaped and continue to shape unique places along Cheonggyecheon by virtue of their materiality, their usage, their trajectory as ingrained in them, their visuality, their legacy – their shifting value. The circuit board as an object that is representative of its social context (the electronics market around Sewoon Sangga) led to observations about the regeneration of the megastructure, the persistence of things within it, and the spatial construction around, and isolation of, things in the context of the museum – driven by these things' historical and cultural value. Inspiring ideas about how items such as electronics are culturally significant as forms of heritage, changing value systems contribute to the adaptation of old spaces and the shaping of new ones within the original context of Sewoon Sangga. A comparable trajectory was found in the object of the scissors from the old sewing village of Changsin-dong. Not a commodity from this place but an essential tool used for the production of apparel, the labour and mastery inscribed in – and symbolized by – it was brought out in its visual display in the since-closed Iumpium: Sewing History Museum. The museum's mediation of the scissors' story in the caption on the wall highlighted the new regime of value this former tool had entered as it was valued not just for what it was but for what it looked like and symbolized. The mechanical pocket watch did not have a museum built around it but, against the same background of urban redevelopment and decreasing small-scale manufacturing, it equally affects its socio-spatial context as it carries, besides economic value, sentimental, personal, and social value, determining a legacy. In an "uncertain world of categories",[85] the three objects described in this chapter – each with "an eventful biography"[86] – offer insight into the interplay between shifting urban contexts and shifting meanings and values of things within these contexts.

Acknowledgements

I am grateful to the people who were willing to be interviewed for the larger research project this chapter draws from, and to the former Iumpium: Sewing History Museum for allowing me to take photos in their museum and use one in this chapter. Most importantly, this research could not have been done without the help of research assistants Haeun Kim and Hyunkyung Go.

Notes

1. Under the democratic leadership of former Seoul Mayor Park Won-soon (2011–20) – and after the enactment of the "Special Act on Promotion of and Support for Urban Regeneration" of the Ministry of Government Legislation in 2013, intended to encourage "sustainable growth of cities [and] recovery of [the] local community, by strengthening the public role in and support for the economic, social, and cultural revitalization of cities" – declining areas of Seoul were selected for urban regeneration. Rather than complete redevelopment, the areas' regeneration involved consideration of their historical and socio-economic makeup and was intended to restore the existing surroundings in conversation with the community. This regeneration approach also implied a certain acknowledgement of the cultural significance of the manufacturing history of certain areas. Seoul's current Mayor Oh Se-hoon (since April 2021) has, however, been steering a different course, leading to the cancellation or alteration of some of the ongoing regeneration projects. The agendas of the former and current leadership,

and the effects of their decisions on particular neighbourhoods and communities, are beyond the scope of this chapter. For more information, see Jiyoun Kim and Mihye Cho, "Creating a Sewing Village in Seoul: Towards Participatory Village-Making or Post-Political Urban Regeneration?", *Community Development Journal* 54, no. 5 (2019): 406–26 and Hyeon-jong Yoon, "'Park Won-soon Legacy' 40% of Seoul Urban Regeneration Centers Closed", *Hankook Ilbo*, 27 December 2022.

2. Ho Soon Choi, "How a High-Modernism Project in South Korea Failed: Sewoon Sangga (1966–1972), the First Experimental Modern Planning", *Archnet-IJAR*, 18, no. 4 (2024): 972–86; Yu-min Joo, *Megacity Seoul: Urbanization and the Development of Modern South Korea* (Routledge, 2019); Soo-chul Kim, "Space, History and Mobility: A Historical Inquiry of Seoul as a Mobile City from 1970 to 2000", PhD dissertation (University of Illinois Urbana-Champaign, 2007); Eyun Jennifer Kim, "The Historical Landscape: Evoking the Past in a Landscape for the Future in the Cheonggyecheon Reconstruction in South Korea", *Humanities* 9, no. 113 (2020): 2–24; Heui-Jeong Kwak, "A Turning Point in Korea's Urban Modernization: The Case of the Sewoon Sangga Development", PhD dissertation (Harvard University, 2002); Manon Mollard, "City Within the City: Sewoon Sangga Renovation in Seoul, South Korea", *The Architectural Review*, 24 January 2018.

3. Dongwon Jo, "Cheonggyecheon Electronics Market, a Technical Culture of Copying, and the Shaping of Digital Culture in Korea", *IDI Urban Research* 11 (2017): 37–78; Jo, "'Bursting Circuit Boards': Infrastructures and Technical Practices of Copying in Early Korean Video Game Industry", *International Journal of Computer Game Research* 20, no. 2 (2020); Jo, "Vernacular Technical Practices Beyond the Imitative/Innovative Boundary: Apple II Cloning in Early-1980s South Korea", *East Asian Science, Technology and Society: An International Journal* 16, no. 2 (2022): 157–80.

4. Jo, "'Bursting Circuit Boards'"; Do-young Song, "Cheonggyecheon gonggusanggae hyongsonggwa ilssangjok gwangyemang" (The Formation and Everyday Networks of the Cheonggyecheon Tool Market), *Seoul Studies Series 12, Cheonggyecheon Stream: Time, Place, People – A Study of the Historical Changes in Seoul in the 20th Century 1*, Seoul Institute of Science and Technology (2001): 55–83; Song, "Cheonggyecheon gonggusanggae hyonggonggwabyonhwa" (The Shape and Changes of the Cheonggyecheon Tool Market), *Seoul Studies Monograph 3, Remembering Cheonggyecheon and the Cheonggye Overpass*, Mati Books, 2009, 81–114.

5. Arjun Appadurai, "Introduction: Commodities and the Politics of Value," in Arjun Appadurai (ed.), *The Social Life of Things: Commodities in Cultural Perspective* (Cambridge University Press, 1986), 3–63.

6. Appadurai, "Introduction", 13–16.

7. Appadurai, "Introduction", 15–17.

8. Appadurai, "Introduction", 5.

9. Svetlana Alpers, *The Museum as a Way of Seeing* (Smithsonian Institution Press, 1990).

10. James Clifford, *The Predicament of Culture: Twentieth-Century Ethnography, Literature, and Art* (Harvard University Press, 1988).

11. Every *gu* (district) is divided into smaller *dongs* (neighbourhoods). There are dongs that are formal administrative divisions and there are smaller legal dongs that fall under the administrative divisions.

12. Hyung Min Kim and Sun Sheng Han, "Seoul", *Cities* 29, no. 2 (2012): 142–54.

13. Sejong-daero is named after Sejong the Great, the fourth ruler of Joseon, who created Hangul, the Korean alphabet.

14. Jong-ro means "bell street" and is named after the bell in the nearby bell pavilion that is called Bosingak today.
15. Kim and Han, "Seoul", 142–54.
16. The Korean government is in the process of moving its government buildings from Seoul to the de facto administrative capital Sejong City (approximately 120 km south of Seoul) in an effort to decentralize and promote regional development. For more information, see Jun-Tae Ko, "Capital Relocation Plan Gains Steam with National Assembly Opening a Branch in Sejong", *The Korea Herald*, 3 October 2021.
17. Kim and Han, "Seoul", 142–54.
18. Song, "The Formation and Everyday Networks", 57.
19. Song, "The Formation and Everyday Networks", 57.
20. Do-yeon Kim, "Goryosidae seoul yongue heureumgwa gwaje" (The Current Studies and Prospect in the Study on Seoul Region in Goryeo Dynasty), *Seoul and History* 100 (2018): 47–84.
21. Dong-hoon Kim, *Eclipsed Cinema: The Film Culture of Colonial Korea* (Edinburgh University Press, 2017).
22. Jieheerah Yun, *Globalizing Seoul: The City's Cultural and Urban Change* (Routledge, 2017), 104.
23. Kim and Han, "Seoul", 143–44.
24. Since the Korean War, women had increasingly become economically active. Those who aspired to develop a trade worked in clothing manufacturing or as hairdressers. Those who had the means became self-employed, running linen shops. Among these women were war widows who had become the breadwinners of their families. See Hye-sung Kim, "Dongdaemun's History as Korea's Fashion Mecca", *The Korea Times*, 14 November 2013 and Hyun-sun Kim, "Life and Work of Korean War Widows During the 1950's", *Review of Korean Studies* 12, no. 4 (2009): 87–109.
25. The increased participation of women in South Korea's labour force and their contributions to the development of South Korea is outside the scope of this chapter. For English-language literature about women's contributions to South Korea's modernity, refer to the book *Women in the Sky: Gender and Labor in the Making of Modern Korea* (Cornell University Press, 2021) by Hwa-sook Nam, which examines women workers' labour activism in colonial and post-colonial Korea. Moreover, a documentary film *Sewing Sisters*, directed by Jung-young Kim and Hyukrae Lee, about women labourers and activists of the 1970s in Pyounghwa Clothing Market debuted in 2020.
26. Yun, *Globalizing Seoul*, 105.
27. Kim and Han, "Seoul", 144.
28. Kim, "Dongdaemun's History as Korea's Fashion Mecca".
29. Jo, "'Bursting Circuit Boards'".
30. Song, "The Shape and Changes", 88.
31. Song, "The Shape and Changes", 88.
32. This all happened under the developmental regime of the military dictatorship of the time.
33. Wonjun Cho and Youngsan Kwon, "The Era of Seoul's Rapid Growth (1960s–1970s): The Role of Ex-military Elite Mayors", *Cities* 110 (2021): 103073.
34. *Pyounghwa* translates to peace, which is a reference to the end of the Korean War. The name is said to be inspired by the many refugees from North Korea who, after the war, sold clothes made of US military uniforms. See Seoul Museum of History, *Cheonggyecheon*

gigyegonggusanggabungoppangteureso ingongwisongkkaji (The Cheonggyecheon Machine Tool Arcade: From Fish-Shaped Cake Moulds to Satellites), Exhibition, Cheonggyecheon Museum, Seoul, 2021–22.

35. Seoul Museum of History, *Meideu in cheonggyecheon: dongdaemunmaegyone sijak pyonghwasijang* (Made in Cheonggyecheon: The Pyounghwa Market, Where Dongdaemun Fashion Begins), Exhibition, Cheonggyecheon Museum, Seoul, 2019.
36. Visit Seoul, "Where Past & Present Collide," Seoulites' Pick.
37. Jiyeoun Song, "The Political Dynamics of South Korea's Human Capital Development Strategy", *Asian Perspective* 44, no. 3 (2020): 461–86.
38. Jin-hai Park, "Changsin-dong Shows Rise, Fall of Sweatshops", *The Korea Times*, 15 April 2018.
39. Suh-yoon Lee, "Euljiro's Last Stand: Redevelopment Rips Through Historic Manufacturing Hub", *The Korea Times*, 9 January 2019.
40. In accordance with the convention of confidentiality in qualitative research, names of interviewees have been withheld.
41. Interview, November 2021.
42. Interview, November 2021.
43. Its build was instigated by "Bulldozer Mayor" Kim Hyeon-ok who was the fourteenth Mayor of Seoul (1966–70).
44. In 1961, Park Chung-hee and his allies who formed the Military Revolutionary Committee successfully carried out a coup d'état. This coup gave rise to a new developmentalist elite as well as to societal struggles and episodes of violence. It was only in 1987 that a more democratic political system was installed in South Korea, in the lead up to which the generation of students of the 1980s played a pivotal and sacrificial role.
45. A squatter area had developed not only along Cheonggyecheon but also along much of the strip of land that Sewoon Sangga was built on. This was a vacant strip of land created at the end of Korea's occupation by Japan, to prevent fire from spreading in case of air raids. See, Mollard, "City Within the City".
46. Due to the rise of commercial areas such as Yongsan and Gangnam.
47. Seoul Museum of History, *Seunsanggawa geu iuttteul: Sanopwae gisueso jonjamanmulsijangkkaji* (Sewoon Sangga and its Neighbours: From Flagship of Industrialization to Electronics Market), Research Department, 2010, 43–71.
48. Jo, "'Bursting Circuit Boards'".
49. Jo, "Cheonggyecheon Electronics Market".
50. In the 2000s, plans were made for the complete demolition of the building, which were later revised.
51. Seoul Metropolitan Government, "Seoul to Reinvigorate Sewoon Sangga with 'Urban Regeneration Plan,'" *City News*, 26 February 2015.
52. This chapter does not intend to assess whether these efforts have been successful.
53. Makercity Sewoon. "The re:Sewoon Project", *Sewoon Made*.
54. Seoul Metropolitan Government, "Introducing Sewoon Electronics Museum! Sewoon Shopping Mall Was Born as Korea's First Electronics and Electrical Specialty Shopping Mall", *Press Release*, 29 May 2018.
55. A Korean musical genre that originates in the Japanese colonial period and has developed over the decades.

56. John Lie, "What Is the K in K-Pop? South Korean Popular Music, the Culture Industry, and National Identity", *Korea Observer* 43, no. 3 (2012): 343–49.

57. It is outside the scope of this chapter to elaborate on the history of Korean pop music. For detailed accounts of the post-war development of the Korean music industry, refer to Gooyong Kim, *From Factory Girls to K-Pop Idol Girls: Cultural Politics of Developmentalism, Patriarchy, and Neoliberalism in South Korea's Popular Music Industry* (Lexington Books, 2019); Ingyu Oh, "The Globalization of K-Pop: Korea's Place in the Global Music Industry", *Korea Observer* 44, no. 3 (2013): 389–409; or Lie, "What Is the K in K-Pop?".

58. "Suri Suri" is a wordplay referring to "suri" (수리), which means repair in Korean, and to "Suri Suri Maha Suri" (수리수리 마하수리), which is an expression similar to "abracadabra" or "hocus pocus".

59. Makercity Sewoon. "Jingong-gwan aempeulo deudneun keullaesig eum-aghoe" (Listening to a Classical Concert with a Vacuum Tube Amplifier), *Event News*.

60. Makercity Sewoon, "Listening to a Classical Concert".

61. Naver Knowledge iN. "Dapppyon: Hanjajilmunjom butaktteuryoyo" (Answer: Question about Hanja Characters).

62. HEGA Corporation. "Greetings", Company Introduction.

63. Eun-kyung Kang, "Bagwonsun jiugi mamuri susun? Dosijaesaeng sangjing changsindong bongjeyokssagwan pyegwan" (The Final Step of "Remove Park Won Soon"? Closure of the "Sewing History Museum" in Changsin-dong, a Symbol of Urban Regeneration), *Biz Hankook*, 21 February 2023.

64. Cho and Kwon, "The Era of Seoul's Rapid Growth".

65. This unionization was incited by the self-immolation of tailor and activist Chun Tae-il.

66. Hwasook Nam, "Reading Chun Tae-il: Making Sense of a Worker Self-Immolation in 1970s South Korea", in Charles R. Kim, Jungwon Kim, Hwasook Nam and Serk-Bae Suh (eds.), *Beyond Death: The Politics of Suicide and Martyrdom in Korea* (University of Washington Press, 2019), 167–201.

67. Kim and Cho, "Creating a Sewing Village in Seoul", 408.

68. Seoul Metropolitan Government, "Introducing Sewoon Electronics Museum!".

69. Appadurai, "Introduction".

70. Alpers, *The Museum as a Way of Seeing*, 26–27.

71. Clifford, *The Predicament of Culture*, 220.

72. Clifford, *The Predicament of Culture*, 220.

73. Alpers, *The Museum as a Way of Seeing*, 30.

74. Alpers, *The Museum as a Way of Seeing*, 30.

75. Not all cultures have representative material objects; the power of selecting certain objects over others lies with those running museum spaces, etc.

76. Alpers, *The Museum as a Way of Seeing*, 30–32.

77. Mi-young Jeon, "San-eobhwa 'neomeo'ui jag-eobjang: yejidong sigyegolmog-ui gisulgwa munhwa" (Workplace "Beyond" Industrialization: Technology and Culture of Yeji-dong Clock Alley), Master's thesis (Seoul National University, 2020).

78. Seoul Museum of History, "The Cheonggyecheon Machine Tool Arcade".

79. Lee, "Euljiro's Last Stand".

80. Interview, November 2021.

81. Interview, November 2021.
82. Interview, November 2021.
83. The engineer from Sewoon Square already experienced this regarding cuckoo clocks as, today, he appears to be one of few people who has the ability to perform their repair.
84. Interview, November 2021.
85. Igor Kopytoff, "The Cultural Biography of Things: Commoditization as Process", in Arjun Appadurai (ed.), *The Social Life of Things: Commodities in Cultural Perspective* (Cambridge University Press, 1986), 90.
86. Kopytoff, "The Cultural Biography of Things", 90.

References

Alpers, Svetlana. *The Museum as a Way of Seeing*, Smithsonian Institution Press, 1990.
Appadurai, Arjun. "Introduction: Commodities and the Politics of Value", in Arjun Appadurai (ed.), *The Social Life of Things: Commodities in Cultural Perspective*, Cambridge University Press, 1986.
Cho, Wonjun and Youngsang Kwon. "The Era of Seoul's Rapid Growth (1960s–1970s): The Role of Ex-military Elite Mayors", *Cities* 110 (2021): 103073. https://doi.org/10.1016/j.cities.2020.103073.
Choi, Ho Soon. "How a High-Modernism Project in South Korea Failed: Sewoon Sangga (1966–1972), the First Experimental Modern Planning", *Archnet-IJAR*, 18, no. 4 (2024): 972–86. https://doi.org/10.1108/ARCH-07-2023-0188.
Clifford, James. *The Predicament of Culture: Twentieth-Century Ethnography, Literature, and Art*, Harvard University Press, 1988.
HEGA Corporation. "Greetings", Company Introduction. http://www.hegacorp.com/page.php?p_id=greetings (accessed 20 August 2023).
Jeon, Mi-young. "San-eobhwa 'neomeo'ui jag-eobjang: yejidong sigyegolmog-ui gisulgwa munhwa" (Workplace "Beyond" Industrialization: Technology and Culture of Yeji-dong Clock Alley), Master's thesis, Seoul National University, 2020. http://dcollection.snu.ac.kr/common/orgView/000000159168.
Jo, Dongwon. "Cheonggyecheon Electronics Market, a Technical Culture of Copying, and the Shaping of Digital Culture in Korea", *IDI Urban Research* 11 (2017): 37–78. https://doi.org/10.34165/urbanr.2017..11.37.
Jo, Dongwon. "'Bursting Circuit Boards': Infrastructures and Technical Practices of Copying in Early Korean Video Game Industry", *International Journal of Computer Game Research* 20, no. 2 (2020). https://gamestudies.org/2020/articles/jo.
Jo, Dongwon. "Vernacular Technical Practices Beyond the Imitative/Innovative Boundary: Apple II Cloning in Early-1980s South Korea", *East Asian Science, Technology and Society: An International Journal* 16, no. 2 (2022): 157–80.
Joo, Yu-min. *Megacity Seoul: Urbanization and the Development of Modern South Korea*, Routledge, 2019.
Kang, Eun-kyung. "Bagwonsun jiugi mamuri susun? Dosijaesaeng sangjing changsindong bongjeyokssagwan pyegwan" (The Final Step of "Remove Park Won Soon"? Closure of the "Sewing History Museum" in Changsin-dong, a Symbol of Urban Regeneration), *Biz Hankook*, 21 February 2023. http://www.bizhankook.com/bk/article/25240.
Kim, Do-yeon. "Goryosidae seoul yongue heureumgwa gwaje" (The Current Studies and Prospect in the Study on Seoul Region in Goryeo Dynasty), *Seoul and History* 100 (2018): 47–84. https://doi.org/10.22827/seoul.2018..100.002.

Kim, Dong-hoon. *Eclipsed Cinema: The Film Culture of Colonial Korea*, Edinburgh University Press, 2017.
Kim, Eyun Jennifer. "The Historical Landscape: Evoking the Past in a Landscape for the Future in the Cheonggyecheon Reconstruction in South Korea", *Humanities* 9, no. 113 (2020): 2–24. https://doi.org/10.3390/h9030113.
Kim, Gooyong. *From Factory Girls to K-Pop Idol Girls: Cultural Politics of Developmentalism, Patriarchy, and Neoliberalism in South Korea's Popular Music Industry*, Lexington Books, 2019.
Kim, Hye-sung. "Dongdaemun's History as Korea's Fashion Mecca", *The Korea Times*, 14 November 2013. https://www.koreatimes.co.kr/www/culture/2020/02/199_146241.html.
Kim, Hyun-sun. "Life and Work of Korean War Widows During the 1950s", *Review of Korean Studies* 12, no. 4 (2009): 87–109.
Kim, Hyung Min and Sun Sheng Han. "Seoul", *Cities* 29, no. 2 (2012): 142–54. https://doi.org/10.1016/j.cities.2011.02.003.
Kim, Jiyoun and Mihye Cho. "Creating a Sewing Village in Seoul: Towards Participatory Village-Making or Post-Political Urban Regeneration?", *Community Development Journal* 54, no. 5 (2019): 406–26. https://doi-org.libproxy.hongik.ac.kr/10.1093/cdj/bsx051.
Kim, Jung-young and Hyukrae Lee, directors. *Sewing Sisters*, 2020. 1 hour, 50 min.
Kim, Soo-chul. "Space, History and Mobility: A Historical Inquiry of Seoul as a Mobile City from 1970 to 2000", PhD dissertation, University of Illinois Urbana-Champaign, 2007.
Ko, Jun-tae. "Capital Relocation Plan Gains Steam with National Assembly Opening a Branch in Sejong", *The Korea Herald*, 3 October 2021. https://www.koreaherald.com/view.php?ud=20211002000077.
Kopytoff, Igor. "The Cultural Biography of Things: Commoditization as Process", in Arjun Appadurai (ed.), *The Social Life of Things: Commodities in Cultural Perspective*, Cambridge University Press, 1986.
Kwak, Heui-Jeong. "A Turning Point in Korea's Urban Modernization: The Case of the Sewoon Sangga Development", PhD dissertation, Harvard University, 2002.
Lee, Suh-yoon. "Euljiro's Last Stand: Redevelopment Rips through Historic Manufacturing Hub", *The Korea Times*, 9 January 2019. https://www.koreatimes.co.kr/www/nation/2023/10/113_261640.html.
Lie, John. "What Is the K in K-Pop? South Korean Popular Music, the Culture Industry, and National Identity", *Korea Observer* 43, no. 3 (2012): 339–63.
Nam, Hwasook. "Reading Chun Tae-il: Making Sense of a Worker Self-Immolation in 1970s South Korea", in Charles R. Kim, Jungwon Kim, Hwasook Nam and Serk-Bae Suh (eds.), *Beyond Death: The Politics of Suicide and Martyrdom in Korea*, University of Washington Press, 2019, 167–201.
Nam, Hwasook. *Women in the Sky: Gender and Labor in the Making of Modern Korea*, Cornell University Press, 2021.
Makercity Sewoon. "The re:Sewoon Project", *Sewoon Made*. https://sewoon.org/eng_overview (accessed 14 April 2023).
Makercity Sewoon. "Jingong-gwan aempeulo deudneun keullaesig eum-aghoe" (Listening to a Classical Concert with a Vacuum Tube Amplifier), *Event News*. https://sewoon.org/event/?q=YToyOntzOjEyOiJrZXl3b3JkX3R5cGUiO3M6MzoiYWxsIjtzOjQ6InBhZ2UiO2k6Mzt9&bmode=view&idx=12045990&t=board (accessed 12 August 2023).
Ministry of Government Legislation. "Special Act on Promotion of and Support for Urban Regeneration", Korean Law Information Center. https://www.law.go.kr/eng/engLsSc.do?menuId=2&section=lawNm&query=Special+Act+on+Promotion+of+and+Support+for+Urban+Regeneration&#x=0&y=0#liBgcolor1 (accessed 23 August 2023).
Mollard, Manon. "City Within the City: Sewoon Sangga Renovation in Seoul, South Korea", *The Architectural Review*, 24 January 2018. https://www.architectural-review.com/buildings/city-within-the-city-sewoon-sangga-renovation-in-seoul-south-korea.

Naver Knowledge iN. "Dapppyon: Hanjajilmunjom butaktteuryoyo" (Answer: Question about Hanja Characters). https://kin.naver.com/qna/detail.naver?d1id=11&dirId=11080201&docId=363437631&qb (accessed 1 February 2023).

Oh, Ingyu. "The Globalization of K-Pop: Korea's Place in the Global Music Industry", *Korea Observer* 44, no. 3 (2013): 389–409.

Park, Jin-hai. "Changsin-dong Shows Rise, Fall of Sweatshops", *The Korea Times*, 15 April 2018. http://www.koreatimes.co.kr/www/culture/2018/04/317_247300.html.

Seoul Metropolitan Government. "Seoul to Reinvigorate Sewoon Sangga with 'Urban Regeneration Plan'", *City News*, 26 February 2015. https://english.seoul.go.kr/seoul-reinvigorate-sewoon-sangga-urban-regeneration-plan/.

Seoul Metropolitan Government. "Introducing Sewoon Electronics Museum! Sewoon Shopping Mall Was Born as Korea's First Electronics and Electrical Specialty Shopping Mall", *Press Release*, 29 May 2018. https://uri.seoul.go.kr/web/main/bbs/info_graphics/1441?cp=25&pageSize=6&sortOrder=BA_REGDATE&sortDirection=DESC&bcId=info_graphics&baNotice=false&baCommSelec=false&baOpenDay=false&baUse=true.

Seoul Museum of History. *Seunsanggawa geu iuttteul: Sanopwae gisueso jonjamanmulsijangkkaji* (Sewoon Sangga and its Neighbours: From Flagship of Industrialization to Electronics Market), Research Department, 2010.

Seoul Museum of History. *Meideu in cheonggyecheon: dongdaemunmaegyone sijak pyonghwasijang* (Made in Cheonggyecheon: The Pyounghwa Market, Where Dongdaemun Fashion Begins), Exhibition, Cheonggyecheon Museum, Seoul, 2019. https://museum.seoul.go.kr/CHM_HOME/jsp/MM03/vr/122/index.html.

Seoul Museum of History. *Cheonggyecheon gigyegonggusanggabungoppangteureso ingongwisongkkaji* (The Cheonggyecheon Machine Tool Arcade: From Fish-Shaped Cake Moulds to Satellites), Exhibition, Cheonggyecheon Museum, Seoul, 2021–22. https://museum.seoul.go.kr/CHM_HOME/jsp/MM03/vr/the_cheonggyecheon_machine_tool_arcade/index.html (accessed 20 December 2023).

Song, Do-young. "Cheonggyecheon gonggusanggae hyongsonggwa ilssangjok gwangyemang" (The Formation and Everyday Networks of the Cheonggyecheon Tool Market), *Seoul Studies Series 12, Cheonggyecheon Stream: Time, Place, People – A Study of the Historical Changes in Seoul in the 20th Century 1*, Seoul Institute of Science and Technology (2001): 55–83. https://db.history.go.kr/id/hb_115_01_000613.

Song, Do-young. "Cheonggyecheon gonggusanggae hyonggonggwabyonhwa" (The Shape and Changes of the Cheonggyecheon Tool Market), *Seoul Studies Monograph 3, Remembering Cheonggyecheon and the Cheonggye Overpass*, Mati Books, 2009, 81–114.

Song, Jiyeoun. "The Political Dynamics of South Korea's Human Capital Development Strategy", *Asian Perspective* 44, no. 3 (2020): 461–86. https://dx.doi.org/10.1353/apr.2020.0020.

Visit Seoul. "Where Past & Present Collide", Seoulites' Pick. https://english.visitseoul.net/editorspicks/Find-the-Past--Present-of-Shopping-and-Fashion-at-the-Dongdaemun-Fashion-Cluster_/32571 (last modified 31 August 2023).

Yoon, Hyeon-jong. "'Park Won-soon Legacy' 40% of Seoul Urban Regeneration Centers Closed", *Hankook Ilbo*, 27 December 2022). https://www.hankookilbo.com/News/Read/A2022122311240000294.

Yun, Jieheerah. *Globalizing Seoul: The City's Cultural and Urban Change*, Routledge, 2017.

PART II
DESIGN, MATERIAL CULTURE, AND MEDIATION

CHAPTER 4
HEALTH BOOMS AND BUBBLY BODIES: *HANAKO* MAGAZINE, WOMEN, AND BEAUTY IN THE 1980S JAPANESE BUBBLE ECONOMY
Hui-Ying Kerr

Introduction

In the late 1980s, "Girls, be ambitious!" was the rallying cry that accompanied the period optimistically pronounced as the *onna no jidai*, or "women's decade".[1] Highly visible in leisure and as a consumer market, young women appeared to be the main winners when it came to enjoying the benefits of the Japanese Bubble Economy. Yet with only 1.3 per cent of working women able to enter corporate managerial track work,[2] and high levels of sexism in working practices,[3] it could be said that women's conditions had not improved that much when it came to structural change. During this time, new women's magazines aimed at the modern working woman documented this dichotomy between cultural and professional presence, becoming a key indicator for many of the changes happening in the cultural and social sphere of the Bubble Economy. Through the lens of *Hanako* magazine, this chapter will explore how women, through their consumption and presentation of themselves, became a key battleground in the Japanese economic bubble, as receiver of consumer strategies and instigator of rebellion and change.

The Bubble, women, and *Hanako* magazine

In the 1980s, Japan experienced a massive account surplus that propelled it to being the second largest economy in the world, second only to the United States. In response to international pressure, Japan signed the 1985 Plaza Accord, agreeing to an artificial yen appreciation and the opening up of its economy to international markets that directly led to the massive asset boom known as the Bubble Economy. During this period, property, stocks, and shares all escalated rapidly as cheaper financing became available, with a correspondent boom in consumer markets, notably leisure. This feverish "bubbly" culture of financial and material exuberance is what characterized the Bubble Economy, slowing down only when interest rates started to rise in 1989, when land prices peaked in 1991, and finally ending culturally by 1995 when the disasters of the sarin gas attacks and the Kobe earthquake put to rest any lingering feelings of celebratory optimism.[4]

In line with international pressure to open the Japanese market was the 1986 Maekawa Report, which recommended encouraging the domestic consumer market as a way to promote international relations through reducing Japan's account surplus, as well as improving the work-life balance through changes to Japanese lifestyle and leisure.[5] As a result, one of the more prominent consumer trends during the Bubble was that of young women, who were seen as a new burgeoning market to promote these changes. Entering the workforce in large numbers, young women were encouraged to work, through the passing of the 1986 Equal Employment Opportunity Law (EEOL)[6] and encouraged to spend their earnings through structural mechanisms that were both the result of gender norms in employment and culture. For despite having high representation in the workforce, young women had few long-term career opportunities, with the cultural norm being that women would work until either marriage or maternity, preferably within their twenties, before re-entering the labour market as older women in what is known as the "m-curve" of women's employment in Japan, often in lower-waged, lower-skilled work such as supermarket and convenience store workers.[7] With such high turnover, most roles for women were therefore administrative (*ippanshoku*), with only one per cent attaining managerial-track positions (*sōgōshoku*). Known as Office Ladies (OLs), or the female working counterpart to the corporate "salarymen" or corporate male office workers, these young women were perfect consumers for the time. Still living at home with largely disposable incomes, young women had no real incentive to save up or work on their career, with the added imperative to enjoy themselves before settling down for marriage. As such, with disposable income and time, they were the perfect recipients for shoring up the declining parts of the Japanese economy and pushing forward the recommendations of the Maekawa Report to increase Japanese leisure and quality of life, moving society to a more consumer-based economy. These included the reduction of working hours from around 2,100 to 1,800 hours per annum, transforming industry to expand domestic demand and improve market access for manufactured goods and services.[8]

It is against this background that *Hanako* magazine was created. From the beginning of the twentieth century, Japanese magazines have a long history as markers of social change, and women's magazines in particular have informed scholarly study that charts their influence as educators of women as housewives to empowered female consumers of goods and information.[9] Moreover, the magazine market in Japan is highly specialized and segmented according to gender and age, with a rapid changeover of titles reflecting the dynamic tastes of a rapidly expanding consumer market, making it an excellent arbiter of social and cultural influences.

It was into this mix that *Hanako*, first published by Magazine House in 1988 at the height of the Bubble and still in circulation today, broke new ground for Japanese women's magazines by focusing not on fashion, but on leisure, targeting those OLs at whom so much leisure policy was aimed. In this it heralded a more lifestyle-oriented type of magazine that recognized women's increased consumer power. With bi-weekly publication and a readership of around 300,000, it was primarily aimed at a Tokyo metropolitan audience of young, single working women who made up the OLs. However, as White notes,[10] magazines such as *Hanako* have a pervasive trickle-out effect into surrounding readerships wanting to keep abreast of trends in the capital, while *Hanako* was specifically observed to function as a popular tour guide[11] among visiting young women abroad, meaning its exposure and influence was more significant than just among the direct readership. Featuring everything from travel to restaurants, shopping to spas, *Hanako* was an unabashed magazine of the Bubble, and represented the new way of living that was promised by the possibilities (and excesses) of the Bubble Economy, or the "Bubbly Life".

The *Hanako* woman

While *Hanako* focused on lifestyle rather than fashion, beauty was a natural focus for *Hanako*'s demographic. Though broadly translating as administrative clerical roles, OL duties also extended to general services such as making tea for their male colleagues, keeping the office tidy by clearing desks and emptying ashtrays, greeting clients, and being the presentable service-related face of the company. As such, standards of appearance through prescribed hairstyles, make-up, uniforms, and even – in some of the larger corporations – etiquette classes, were required of women, with an essential part of their job being decorative – or to brighten up the office with their female presence as "office flowers".[12] At the height of their marital eligibility, OLs were also seen as potential marriage partners for their male colleagues; not only by management as a positive stabilizing force on their male workforce, but also by the OLs themselves, keen to secure their future with a good match.[13] Beauty and appearance were thus of prime importance to the *Hanako* demographic, not only for their work, but more importantly for their longer-term marital prospects.

However, how the Japanese woman was represented in *Hanako* magazine differs from this corporate and marital view of Japanese female womanhood. Strikingly, within *Hanako* the image of the Japanese woman does not appear that often. While there is still beauty present, this is notably in the form of elegantly poised Western or Eurasian models to be gazed at. Instead, how the magazine can be interpreted is that the Japanese woman *is* the gaze looking out at the world, and so the magazine is filled with things to do and see, from domestic and international locations for travel, leisure, and entertainment, to activities that span drinking, eating, shopping, and sports.

Where Japanese women do appear, they are often portrayed doing something, and instead of standalone, being looked at, they are active or in groups, looking out. Thus, rather than the demure tea-serving "office flower", *Hanako* women are bold, bright, and colourful; frequently depicted outside and having fun, these women are stylish, modern, and ambitious. Even when depicted in a professional context, they are not of the conventional OL with her corporate uniform and prescribed hairstyle, but dynamic career women, magnetic in their independence and self-assured freedom.

An example of this can be seen in Figure 4.1, for one of the regular "After Hours" articles featuring an extensive "recommendation" for the drink, Bacardi and Coke.[14] Taking centre-stage are three Japanese professional women, notably not in company uniform, but presented stylishly, with modern hairstyles, accessories, make-up, and

Figure 4.1 *Hanako* magazine, issue 125, 6 December 1990 (Magazine House, Tokyo, 1990), 102–3.

clothing. Seated around a marble-topped table in a bar furnished with luxurious modern décor and soft, low lighting, the three women are clearly relaxing and enjoying themselves in the evening, appearing carefree and enjoying each other's company. In this, we see not necessarily the direct experience of the OL readership, but more an idealized version of the modern Japanese working woman, dynamic and liberated from the reality of professional life.

Taking things further away from reality, encapsulating the energetic and at times zany zeitgeist of the Bubble, in some of the advertisements and articles in *Hanako*, Japanese women don outlandish costumes and are presented in contexts at odds with conventional views of traditional Japanese femininity. An example of this can be seen in an advertisement for rental telephones (Figure 4.2), in which the woman at the centre is bright and attention-grabbing, not only through the use of the bold yellow palate and unusual hairstyle, but also in her very expressive face and vocality. Wide-eyed and mouth open, the Japanese model appears loud both visually and metaphorically, the social indecency of her open expression and loud clothing explained by the "crazy" in the accompanying copy. In a wider sense, the woman's brashness and surrealness can be seen as reflective of – and accepted as – the strange brash cultural atmosphere of the Bubble Economy in which property prices were astronomical, everyone was flush with money, and the possibility of the high life could be had by all.

This "chattiness" of the woman is something reflected in other mediums of the time, notably in the popular manga, *OL Shinkaron* (OL Evolution), which was first published in 1989 at the peak of the Bubble Economy. Here, OLs display comic characteristics such

Health Booms and Bubbly Bodies

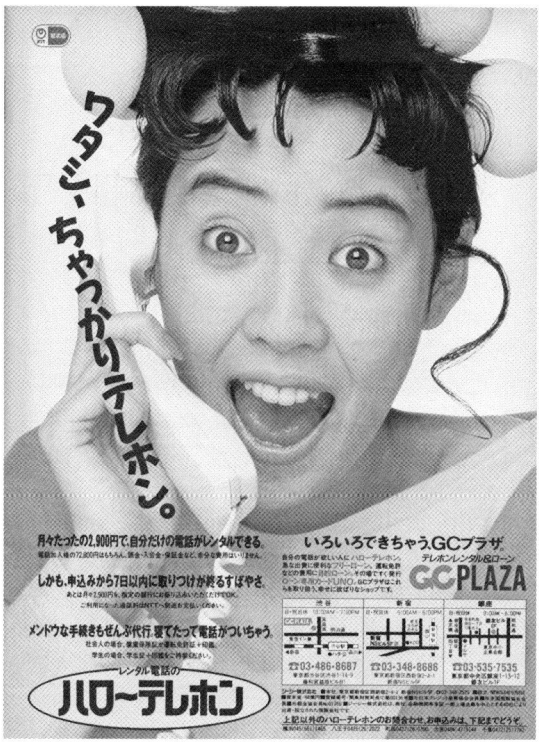

Figure 4.2 Kutashi "Crazy Telephone" advertisement, *Hanako* magazine, issue 32, 19 January 1989 (Magazine House, Tokyo, 1989), 84.

as mischievousness, loving gossip, playing the system, and having fun. In Figure 4.3,[15] two OLs discuss how to gently let down a potential marriage suitor by signalling their unsuitability through wearing "playgirl" attire: revealing clothes, bold leopard-skin prints, and excessive make-up – the punchline being revealed that this is the normal dress of the OL giving the advice. Here we see the coded use of dress and appearance to signal not only the strategy and mischievousness of the OLs in navigating social situations, but also the emphasis on having fun, and their relative freedom to do so outside of work as single working women before settling down for marriage. In a wider sense, what *OL Shinkaron* does is lift the lid on the working practices and thoughts of OLs, revealing a much more human and expansive reality underneath the carefully constructed veneer of OL professionalism and Japanese femininity.

However, while endearing and funny, at its heart, it is important to note that this more expressive and loud female identity was at odds with the tradition of Japanese feminine modesty predicated on silent mystique and passivity. In the dynamic arena of the Bubble Economy, older, traditional forms of Japanese femininity were making way for cheerier characteristics more useful not only in brightening up the office, but also for the hustle and bustle of international corporate business. In addition to qualities such as cleanliness, elegance, and moderation, other terms such as sparkle and radiance (*kagayaku*),

Figure 4.3 *OL Shinkaron*, Risu Akizuki (Magazine House, Tokyo, 1989), 20.

cheerfulness (*akarui*), and brisk efficiency (*haki haki suru*) were emphasized as qualities ideal for OLs.[16] In this way, OLs were at the forefront of a gradual evolution of less restrictive Japanese femininity facilitated by the workplace. However, it must be remembered that this "bright and bubbly" nature was also being encouraged to ultimately further the needs of the Japanese economy, with Japanese women co-opted for wider economic gains they were mostly directly excluded from.

Beautiful things

While light on the visibility of Japanese women, *Hanako* is, of course, resplendent with many beautiful goods. From beauty products such as make-up, facial creams, and beauty treatments, to clothes, fashion accessories, jewellery, and household goods such as porcelain tea sets, coffee makers, and even cars. Taken collectively, these items describe a lifestyle that chimes with the emphasis on consumption as national good, tailored to young working Japanese women as the new promising consumer market, and natural participants of the Bubble Economy. During the 1980s, the enthusiastic uptake of luxury consumer goods and brands was part and parcel of the culture of the Bubble Economy, facilitated by the artificial upward revaluation of the yen as well as the liberalization of the financial and consumer markets as set out in the Plaza Accord. It was also a convenient way to offset the international and trading issues brought on by Japan's high account surplus, and ordinary Japanese consumers were encouraged to buy foreign goods by no less than the prime minister himself.[17] Practically speaking, among OLs, this most often manifested in a collective desire for international luxury fashion items such as Louis Vuitton, Tiffany open-heart necklaces, and Hermés scarves that themselves were elevated into a kind of OL mythology and typecasting. However, what *Hanako* magazine shows is that this emphasis on consumption was not restricted to luxury fashion alone, but extended out to all kinds of goods made available to their female readers.

On an individual readership level, the magazine operates in the traditional instructional sphere of women's magazines, giving advice on fashion and goods that includes not only the images, but also the pricing, locations, and retailers. In this way, consumption is moved from the dreamscape of luxurious consumption and the fantasy of being rich in a first-world economy, to the practicalities of materializing such wealth to incorporate it into everyday life. Thus, while there are images of desirable goods advertised in conventional luxurious layouts framed by negative space, these are more often crowded out by the plethora of products and accompanying information amassed onto pages, clamouring for the reader's attention. As such, the magazine becomes educational, imparting knowledge of product and brand value, as much as what to buy and where to buy it.

Furthermore, despite the inequalities of men and women's working arrangements, the pressure to achieve matrimony and OLs' dependence on their appearance for their work, *Hanako* magazine does not seem to frame its articles on gaining the attention of men. Rather, the goods displayed appear to describe a beautiful life to be enjoyed for its own sake, at a time of national plenty and international possibility. Rather than merely beautifying oneself through clothes, make-up, and accessories, it creates an entire world in which the Japanese woman is redrawn as the prime instigator and consumer of a new lifestyle, governed by abundance. In this way, it not only encourages the female readers to participate in the Bubble as a new consumer market, but also taps into the zeitgeist of the time, captured by the novel, *Somehow Crystal* (*nantonaku kurisutaru*).[18] Winner of the 1980 literary Bungei Prize, the book broke with literary tradition, placing consumer culture centre-stage through the deliberate cataloguing of existing brands, products, shops, and restaurants; in doing so it provided the basis on which the characters formed their identities and captured the spirit of the new, more materialistic generation, even leading to the phenomenon of the *kurisutaru-zoku* (crystal tribe) named after the book. While sparking a certain moralistic disapproval over the new consumer and materialistic lifestyles of the younger generation, termed the *shinjinrui* – or so-called "New Breed" due to their difference in attitudes[19] – young women were also being positioned as a new type of Japanese consumer-citizen, in which Japanese purchasing power could literally buy oneself a beautiful carefree life, embodying the economic prestige and power of the second largest economy in the world.

It is in this way that young women's beauty, rather than internalized or even externalized, is extended further beyond the confines of the body to incorporate an entire beautiful lifestyle of a nation, full of desirable objects within grasp and materialized for easy consumption. Tellingly, however, there are few mentions of interior decorating other than a few articles on apartments to rent – acknowledging the limited participation of working women in the investment of their own real estate before marriage, and thus in the real investment opportunities that characterized the Bubble.

Food for beauty

Even as a new type of femininity was being explored through depiction, how it was being expressed took a variety of forms, with one being the surprisingly prevalent and persistent incorporation of food in *Hanako* magazine. While the traditional role of men was to be the main and often sole breadwinner in society, women's roles were much more practically and intrinsically linked to food, with the main narrative being that of the good wife/wise mother and provider of home-cooked, nutritious meals. Complicating this, however, was the fact that young single women, often still living at home with their parents, were yet to fill this role. Instead, food became a staging ground in the dynamics of dating and romantic games, assessing the viability of potential marriage partners, as well as a way to express their own femininity and reflect upon themselves. The latter took the form of either sophisticated knowledge and experiences, to create an *ojosama* (ladylike) persona, or a deliberately naïve and unsophisticated approach, to create an appealingly innocent and pure *burikko* (childlike) sensibility, both approaches covered in *Hanako* magazine and its extensive articles on food. In this, *Hanako* once again took an instructional approach, with extensive listings of places to eat and types of foods, accompanied by locations, prices, and descriptions. Ranging from restaurants and sophisticated eateries both local and abroad, to cute snacks and foods both Japanese and international, what *Hanako* noticeably didn't provide were recipes on how to make these foods. Focusing solely on pure consumption rather than production, food was for appearance and enjoyment only, accentuating one's sophistication or feminine appeal through eating and presenting one's character through food. In their analysis of Japanese OL working practices in the early 1990s, Ogasawara[20] and Lo[21] both note the importance of food in the presentation of the OLs especially to their male colleagues, as well as in the smooth running of complex office dynamics in the form of gifts, souvenirs, snacks, and treats, especially between genders and superiors and subordinates. In this, foodstuffs are used to display not only the hard power of the men in their ability to buy gifts and treats, but also in the soft power of the women in their ability to signal favour of specific men in the context of romance and the working environment.

Another approach explored in *Hanako* was the link between food and health and beauty, notably in the proliferation of so-called "functional foods", including dieting foods, nutritional foods, health foods, and energy drinks. During this period, there was a boom in health foods and energy drinks, as the frenetic pace of the Bubble Economy took hold. An example of this expansion is that of the energy drink brand, Lipovitan D, its sale of energy drinks increasing from 100 million bottles in 1965 to 400 million bottles in 1980.[22] While these trends have normally been associated with the hectic lives of the hard-working salarymen, adverts for these foods abound in *Hanako*, aimed at women, falling broadly into one of two categories: the transformational and the affirmative.

In promoting a strategy of the transformational, the food and drink advertised offers the promise of additional energy, weight loss, or improving one's health or appearance. While the promise of calorie and weight reduction through diet-related foods is nothing new, and indeed long-aligned with traditional East Asian femininity of smallness, slenderness, and fragility,[23] what is interesting is the appearance of energy drink advertisements in a women's magazine. Normally associated with the triumphalist hegemony of corporate salarymen, energy drinks utilize a different strategy that seeks to enhance rather than reduce the female body through the injection of energy.

For example, in Figures 4.4 and 4.5, we can see two examples of the type of energy drinks marketed to women through *Hanako* magazine. In Figure 4.4, for *Lipovitan D*, a

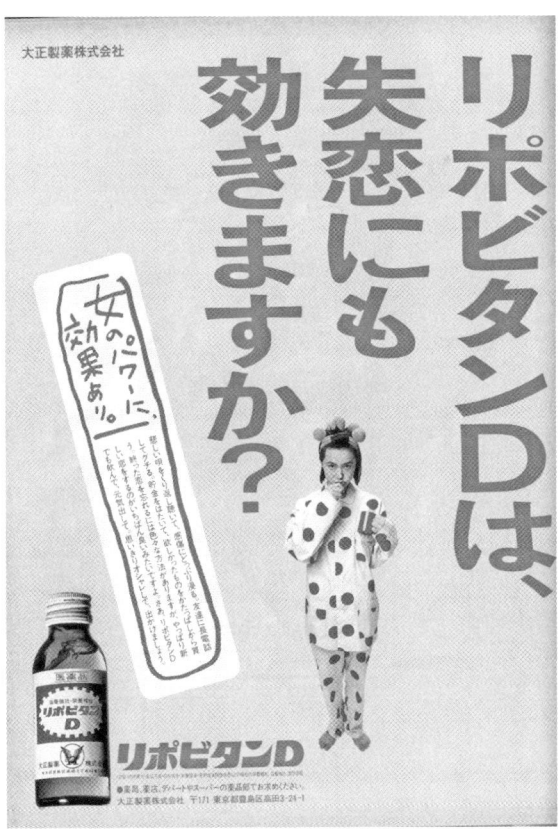

Figure 4.4 *Hanako* magazine, issue 45, 20 April 1989 (Magazine House, Tokyo, 1989), 143.

Figure 4.5 *Hanako* magazine, issue 92, 5 April 1990 (Magazine House, Tokyo, 1990), 50.

young woman in spotted pyjamas, cutely tied-up hair, and soulful upward-looking expression, is shown under the caption, "Do you love Lipovitan D too?", and with a side caption of "Effective for women's power".[24] In Figure 4.5, for the drink *Guronsan Fresh*, a smiling young woman as marionette is pictured behind the tagline, "Firm body. Vitamin and Calcium".[25] In both advertisements, while the women are portrayed with childlike or doll-like attributes, they also have the breezy and cheery aesthetic of modern, commercial OL culture, added to which is the promise of "women's power" in addition to a "firm body" through vitamin and mineral supplements. Coupled with the image of the woman as puppet, accompanying the immediate energy boost from the drink is the implication that this is a strategy of deliberate self-emancipation and empowerment, transforming from the dancing smiling marionette to being an independent self-actualizing woman, simultaneously beautified and emancipated through the medium of the energy drink.

Augmenting this approach is another type of drink advertisement – featuring rehydration drinks and added supplementary vitamin drinks, these advertisements present as part of a complete aspirational lifestyle, covering everything from work to leisure. Figure 4.6 shows an advertisement for PF21, a sports drink from Asahi Beer Co. containing protein and collagen. However, rather than featuring sports, the drink is set

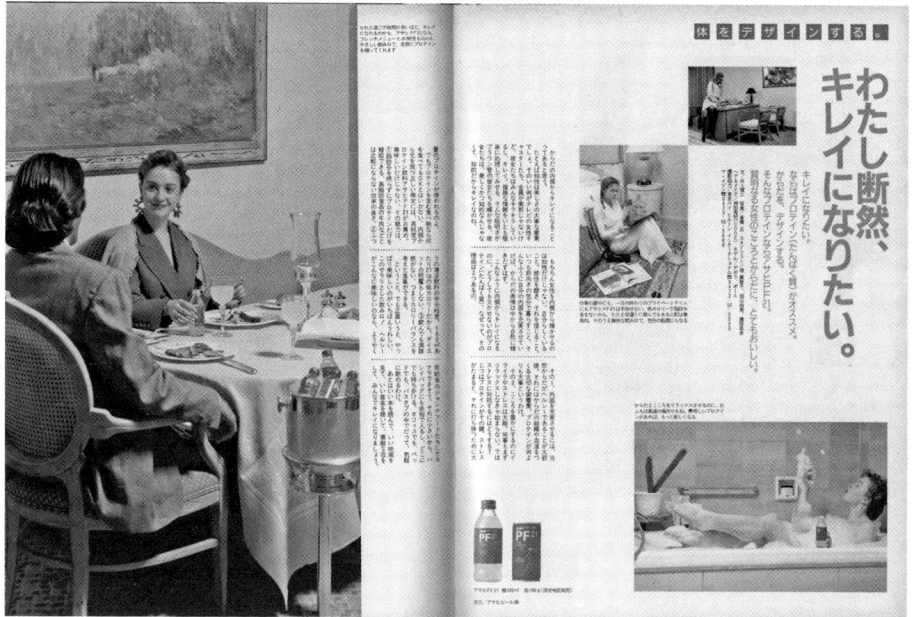

Figure 4.6 *Hanako* magazine, issue 46, 27 April 1989 (Magazine House, Tokyo, 1989), 84–5.

as an integral accompaniment to a complete lifestyle that encompasses fine dining, elegant desk work, and relaxing at home, in the bedroom and in the (luxurious) bath. Headed by the copy, "I definitely want to be beautiful", the emphasis is not on sport, but a type of liberated independent beauty, expanded to include a beautiful lifestyle that, featuring Caucasian women in elegant Western surroundings, places this particular type of femininity within the socially liberated universalist spaces of the West, as compared to the highly stratified context of Japanese social and cultural relations.[26]

Likewise, Figure 4.7, for the coffee drinks company, UCC, features a series of functional food drinks called UCC Works, and individually labelled "Hard Work", "Daily Work", and "After Work". With an attractive Japanese female office worker at her computer (Daily Work), playing golf (Hard Work), and with her side dishes (After Work), accompanied by the copy, "Sending cheers to the urban women for whom work and play are important", it is clear these drinks play out the fantasy of what it means to be an independent Japanese office lady, working hard and playing hard in an environment of meaningful and successful work.

In these examples, apart from an unidentifiable male dining companion, the women are portrayed as mostly solitary, enjoying leisurely time alone, adding to the message of self-determined empowerment, as well as conveniently acting out the fantasy of female agency outside the context of other actors. Furthermore, in control of their time, work, and leisure, and by implication of their dress and inclusion of the functional food beverage, their wellbeing and beauty, the women are portrayed as active agents, able to "have-it-all". Unlike other adverts for energy drinks in which the narrative is about

The Dynamics of Modern Asian Design

Figure 4.7 *Hanako* magazine, issue 92, 5 April 1990 (Magazine House, Tokyo, 1990), 74–5.

helping the man keep at his work, these adverts demonstrate the importance of leisure as much as work to women, with health linked to success, not for a romantic or family life in the context of others, but the individual, using the language of either career advancement (for a non-existent career) or a sophisticated modern lifestyle of the single woman in control of her destiny.

However, while seemingly utilizing the language of female empowerment, with the inclusion of beauty, transformation, and consumption, these functional food advertisements targeted at women can more accurately be seen within the strategy of a post-feminist framework; that of a promise of self-actualization and empowerment through a capitalist lens, or self-realization through consumption. In this, fantasies of power through lifestyle and leisure replace the realities of actual working and social conditions most Japanese women experienced as OLs. For, with only one per cent of Japanese women going on to managerial-track roles, the experience for the majority of OLs was of administrative and menial office tasks that echoed the domestic role of the housewife, alongside an expected short tenure and subsequent lack of career advancement that precluded any sense of career importance or advancement. Even with the leisure portrayed, Japanese women would encounter these as privilege-segregated. Western fine dining and spacious living, for example, would be out of reach for many single women on lower-waged employment and without access to business expense accounts for work, and with golf club memberships highly competitive and symbolic of masculine executive status,[27] women accessing golf was a fantastical aspiration, symbolic of access to a gendered privilege out of reach for many men, let alone women.

Women and sport

Even as food was being used in the service of lifestyle and the body beautiful, along with the Bubble's economic and consumer booms there was a significant one in sport and fitness. Against the context of political consensus to reform Japanese society in the 1980s, sport became increasingly seen as another consumer activity to be developed in accordance with other international trends, benefiting from privatized investment. In particular, previously undeveloped sports in Japan were a focus of this investment, leading to a nearly ten-fold increase in the number of sports clubs between 1981 and 1991, from a rate of 30+ established per year in 1982 to over 200 per year by 1991, and with an increase in market scale from US$2 billion to over US$30 billion between 1982 and 1991.[28]

However, although the sporting boom in the Bubble has usually been identified as the golfing craze that swept Japan in the 1980s and 1990s, privatized sport for the most part was aimed at women who had little access to golf. Thus, while men and their practice of golf (or indeed attempts at gaining access to golf) grabbed headlines, it was other sports, such as skiing, tennis, and aerobics, that were activities in which women were the new frontier and main consumer market, and who were the main customers of the boom in sports clubs and facilities of this time.

In this, the privileges and elitism of sport, as well as its emphasis on the body come to be perfectly positioned for young Japanese women. In order to utilize their disposable income and time, as well as desire for leisure, sport at this point became decoupled from masculinity, adopting a feminine strategy that linked beauty and travel with fitness and enjoyment, building on trends for individuality and spiritual richness that can be traced to strategies in Japanese travel and tourism from the 1970s.[29]

It is this turn away from the hegemonic order, reclaiming space and becoming visible in public, that we see in young women accessing sport, and nowhere is this more visible than in the very physicality of participation. Linked to beauty and health as a feminizing strategy to appeal to female consumers, the body itself becomes emphasized and repackaged through accessories, fashion, and advertising. Epitomized through the aerobics boom, women and their own bodies are sold to themselves through the new medium of sport. While this is nothing new, fashion and beauty being a longstanding feature of control and consumer commodification, it is this new medium of sporting athleticism that proves significant for this period.

An example of this can be seen in Figure 4.8, an advertisement not for sport but for accommodation. Headlined "Tokyo Wave: The Tokyo single girl who crashes on the waves lives in an Itoman Total Housing condominium and apartment", this advertisement deliberately utilizes fun, sporting leisure, and a single girl lifestyle to sell rentals in the popular holiday sub-tropical island of Okinawa at Japan's most south-westerly point. Combining smiling young Japanese women in swimsuits, beach umbrellas, recliners, and active participation in modern water sports of surfing, windsurfing, and jet skiing, the image not only evokes a fun single girl life, but frames it within a world of internationalist, liberated enjoyment, in which normal Japanese OLs are free to enjoy.

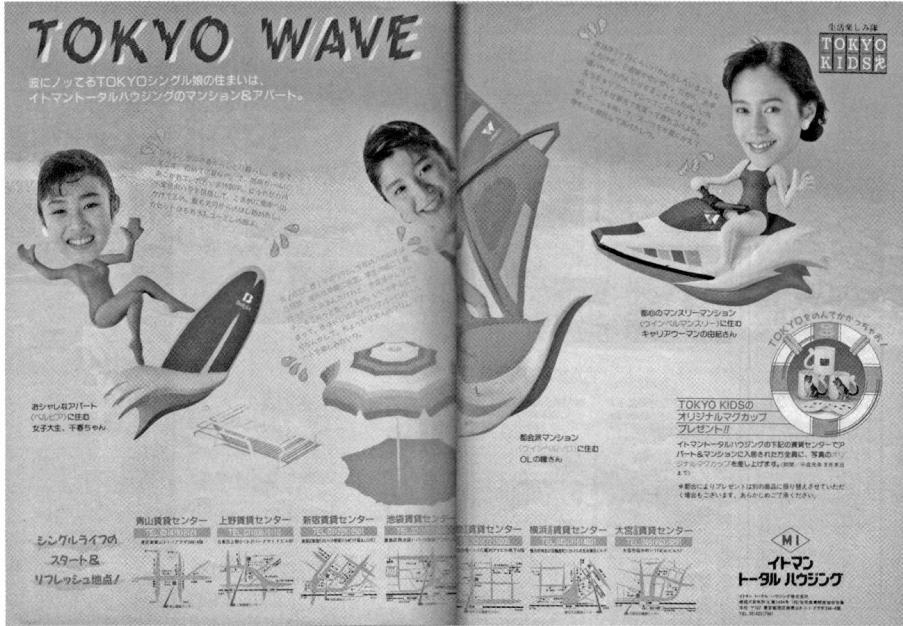

Figure 4.8 *Hanako* magazine, issue 58, 27 July 1989 (Magazine House, Tokyo, 1989), 24–5.

While seemingly everyday in appearance, with jet-skiing women in swimwear nothing new in the global culture of the 1980s, seen in the context of Japanese femininity, these are daring pronouncements to be made, not only culturally with its emphasis on modesty and purity, but also in light of women's roles at work. For alongside restrictions in roles and duties, young women also faced more immediate controls over their appearance and presentation of manner at work, with the most presentable handpicked to serve in the most lucrative departments. More than education and administrative skills, OLs' remit to be "office flowers" that brightened up the office[30] meant that appearance, manner, and ability to "present a culturally condoned front (*omote*) of comforting 'femaleness' to customers and clients"[31] was seen as vital for the smooth running of the Japanese corporate environment. In this, young women's skills and bodies were not only tightly controlled, but also exploited for literal commercial gain, in which stringently prescribed uniforms, make-up, and even year-long etiquette lessons were required of OLs who were seen as physically embodying the ethos of the company through their appearance.

Sport in this sense thus provides not only a relief from the official demands of social control on young women's bodies, but also engenders a type of liberation, claiming back, and to a certain extent rebellion from everyday expectations of modesty and propriety. Although honing the body through sport and cladding it in tight or skimpy sportswear may seem both an exploitative commodification and sexualization of women's bodies, positioned against the context of traditional Japanese demands of feminine modesty, shyness, and virginity, women's deliberate engagement with sport as leisure can be seen as an act of agency, redefining themselves as liberated bodies in the international sphere of modern sport.

Party! The liberated body

Where the emphasis on the physicality of women's bodies – through beauty, food, sport, and fitness – leads to, is the exploration of night-time leisure for women. In addition to international and domestic travel, *Hanako* often depicts women drinking and going out after work, demonstrating the determination of OLs to enjoy themselves before marriage. Regular features such as the "After 5pm Going-Out Guide" showcase real-life OLs eating and drinking in the night-time economy, acting as both instructional and normalizing discourse. While these women in the magazine are photographed more modestly attired, frequent accounts of young women in racy dress illustrate an opening up of a more liberated attitude towards feminine beauty, appearance, and behaviour that echo the fun-loving OLs of OL Evolution. Sporting sticky-up bangs, slinky body-conscious dresses, spectacular make-up, and designer labels, scores of young single women would descend on nightclubs such as Maharaja and Juliana's to dance with their feather-edged fans on a night out. Here, OLs were no longer introverted, modest Japanese ladies, nor professionally elegant Office Ladies, but loud, vivacious, colourful, and sexy.

However, as before, the Japanese woman, not only as bright and energetic, but also loud and sexy, is at odds with traditional views of Japanese femininity through modesty, purity, and adherence of appropriate place. It is this tension that is recognized in an advertisement for *Torabāyu*, where the notion of the professional Japanese OL is directly challenged through dress and accompanying copy (Figure 4.9). Part of a series of advertisements placed in *Hanako* in 1989 for the job magazine, *Torabāyu*, it features an illustration of a young Japanese woman, stylishly but provocatively dressed in a figure-hugging, short dress, big hoop earrings, heels with criss-crossed laces extending up the calf, big hair further framed with a wide-brimmed hat, and visible make-up including bright red lipstick. Moreover, her sensuality is further accentuated by her sitting perched with one leg up, displaying an extent of shapely leg and only just obscuring any visibility of underwear at her crotch in a deliberate act of titillation. Yet, accompanying the image is the copy, "It has become apparent to me that I don't need to depend on my appearance for the company", which coupled with the woman's serious pensive gaze off to the side, indicates not only a depth and melancholia belied by her appearance, but also a sense of determination and rebelliousness apparent in her dress and agentic message of self-actualization. Aimed at the *Hanako* reader and framed in the context of work, this advertisement demonstrates a challenging of professional and cultural norms around acceptable feminine behaviour that appeals to the mainstream.

For while precursors to this liberated sexy Japanese single woman can be seen in her historical predecessors such as the 1920s "modern girl" and the degenerate schoolgirl of the Meiji period (1868–1912),[32] these were always still very marginalized portrayals

Figure 4.9 *Torabāyu* advertisement, *Hanako* magazine, issue 66, 28 September 1989 (Magazine House, Tokyo, 1989), 127.

of Japanese femininity, limited to the small numbers of city-dwelling women of the early twentieth century or girls from elite families allowed an education and the fictions written about them. Instead, from the 1980s, what can be seen is a sudden slippage into the mainstream of female sexual visibility that goes outside night-time leisure and into the day through the very fashions of the OLs themselves. Although at work, OLs were restricted by prescribed uniforms, make-up, and manner, outside in the public sphere they were a very visible presence. Clutching their international designer handbags and dressed in structured power suits accessorized with coordinating heels, Hermés scarves, Tiffany necklaces, and framed with '80s hairstyles of big hair made more imposing with hairspray and sticky-up bangs, these corporate women embodied a visibility that made them emblems of the success of the Japanese economy.[33] Moreover, with many of their luxury items bought for them as gifts from boyfriends, OLs demonstrated the height of female sexual power and desirability conflated with the heady mix of material prosperity and the rising international power and influence of Japan.

It is in this powerful visibility of the Japanese modern woman as working, successful, feminine, and sexually empowered that can be seen early indications of the international post-feminism popularized in the 1990s and beyond. With the passing of the EEOL coupled with the identification of the power of the new female consumer in everything from make-up to consumer electronics, Japanese women's embrace of empowerment was signified by their apparent freedom to enjoy in terms of time, spending, their body (outside of work), and access to leisured activities. This was in stark contrast to the conditions of their male counterparts, the salarymen, who while apparent beneficiaries of the booming economy and patriarchal social and corporate system, in practice felt the constraints of long working hours, obligations in building a corporate career, and a distinct lack of opportunities to enjoy the new leisure landscape of the Bubble Economy.[34] Yet like the mirage of the post-feminist promise, these agentic symbols of self-actualization were not replicated in the actual conditions of working life, nor was there an appetite to actively level-up women's situations. Instead, empowerment and emancipation were signified through an ability to choose within the framework of conspicuous consumption, alongside using gendered division to gain preferential treatment through soft power and gifts. These in turn were enabled by the logic of gender inequality that saw young women on low-waged, unfulfilling work of short-tenure look to maximize their enjoyment as much as possible; at the expense of the men and systems around them, but which ultimately profited off the very gender inequality imposed on women.

Yet, the failings of post-feminism aside in which women's attempts at enacting an empowered life through consumption nevertheless disregarded the fundamental inequalities of gendered relations, seen through the lens of the specific context of Japanese OLs in the 1980s, it is this act of agency and liberation of the body that is both significant and contentious when applied to Japanese women. From the outside, it may be easy to critique Japanese women as either coming under the Western exploitative influence of commercialization, over-sexualization, and objectification of their bodies through revealing outfits, or early post-feminist pronouncements of liberation and self-actualization through spectacular feminine style and material goods. However, positioned against social, professional, and cultural realities that included the confinements of the entrenched Japanese corporate system of gender inequality, company uniforms, and social restrictions on freedoms through cultural expectations of modesty, we can see how trends such as the body-conscious dress, drinking alcohol, going out, and participating in sports and exercise were also part of a greater move towards liberating the female body and the rebellion of Japanese women.

Furthermore, through the very act of being outside and participating in the consumer-leisure boom, whether in sports clubs, resorts, or bars, discos, and restaurants, young women's very visibility in public spaces and financial independence enabled them to transgress specific Japanese social and cultural boundaries and occupy a new space for themselves. While there had been precedent for young unmarried women to be in public through the process of modernization in Japan, from the visibility of Meiji-era schoolgirls in the city to the modern girl (*modan gāru*) of the early twentieth century, typically these phenomena soon sparked moral panics about young women's respectability, with implications for their prospects as future wives and mothers of the nation.[35] An exception to these were the department stores which, as retail spaces, were often viewed as a more natural female environment, and in the 1980s were one of the few employers of women with favourable terms that included maternity leave, onsite childcare facilities, and generous leave and career breaks.[36] However, it must be remembered that for female consumers, department stores historically were mainly available to middle- and upper-class women in the cities with the financial ability and privilege to enjoy leisured consumption in public. Likewise, intellectual or feminist groups that evolved alongside Japanese modernity were limited to women of the educated upper classes, as were the pursuit of the traditional arts as elite leisure activities such as flower arrangement (*ikebana*) and the tea-ceremony (*chadō*), while self-organized housewife collectives were largely exclusive to married women.[37] With increasing numbers of young single women earning their own money in respectable professions and seen as a new female consumer group to cater to, the sheer numbers of unmarried women in public for leisure without censure was unprecedented.

In this enjoyment and active living for themselves, without reference to other actors such as romantic partners or preparation for family life, can be read a rebellion against being what Miller terms, "the progenitor of future salarymen".[38] It is the deliberate denial of the "good wife/wise mother" motif[39] that had framed Japanese feminine discourse over the twentieth century, as can be seen through the rejection of qualities such as purity, cleanliness, hard work, thriftiness, and nurturing, being replaced with a relaxed attitude to work, pleasure in material goods and leisure, and implied sexual and gender liberation through dress (even if not necessarily in practice), that prompted both horror from the Japanese media and envy from their male corporate counterparts alike.

Here we can see the difficulties encountered when applying theories such as post-feminism to non-Western contexts. Following Dosekun's observations[40] on the limitations of post-feminism as derived from the experiences of predominantly white privileged women when applied to those of Nigerian women, so this can also be said in relation to the specific contexts of Japanese women in the Bubble. While helpful in some ways to explain the tensions between apparent displays of empowerment and soft power with the realities of an inflexible gender-segregated system, it also fails in others to stand up to the specific contexts within which Japanese women were operating, and their specific conditions of cultural enmeshment.

Arguably at the peak of their sexual desirability, aligned through work with many of the corporations that provided the national identity of the Japanese Bubble Economy, and with high amounts of time and disposable income to spend on themselves, OLs do fit within the privileged conditions necessary for post-feminism to occur. Yet taking into account Japanese women's overall lack of gender privilege and hard power when it came to employment, public space, and social rights, young women, who also lacked the employment rights of men and the soft power and cultural authority of married housewives, could also be seen as an underprivileged group in Japanese social dynamics. Seemingly occupying the simultaneous positions of privileged and underprivileged, OLs appear to use strategies that are feminist or post-feminist depending on one's position. While using the consumer language of material luxury and spectacular lifestyle to demonstrate self-actualization and empowerment that in themselves were exploitable by wider economic forces, and which were poor substitutes for real engagement in the economy, it could also be argued that taking into account OLs specific conditions of gender inequality in the face of such an inflexible system, any rebellion – from being more visible in terms of designer dress and goods, to immodest dress and behaviours such as going out clubbing and drinking – is a valid rebellion, demonstrating, no matter how small, OLs agentic desire for more.

Conclusion

In exploring how women accessed concepts of beauty through portrayals of appearance and lifestyle in the magazine *Hanako*, we can see how young single women were key players in the Bubble Economy, defining the consumer landscape even as men defined the economic one. Benefiting from policies that ranged from encouraging women to work through the EEOL to ones that promoted leisure such as the Maekawa Report, young women, and especially OLs, became a cornerstone in promoting national interests in domestic and international policies governing lifestyle and the economy. From developing a new feminine persona of energetic dynamism to being a market for beautiful consumption, OLs were at the forefront of and the visible face of the benefits of the Bubble Economy. Yet even as their disposable income and time were being used to fuel the zeitgeist of the economy, so female culture was changing to incorporate these new visions of femininity. Independence, equality, sporting athleticism, emancipation, and empowerment, all were qualities also present in the portrayal of the new female consumer and her participation in relevant industries, preparing the ground for wider discussions on women's participation in public life.

However, it must be remembered that although Japanese young women may be posited as liberating pioneers and beneficiaries of various consumer booms in the Bubble Economy, these conditions were predicated on their very lack of participation and agency in the wider economy. Shut-out from managerial track work, their disposable income and time were the result of being excluded from meaningful economic participation, both in employment and investment. Instead, what they were left with was a short-term urgency to enjoy while they were single and working, and exploited to fuel the leisure industries that were in turn fuelling the consumer economic bubble. Thus, like the sexualization of women's bodies where Japanese women were both claiming liberation from Japanese conformity whilst also buying into Western norms of female objectification, so the trends in women's beauty, fashion, and leisure were both being claimed and enjoyed by Japanese women whilst also being used to fund national and predominantly male economic prosperity.

Nevertheless, this period marks a real sea-change in the way in which young Japanese women presented themselves and were perceived. The opportunity to participate in open public spaces and be visible in self-determined action, dress, and activities, enabled young women to self-determine and negotiate additional socially acceptable ground that was both international and Japanese. In this, Japanese women in the 1980s were at the forefront of a new kind of East Asian identity, articulating a new wave of femininity that was both modern and culturally grounded. Creating a language of liberation, they appropriated selected international elements for local purposes, retranslating Western concepts to create a negotiated East Asian femininity suitable for a postmodern age. While not perfect, it is these legacies of modernity played out on the female body that continued after the Bubble burst, to create conditions for subversions and subcultural style that make up the vibrancy of Japanese modern culture in the 1990s onwards.

Notes

1. Joseph Jay Tobin (ed.), *Re-Made in Japan: Everyday Life and Consumer Taste in a Changing Society* (Yale University Press, 1992), 145; Ulrike Wöhr, Barbara Hamill Sato and Sadami Suzuki (eds.), *Gender and Modernity: Rereading Japanese Women's Magazines* (International Research Centre for Japanese Studies, 1998), 144.
2. Tomoko Kurihara, *Japanese Corporate Transition in Time and Space* (Palgrave Macmillan, 2009), 60.
3. Mary C. Brinton, *Women and the Economic Miracle: Gender and Work in Postwar Japan* (University of California Press, 1993); Brian J. McVeigh, *Life in a Japanese Women's College: Learning to Be Ladylike* (Routledge, 1997).
4. Thomas F. Cargill and Takayuki Sakamoto, *Japan since 1980* (Cambridge University Press, 2008); Carl Mosk, *Japanese Economic Development: Markets, Norms, Structures* (Routledge, 2008); Kōichi Hamada, Anil K. Kashyap and David E. Weinstein, *Japan's Bubble, Deflation, and Long-Term Stagnation* (MIT Press, 2011).
5. David Richard Leheny, *The Rules of Play: National Identity and the Shaping of Japanese Leisure* (Cornell University Press, 2003).
6. Brinton, *Women and the Economic Miracle*; Laura Dales, *Feminist Movements in Contemporary Japan* (Routledge, 2009); Beverley Bishop, *Globalisation and Women in the Japanese Workforce* (Routledge Curzon, 2005); Matthew Allen and Rumi Sakamoto (eds.), *Japanese Popular Culture, vol. IV: Globalising Japanese Popular Culture: The Coolness of Japan*, Critical Concepts in Asian Studies (Routledge, 2014).
7. Brinton, *Women and the Economic Miracle*; Sumiko Iwao, *The Japanese Woman: Traditional Image and Changing Reality* (Free Press, 1993); Anne E. Imamura (ed.), *Re-Imaging Japanese Women* (University of California Press, 1996); Makoto Ohtsu and Tomio Imanari, *Inside Japanese Business: A Narrative History, 1960–2000* (M.E. Sharpe, 2002); Ross E. Mouer and Hirosuke Kawanishi, *A Sociology of Work in Japan* (Cambridge University Press, 2005).
8. Leheny, *The Rules of Play*; Masahiko Ishizuka (ed.), *Japan Economic Almanac 1988: The Japan Economic Journal* (Nihon Keizai Shimbun, 1988).
9. Brian Moeran, *Japanese Advertising Agency: An Anthropology of Media and Markets*, Consumasian Book Series (Routledge, 1996); Dolores P. Martinez, *The Worlds of Japanese Popular Culture; Gender, Shifting Boundaries and Global Cultures* (Cambridge University Press, 1998); Penelope Francks and Janet Hunter (eds.), *The Historical Consumer: Consumption and Everyday Life in Japan, 1850–2000* (Palgrave Macmillan, 2012).

10. Merry I. White, *The Material Child: Coming of Age in Japan and America* (Maxwell Macmillan, 1993).
11. Lise Skov and Brian Moeran (eds.), *Women, Media, and Consumption in Japan* (Curzon Press and The University of Hawaii Press, 1995).
12. Brinton, *Women and the Economic Miracle*; Imamura (ed.), *Re-Imaging Japanese Women*; McVeigh, *Life in a Japanese Women's College*.
13. Jeannie Lo, *Office Ladies, Factory Women: Life and Work at a Japanese Company* (M.E. Sharpe, 1990); Yuko Ogasawara, *Office Ladies and Salaried Men: Power, Gender, and Work in Japanese Companies* (University of California Press, 1998).
14. Tie-up articles featuring a specific product, store, or service are common advertising strategies in the Japanese magazine landscape, blurring the boundaries between paid-for advertising and consumer instructional advice.
15. Risu Akizuki, *OL Shinkanron* (Survival in the Office: The Evolution of Japanese Working Women), vols. 1 and 3, trans. Dominic Young and Jules Young (Kodansha America, 1999), 20.
16. McVeigh, *Life in a Japanese Women's College*, 158.
17. Leheny, *The Rules of Play*.
18. Yasuo Tanaka, *Somehow Crystal* (Kawade Shobo Shinsha, 1981).
19. Gordon Matthews and Bruce White (eds.), *Japan's Changing Generations: Are Young People Creating a New Society?* (Routledge, 2004).
20. Ogasawara, *Office Ladies and Salaried Men*.
21. Lo, *Office Ladies, Factory Women*.
22. Svend Hollensen, *Essentials of Global Marketing* (Prentice Hall, 2008); Ken Belson, "Japanese Energy Drink Is in Need of a Boost – The New York Times", *The New York Times*, 19 July 2002.
23. Jesper Andreasson and Thomas Johansson, "The New Fitness Geography: The Globalisation of Japanese Gym and Fitness Culture", *Leisure Studies* 36, no. 3 (2017): 383–94.
24. *Hanako* magazine, Issue 45 (Magazine House, 1989), 143.
25. *Hanako* magazine, Issue 92 (Magazine House, 1990), 50.
26. Karen Kelsky, "Self as Other: Internationalism as Resistance among Japanese Women", in David Blake Willis and Stephen Murphy-Shigematsu (eds.), *Transcultural Japan: At the Borderlands of Race, Gender and Identity* (Routledge, 2008).
27. John Horne, "The Politics of Sport and Leisure in Japan: Global Power and Local Resistance", *International Review for the Sociology of Sport* 33, no. 2 (1998): 171–82; Angus Lockyer, "From Corporate Playground to Family Resort: Golf as Commodity in Post-War Japan", in Penelope Francks and Janet Hunter (eds.), *The Historical Consumer: Consumption and Everyday Life in Japan, 1850–2000* (Palgrave Macmillan, 2012).
28. Takayuki Yamashita, "The Changing Field of Japanese Sport", in Joseph Maguire and Masayoshi Nakayama (eds.), *Japan, Sport and Society: Tradition and Change in a Globalizing World* (Routledge, 2006).
29. Marilyn Ivy, *Discourses of the Vanishing: Modernity, Phantasm, Japan* (University of Chicago Press, 1995).
30. McVeigh, *Life in a Japanese Women's College*.
31. Brinton, *Women and the Economic Miracle*, 152.

32. Barbara Sato, *The New Japanese Woman: Modernity, Media, and Women in Interwar Japan* (Duke University Press, 2003); Laura Miller and Jan Bardsley (eds.), *Bad Girls of Japan* (Palgrave Macmillan, 2005).
33. Ofra Goldstein-Gidoni, "Consuming Domesticity in Post-Bubble Japan", in Katarzyna J. Cwiertka and Ewa Machotka (eds.), *Consuming Life in Post-Bubble Japan: A Transdisciplinary Perspective* (Amsterdam University Press, 2018).
34. Hui-Ying Kerr, "Envisioning the Bubble: Creating and Consuming Lifestyles through Magazines in the Culture of the Japanese Bubble Economy (1986–1991)", PhD thesis (Royal College of Art and Design, 2017).
35. Sato, *The New Japanese Woman*; Melanie Czarnecki, "Bad Girls from Good Families: The Degenerate Meiji Schoolgirl", in Laura Miller and Jan Bardsley (eds.), *Bad Girls of Japan* (Palgrave Macmillan, 2005).
36. Millie R. Creighton, "Marriage, Motherhood, and Career Management in a Japanese 'Counter Culture'", in Anne E. Imamura (ed.), *Re-Imaging Japanese Women* (University of California Press, 1996), 192–220.
37. Machiko Matsui, "Evolution of the Feminist Movement in Japan", *NWSA Journal* 2, no. 3 (1990): 435–49; Barbara Lynne Rowland Mori, "The Traditional Arts as Leisure Activities for Contemporary Japanese Women", in Anne E. Imamura (ed.), *Re-Imaging Japanese Women* (University of California Press, 1996); Dina Lowy, *The Japanese "New Woman": Images of Gender and Modernity* (Rutgers University Press, 2007); Ki-Young Shin, "The Women's Movements", in Alisa Gaunder (ed.), *The Routledge Handbook of Japanese Politics* (Routledge, 2011).
38. Laura Miller, *Beauty Up: Exploring Contemporary Japanese Body Aesthetics* (University of California Press, 2006), 174.
39. Brinton, *Women and the Economic Miracle*; Andrea Germer, Vera C. Mackie and Ulrike Wöhr, *Gender, Nation and State in Modern Japan* (Routledge, 2014); Michelle H.S. Ho, "Is Nadeshiko Japan 'Feminine?' Manufacturing Sport Celebrity and National Identity on Japanese Morning Television", *Journal of Sport and Social Issues* 38, no. 2 (2014): 164–83.
40. Simidele Dosekun, *Fashioning Postfeminism: Spectacular Femininity and Transnational Culture* (University of Illinois Press, 2020).

References

Akizuki, Risu. *OL Shinkanron* (Survival in the Office: The Evolution of Japanese Working Women), vols. 1 and 3, trans. Dominic Young and Jules Young, Kodansha America, 1999.

Allen, Matthew and Rumi Sakamoto (eds.). *Japanese Popular Culture, vol. IV: Globalising Japanese Popular Culture: The Coolness of Japan*, Critical Concepts in Asian Studies, Routledge, 2014.

Andreasson, Jesper and Thomas Johansson. "The New Fitness Geography: The Globalisation of Japanese Gym and Fitness Culture", *Leisure Studies* 36, no. 3 (2017): 383–94.

Belson, Ken. "Japanese Energy Drink Is in Need of a Boost – The New York Times", *The New York Times*, 19 July 2002. https://www.nytimes.com/2002/07/19/business/japanese-energy-drink-is-in-need-of-a-boost.html.

Bishop, Beverley. *Globalisation and Women in the Japanese Workforce*, Routledge Curzon, 2005.

Brinton, Mary C. *Women and the Economic Miracle: Gender and Work in Postwar Japan*, University of California Press, 1993.

Cargill, Thomas F. and Takayuki Sakamoto. *Japan since 1980*, Cambridge University Press, 2008.
Creighton, Millie R. "Marriage, Motherhood, and Career Management in a Japanese 'Counter Culture'", in Anne E. Imamura (ed.), *Re-Imaging Japanese Women*. University of California Press, 1996, 192–220.
Czarnecki, Melanie. "Bad Girls from Good Families: The Degenerate Meiji Schoolgirl", in Laura Miller and Jan Bardsley (eds.), *Bad Girls of Japan*, Palgrave Macmillan, 2005.
Dales, Laura. *Feminist Movements in Contemporary Japan*, Routledge, 2009.
Dosekun, Simidele. *Fashioning Postfeminism: Spectacular Femininity and Transnational Culture*, University of Illinois Press, 2020.
Francks, Penelope and Janet Hunter (eds.). *The Historical Consumer: Consumption and Everyday Life in Japan, 1850–2000*, Palgrave Macmillan, 2012.
Germer, Andrea, Vera C. Mackie and Ulrike Wöhr. *Gender, Nation and State in Modern Japan*, Routledge, 2014.
Goldstein-Gidoni, Ofra. "Consuming Domesticity in Post-Bubble Japan", in Katarzyna J. Cwiertka and Ewa Machotka (eds.), *Consuming Life in Post-Bubble Japan: A Transdisciplinary Perspective*, Amsterdam University Press, 2018.
Hamada, Kōichi, Anil K. Kashyap and David E. Weinstein. *Japan's Bubble, Deflation, and Long-Term Stagnation*, MIT Press, 2011.
Hanako magazine, Issue 45, Magazine House, 1989.
Hanako magazine, Issue 92, Magazine House, 1990.
Ho, Michelle H.S. "Is Nadeshiko Japan 'Feminine?' Manufacturing Sport Celebrity and National Identity on Japanese Morning Television", *Journal of Sport and Social Issues* 38, no. 2 (2014): 164–83.
Hollensen, Svend. *Essentials of Global Marketing*, Prentice Hall, 2008.
Horne, John. "The Politics of Sport and Leisure in Japan: Global Power and Local Resistance", *International Review for the Sociology of Sport* 33, no. 2 (1998): 171–82.
Imamura, Anne E. (ed.). *Re-Imaging Japanese Women*, University of California Press, 1996.
Ishizuka, Masahiko (ed.). *Japan Economic Almanac 1988: The Japan Economic Journal*, Nihon Keizai Shimbun, 1988.
Ivy, Marilyn. *Discourses of the Vanishing: Modernity, Phantasm, Japan*, University of Chicago Press, 1995.
Iwao, Sumiko. *The Japanese Woman: Traditional Image and Changing Reality*, Free Press, 1993.
Kelsky, Karen. "Self as Other: Internationalism as Resistance among Japanese Women", in David Blake Willis and Stephen Murphy-Shigematsu (eds.), *Transcultural Japan: At the Borderlands of Race, Gender and Identity* (Routledge, 2008).
Kerr, Hui-Ying. "Envisioning the Bubble: Creating and Consuming Lifestyles through Magazines in the Culture of the Japanese Bubble Economy (1986–1991)", PhD thesis, Royal College of Art and Design, 2017.
Kurihara, Tomoko. *Japanese Corporate Transition in Time and Space*, Palgrave Macmillan, 2009.
Leheny, David Richard. *The Rules of Play: National Identity and the Shaping of Japanese Leisure*, Cornell University Press, 2003.
Lo, Jeannie. *Office Ladies, Factory Women: Life and Work at a Japanese Company*, M.E. Sharpe, 1990.
Lowy, Dina. *The Japanese "New Woman": Images of Gender and Modernity*, Rutgers University Press, 2007.
Martinez, Dolores P. *The Worlds of Japanese Popular Culture: Gender, Shifting Boundaries and Global Cultures*, Cambridge University Press, 1998.
Matsui, Machiko. "Evolution of the Feminist Movement in Japan", *NWSA Journal* 2, no. 3 (1990): 435–49.
Matthews, Gordon and Bruce White (eds.). *Japan's Changing Generations: Are Young People Creating a New Society?*, Routledge, 2004.

McVeigh, Brian J. *Life in a Japanese Women's College: Learning to Be Ladylike*, Routledge, 1997.
Miller, Laura. *Beauty Up: Exploring Contemporary Japanese Body Aesthetics*, University of California Press, 2006.
Miller, Laura and Jan Bardsley (eds.). *Bad Girls of Japan*, Palgrave Macmillan, 2005.
Moeran, Brian. *Japanese Advertising Agency: An Anthropology of Media and Markets*, Consumasian Book Series, Routledge, 1996.
Mosk, Carl. *Japanese Economic Development: Markets, Norms, Structures*, Routledge, 2008.
Mouer, Ross E. and Hirosuke Kawanishi. *A Sociology of Work in Japan*, Cambridge University Press, 2005.
Ogasawara, Yuko. *Office Ladies and Salaried Men: Power, Gender, and Work in Japanese Companies*, University of California Press, 1998.
Ohtsu, Makoto and Tomio Imanari. *Inside Japanese Business: A Narrative History, 1960–2000*, M.E. Sharpe, 2002.
Rowland Mori, Barbara Lynne. "The Traditional Arts as Leisure Activities for Contemporary Japanese Women", in Anne E. Imamura (ed.), *Re-Imaging Japanese Women*, University of California Press, 1996.
Sato, Barbara. *The New Japanese Woman: Modernity, Media, and Women in Interwar Japan*, Duke University Press, 2003.
Shin, Ki-Young. "The Women's Movements", in Alisa Gaunder (ed.), *The Routledge Handbook of Japanese Politics*, Routledge, 2011.
Skov, Lise and Brian Moeran (eds.). *Women, Media, and Consumption in Japan*, Curzon Press and The University of Hawaii Press, 1995.
Tanaka, Yasuo. *Somehow Crystal*, Kawade Shobo Shinsha, 1981.
Tobin, Joseph Jay. (ed.). *Re-Made in Japan: Everyday Life and Consumer Taste in a Changing Society*, Yale University Press, 1992.
White, Merry I. *The Material Child: Coming of Age in Japan and America*, Maxwell Macmillan, 1993.
Willis, David Blake and Stephen Murphy-Shigematsu (eds.). *Transcultural Japan: At the Borderlands of Race, Gender and Identity*, Routledge, 2008.
Wöhr, Ulrike, Barbara Hamill Sato and Sadami Suzuki (eds.). *Gender and Modernity: Rereading Japanese Women's Magazines*, International Research Centre for Japanese Studies, 1998.
Yamashita, Takayuki. "The Changing Field of Japanese Sport", in Joseph Maguire and Masayoshi Nakayama (eds.), *Japan, Sport and Society: Tradition and Change in a Globalizing World*, Routledge, 2006.

CHAPTER 5
ADORNMENT AND THE SELF: ORNAMENTAL DESIGN AND THE MODERN WOMAN IN CHINA
Sandy Ng

Introduction

In the early twentieth century, China sought to define its unique modern characteristics, a time when anxieties over ideals of womanhood began to surface alongside the tensions over modernity. Two kinds of women began to be perceived in the visual cultures of the time. The first was the Modern Woman (also termed "New Woman" in literature on the subject) who advanced modernity through courage and humility. In this representation, she was educated, patriotic, and a responsible citizen. The second type of woman was the Modern Girl with fun-loving and materialistic characteristics who represented modernity's ambiguities and individualized alienation. This chapter traces how women asserted their identities through adornment and the use of designs that affirmed their sense of self and increased their visibility in the modern era. It discusses how women negotiated social changes and identity formation in the early modern period and the twentieth century.[1] This chapter explores how ornamental designs such as accessories, cosmetic cases, and dressing tables affirmed female identity and self-perceptions.[2] Designs dictated usage and the ways the owner used the object, which in turn guided her behaviour. Thus, the object carried an instructive function, directing the user in exercising proper conduct. The accessories, cosmetic cases, and dressing tables specifically created for women not only aided them in enhancing their appearances, they also encouraged self-improvement and cultivation. Perfecting one's countenance was not simply a frivolous act. Ornamental designs articulated modern women's progressive social status.

Participation in consumer culture in the twentieth century empowered women in the family and the wider social structure. Advertisements and photographs associated middle-class women with materialistic lifestyles, filled with desirable imported designs such as wristwatches and high-heeled shoes that altered their lifestyles and redefined their identities. Taste domesticated unfamiliar designs in China and stylish women as tastemakers made this transition visible in modern material culture. To further understand women's cultural and social roles in China in the early twentieth century, accessories, cosmetics cases, and dressing tables, alongside advertisements and photographs will be examined in relation to Pierre Bourdieu's (1930–2002) concept of aesthetic judgements and cultural capital.[3] Modern designs for women were instrumental in asserting their identities, and ornamentation in design helps articulate cultural and social functions.

The impact of modernity on women in Republican China

In the early twentieth century, Chinese intellectuals began to question the viability of traditional culture. The fall of the Qing dynasty in 1911 and subsequent social movements for change, of which the May Fourth in 1919 is the most well-known, introduced a new era in the development of modern Chinese cultural and social history.[4] Apart from various projects for social reform, the end of the Qing dynasty signalled a radical reshaping of the whole concept of cultural character and a search for a new identity. Women's appearance became the focus of debates about gender roles and identities.

Urban-educated women were recognized as archetypes of the Modern Woman in the early Republican period (1911–24). Unlike their ancestors, they could enter public domains such as school campuses and parks, as well as participate in street demonstrations. Their presence was prevalent in newspapers, fictional literature, films, and popular advertising posters, better known as "calendar posters".[5]

In the past, only daughters from affluent and open-minded families were educated by private tutors. This practice changed with the establishment of public schools in the early twentieth century when more women could leave their homes and study in a shared environment. Female students entered the realm of mass education previously reserved for men, challenging accepted patriarchal social structures. This change marked a reformation of Chinese society that was based on a reinterpreted Confucian philosophical system, dictating how women of differing ages ought to behave. Chen Duxiu (1879–1942), editor of *New Youth* (*Xin Qingnian*), the most influential periodical of the time, proclaimed that it was essential to support women's liberation. Fervent calls to intensify progress only grew as young women became aware of their new citizenry responsibilities. These transformations defied the traditional familial structure that had kept women almost completely naïve about their social surroundings and rights, coinciding with the re-evaluation of women's rights, and an expansion of their roles beyond the domestic contexts of motherhood and housewifery.[6] The potential liberation released women from long-held social restrictions or at least gave them hope that they could be freer than their predecessors.

Redefining a woman's place became symbolic of the nation's struggle. "For the rise and fall of the country", it was proclaimed by politicians and the intelligentsia, "women's adornment bears responsibility".[7] While fashionable appearance became popular in the cities and debates about women's education intensified, those living in the countryside did not benefit from these changes, which were largely connected with urban improvements in education, social progress, and wealth. Many continued to live under strict rules dictated by tradition and social constraints.[8]

Despite debates on gender equality, many young women continued to focus on their appearance, fascinated with adornment rather than intellectual engagements. School headmistresses were frustrated by female students' lack of motivation to educate themselves; their attention was focused instead on make-up and jewellery. This return to feminine appearance was promulgated by the Nationalists as a medium to re-inscribe their version of Confucian ideals of social behaviour – a woman ought to display her feminine attributes as a mark of her gender.[9]

Seductively dressed women were deemed frivolous, affirming the impact of fashion magazines and movies, and the heightened sensuality of printed images was what dominated the public's impression.[10] Ultra-feminine women overshadowed female students who chose to represent gender equality rather than enhancing their appearance in a way that drew attention to their bodies. Clearly, despite the serious appearance of female students, many women were not keen to give up the luxury of adornment. Decorating the body was regarded as shallow, obstructing natural beauty and intellectual development. Women were encouraged by the conservatives in society at that time to give up their imported perfume, jewellery, and high heels while plain garments and simple hairstyles were advocated. The challenge to convince them to abandon their habits prompted the writer Xu Dishan (1893–1941) to advocate a complete revamp of the woman's wardrobe in his 1920 essay "Women's Dress".[11] Skirts, earrings, and long hair were signs of obedience in a patriarchal society, binding women to depend on men. He asserted, "If women want to be active in a new society, they must first reform their clothing".[12] Xu favoured a total abandonment that would free a woman's body and mind; provocative fashion would only contribute to the stereotype of women as materialistic playthings. He went on to suggest that women should dress like men to erase gender differences and to save them from wasting time adorning themselves when they could accomplish more useful tasks.[13] In a larger social context, prudent women help to contribute to the wealth of the nation. At the same time, a woman's virtue was epitomized through the material culture in her daily life.

Women's adornments and female identity

The use of cosmetic cases by Chinese women dates back to the Western Zhou dynasty (1046–771 BC) and reached its peak during the Qing period (1636–1912).[14] In ancient China, cosmetic cases (妝奩 zhuāng lián) were used to store cosmetic and ornamental items. Starting out as symbolic artefacts of imperial power, the cases gradually developed into practical designs reflecting the lifestyle of inner quarters that defined Chinese women's domestic lives shaped by marriage.[15] Historically, women tended to stay indoors to fulfil domestic duties and avoid participating in outdoor social activities. Gradually, cosmetic cases that were prevalent among the affluent offered respectable indoor pastimes.[16] Women were encouraged to utilize various objects such as mirrors, combs, makeup items including fragrance powder, and brushes stored in cosmetic cases for adornment. They enhanced their appearances whilst respecting societal boundaries. Cosmetic cases became instrumental in establishing a lifestyle of the inner quarters. Beyond beautifying themselves, women attended to their interests and adhered to patriarchal familial principles through activities associated with cosmetic cases.

Chinese women followed the "Thrice Following to Three Obedience", which did not restrict them all in the same way because each family enforced the rules differently.[17] Women, particularly those from privileged families, were able to negotiate their social identities. The extent of freedom a woman could exercise depended on her social position, her education and skills, and her position in the life cycle. Their roles as household managers and educators of children allowed them to shape family affairs. Women's education in the seventeenth century created a cohort of gentry women with literary and classical education, which helped them to develop their intellectual circles.[18] Their lives were complex and not simply subjugated by men. Women often used cosmetic cases to read, write, and safeguard their properties. Personal seals, for example, were also stored in cosmetic cases. They used cosmetic cases to read various texts as printing had made a wide range of written materials, including novels and poetry, available. In the Qing dynasty, cases were designed with a folding holder on top for mirrors or books so that women could adorn themselves and practise calligraphy with copybooks.[19] Beyond their functions, cosmetic cases epitomized how Chinese women adapted their lives under patriarchal authority.

The function of cosmetic cases went beyond mere storage. Chinese women were excluded from general property rights, an exception being the cosmetic case, which formed part of a woman's personal property. Brides received them as dowries (嫁妆 *jià zhuāng*), permitting them to inherit properties from male family members such as fathers and brothers by incorporating them in the cases.[20] Cosmetic cases became an integral part of women's personal belongings and private lives. Domestically, they fulfilled their aesthetic and emotional needs. Socially, they expressed their social identities by symbolizing family wealth.

Substantial dowries were prevalent in China. Beginning in the middle of the Ming dynasty (1368–1644), families offered substantial and lavish dowries to display their social status.[21] As a result, the Ming court drafted a law forbidding families from providing and accepting hefty dowries. People were eager to marry their daughters off with generous gifts, and cosmetic cases that were part of the dowries became grander than before. A good example is the "Official head-shaped cosmetic case" (Figure 5.1) that takes inspiration from the official cap chair design, a piece of furniture making visible the social status of court officials. Intellectual elites participated directly in the design of furniture during the Ming period.[22] Their sense of aesthetics inspired the style of cosmetic cases, especially when Ming furniture was construed to reflect the aesthetic ideals of intellectual elites who were highly esteemed.

The folding cosmetic case (Figure 5.2) embodied women's engagement with cultural life. The folding frame on the top was used for holding a mirror and books for women to read and practise calligraphy. Interestingly, women combined the irrelevant functions, namely making up and reading, into one object. One may regard makeup items as a distraction when reading or practising calligraphy. Considering the social propriety observed by women in the past, reading on cosmetic cases disassociated intellectual activity from a serious commitment, making such a habit appear more akin to a leisurely activity when women were in fact dedicated to their learning.

The transformation of cosmetic cases to dressing tables signals that women's adornment became an integral part of domestic life and furniture design. This adaptation demonstrates ornamental style is related to change in social status. Historically, Chinese women used separate mirrors on tables in bedrooms for dressing and making-up when

Adornment and the Self

Figure 5.1 Cosmetics case, mirror stand, and screen, late sixteenth to early seventeenth century. Liang Yi Museum, Hong Kong.

Chinese furniture did not include dressing tables.[23] In the Republican period (1912–1949), fashionable women began using dressing tables imported from Europe as part of their bedroom furniture.[24] After the Opium War (1840–42), furniture was imported from England and Germany through Xiamen, Guangzhou, and other thriving treaty ports.[25] European companies established their headquarters in China to import and manufacture furniture in factories for the Chinese market.[26] Furniture makers in Shanghai began to make European-style furniture to meet the growing market of the Chinese privileged class who favoured European designs. Local craftsmen such as Zhang Wanli (张万利) (dates unknown) from Shanghai Mahogany Furniture adapted the structure and appearance of European-style furniture. By the middle of the Republican period, a small number of Chinese designers who were educated in Europe, the United States, and Japan began to design for Chinese consumers.[27] Japan was regarded as an Asian culture that had advanced itself through its adaptation of European ideas. In the early twentieth century, Chinese intellectuals, including designers, studied in Japan to learn new and innovative ideas.

Figure 5.2 Cosmetics chest with a folding mirror stand, seventeenth century. Liang Yi Museum, Hong Kong.

The dressing table made of wood, identified by the Hong Kong Museum of History as an early twentieth-century example, is a typical design (Figure 5.3). It is composed of two parts of carved shelf with a mirror and four carved chests of drawers. The carved shelf resembles the official head-shaped cosmetic case (Figure 5.1) and the ensemble looks like an enlarged cosmetic case that offers storage space. Its presence is robust, providing a considerable amount of interior space.

Styles of dressing tables are diverse, and amalgamate features from different periods, such as Art Nouveau (c. 1890–1920) and Art Deco (1920s) combined with Chinese design characteristics. Dressing tables were particularly important in Republican period furniture.[28] There was no such thing as dressing tables in China before the arrival of Western-style ones. Previously, women used cosmetic cases that were portable and relatively small in size. The dressing table became a notable piece of domestic furniture because it represented the localization of modern Western aesthetic. It was a new category of furniture, specifically designed for women. Historically, female furniture (坤雅 *Kunya* furniture – *Kun* translates as "female" and *Ya* as "elegance") lacked the

Figure 5.3 Dressing table, c. 1900. Hong Kong History Museum.

functionality that fulfilled women's needs. Designs such as stools and chairs were crafted with graphic patterns like flowers and butterflies, which expressed women's aesthetic preferences rather than functionality.[29] Dressing tables were designed to facilitate women's daily lives and the modernization of domestic life. Chinese women have a long history of wearing make-up, yet exclusive furniture for cosmetic application did not appear until the late Qing dynasty and early Republican period. The basic functions of small cosmetic cases were poorly designed. Mirrors in traditional cosmetic cases were made of expensive bronze, which produced inferior imaging effects that could lead to dizziness. In the Republican era, inexpensive glass was first introduced in making larger mirrors on dressing tables, demonstrating that furniture design had started to take into account women's needs.[30] Dressing tables epitomized Western feminist values that considered women as independent individuals whose needs should be respected and made visible. More importantly, the visibility of large-sized dressing tables in domestic interiors embodied the increasing influence of women in their families. Women required autonomy in their living spaces, including the bedroom. They adopted Western lifestyles and self-awareness through the use of dressing tables. Their social status and identities had altered and dressing tables provided more room for various cosmetic products and accessories that could not fit into a traditional cosmetic case, which also emphasized women's social significance and their increased practical needs. This liberated attitude also brought awareness of gender equality in a patriarchal society. Such values were reflected in the lifestyles, behaviours, and education of women in the Republican period as discussed earlier. Chinese women's adaptation of the modern style of dressing up and self-presentation with the use of dressing tables articulated modern femininity and gradual social change.

Modern women and accessories

In the modern era, accessories such as jewellery and portable cosmetic cases became central in defining a woman's identity. Adornment assumed new meanings as women became more liberated than their predecessors. As they spent more time socializing, accessories that carried cosmetic items became necessities for their functional and symbolic values. *Necessaires* were ornamental cases for small items such as tweezers and pencils. They were made in Paris in the 1920s with around a thousand workshops in the city manufacturing goods that were sold in France and other urban cities including Shanghai. The work required to create these intricate cases demanded numerous specialists and craftspeople, such as goldsmiths, lapidaries, metal chasers and engravers, stone setters, lacquerers, guillocheurs, enamellers, and designers. Each fashion house had a studio workshop with specialist designers. Outside artists were used occasionally, most often by large houses like Cartier and Van Cleef & Arpels. Smaller avant-garde jewellers drafted ideas on paper, relying on external workshops to prepare detailed sketches that craftsmen depended on.[31]

A typical example of a small ornamental case is a rectangular beauty compact with oval sections in gold, enamel, diamond, and pearl (Figure 5.4). A landscape in Chinese ink painting style is rendered on the lid, set in two rows of rose-cut diamonds. The landscape in gold is highlighted by the red enamel. *Shou* (壽), the Chinese ideogram for birthday, is set in rose-cut diamonds in the upper right corner. Internal fittings and accessories include a mirror on the reverse of the lid. Two compartments of unequal size are furnished with hinged lids in gold with enamelled black flowerets and catches in the shape of collar studs.[32] Regardless of the owner of the case, whether Chinese or European, the landscape in Chinese ink painting style expresses cultural knowledge. The craftsmanship required to render the delicate design demonstrates the techniques of the craftsman and the wealth, social status, and taste of the woman who used the object.

Women adorning themselves with new commodities and their consumer experiences expressed a sense of new and modern taste.[33] French sociologist Pierre Bourdieu proclaims that aesthetic judgements are divided between the pure aesthetics of the dominant elite class and the popular aesthetics of the working class. The dominant aesthetic taste constitutes various factors such as represented ideas, immediacy of the

Adornment and the Self

Figure 5.4 Lacloche Frères, *Compact*, c. 1925. Liang Yi Museum, Hong Kong.

experiences, and personal interest that inform the user's engagement with the objects. Aesthetic judgements and experiences must be socially and historically situated. The privileged social position achieved through the possession of economic capital keeps aesthetics from becoming a form of necessity. Bourdieu asserts that the working class lacks economic capital; their taste is based on necessity and cultural objects must offer value for money. While the working class could only possess what they could afford, the bourgeoisie's tastes were based on luxury and freedom enabled by economic and cultural capital. Taste distinguishes class, further reinforced by his famous statement: "Taste classifies, and it classifies the classifier".[34] Fashionable women are the "markers of class" who create aspiration in their peers and spectators to gain economic capital that can be turned into cultural capital. Designed objects can be reproduced in a variety of styles in different price ranges. Even when a consumer cannot afford luxurious design, she can purchase a look-alike and create a similar style that shows she possesses the taste for the latest trend. It is knowledge and judgement that distinguishes people with taste.

Women in early twentieth-century China developed better aesthetic judgement and acquired new tastes by discovering the latest trends from popular magazines or visiting boutiques and department stores. Acquisition of taste became challenging as the latest trends and new material goods changed rapidly. Magazines offered guidance on how to choose the newest commodities and stylish accessories that would beautify women's appearances and articulate their identities.[35] Advertisements provided information on new designs and their usage that were critical in defining new roles for women. In an

The Dynamics of Modern Asian Design

Figure 5.5 Advertisement for the Central Automobile Company, *Shun Pao* newspaper (*Shanghai News*), 20 April 1924.

automobile advertisement featuring a woman seated at a dressing table (Figure 5.5), the car reflected in the mirror is her "Dreamed Object" according to the caption. The text emphasizes the automobile is one of the first batch of models to arrive in town, inviting the spectators to test drive it. This advertisement, like many others, offers very little information about the commodity; its focus is its desirability, enticing spectators by offering a trial run of the product. Advertising played a role in strengthening women's purchasing desire, inventing a lifestyle in which the possession of designed objects would play a key role in identity formation. Images of advertising fantasy are to embolden the modern woman as consumption provides her with freedom of choice.

The automobile *necessaire* (Figure 5.6) made of silver and enamel would have further affirmed the modern woman's progressive social status as it epitomized technological advancement, wealth, modernity, and desire depicted in the advertisement (Figure 5.5). Its creation highlighted liberation and the excitement of emancipation enjoyed by privileged urban women who were the drivers or passengers of automobiles. Modern design generated fantasies that symbolized women's social participation in modernity, and permitted them to fulfil the fantasy of liberation.[36]

Figure 5.6 *Necessaire*, c. 1925, silver and enamel. Liang Yi Museum, Hong Kong.

To further understand the correlation between adornment and female identity formation in visual culture, photographs of modern women and accessories including jewellery and dressing tables in *Ling Long* pictorials, a popular journal for female readers, provide evidence.[37] The magazine issues combined images and editorial with diverse topics including perspectives on marriage, romance, women's social status (including women in America, India, and Germany), abortion, child care, advice on hygiene and health, difficulties encountered by women (i.e. trouble with in-laws), and Hollywood and local entertainment news. Images featured Hollywood and Chinese actresses, Chinese socialites, university faculty members and students, and Western entertainers, including dancers. Editorials revealed women's awareness of their social positions and individual identities, while the images illustrated glamourous women and educated ladies, both of whom were role models for readers. The combination of editorial content and confident fashionable women must have impacted how female readers regarded their appearances. Adorning oneself, social awareness, and an educated mind were important characteristics for modern women. Examples can be found in many issues of *Ling Long*, for example, in 1934, issue no.148, a well-dressed young woman with bobbed hair and trousers is featured with an automobile, illustrating the freedom women enjoyed beyond the domestic confines. In the same issue, a photograph of a Chinese woman seated at an Art Deco-style dressing table is accompanied by a Hollywood actress photographed standing in front of a large mirror. The commentary discusses indoor and outdoor lifestyles of ladies who adorned themselves, and women (featured on an opposite page) who displayed their healthy bodies and joyful attitudes through engaging in sport. These photographs illustrated the diverse lifestyles enjoyed by modern women and their identities affirmed by the featured commodities.[38]

Glamorous photographs in popular magazines like *Ling Long* were likely the inspiration for studio photography that was popular among urban Chinese citizens. A

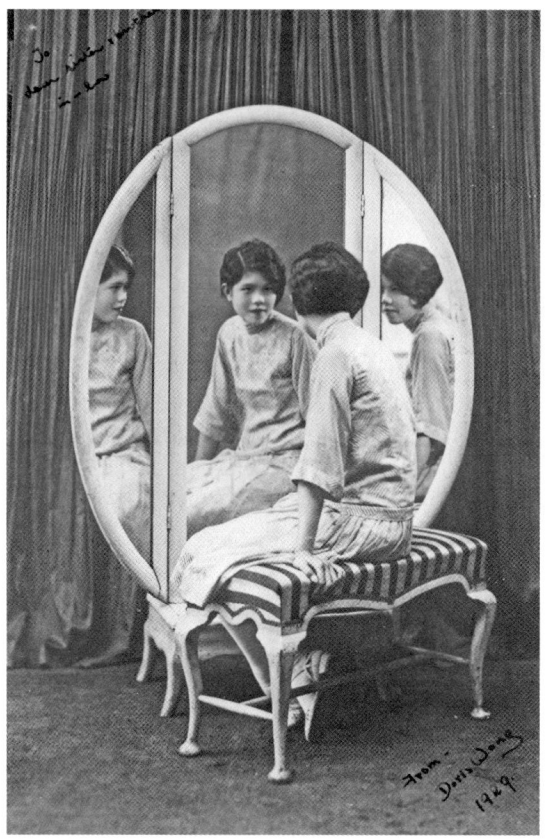

Figure 5.7 Photo taken in a studio, early twentieth century, China. Hong Kong History Museum.

genteel lady gazes into the mirror situated in an arrangement that resembles a dressing table, emphasizing the parallel between adornment and identity formation (Figure 5.7). Her expression denotes pleasure and ease. Adornment does not simply beautify, and the space where a woman attends to her appearance also enhances her self-perception. It is an essential social act that enables women to present themselves respectably. Eileen Chang (1920–1995), an acclaimed modern Chinese novelist who correlated adornment with foreign designs and modernity, observed in her essay, "Chinese Life and Fashions": "The indiscriminate importation of things foreign went to such an extent that society girls and professional beauties wore spectacles as ornament since spectacles were a sign of modernity".[39] The spectacles' function became secondary to the nature of ornamentation that denoted the wearer's taste and fashion sense.

Ornamentation and female identity

Historically, social ranks were predetermined, and the maintenance of multiple roles by an individual was unusual. Gradual changes in the social order starting in the early modern period required new ways of presenting oneself. The folding cosmetic case (Figure 5.2) embodied a woman's engagement with cultural life where she could adorn herself whilst enriching her education. Her dual identities were not contradictory. A proper lady was expected to be concerned about adorning her appearance and expanding her mind. Though women had to adhere to social etiquette, their status improved steadily when social changes allowed new ideas to be adopted into local customs. Cosmetic case design expanded as families assigned more precious possessions to daughters to prepare them for married life. The elaborate case design, coupled with valuable possessions, assured women of their status in their parents' home and a better sense of identity as they entered the in-law's household in hopes that they would be treated with respect. The adaptation of cosmetic cases to dressing tables illustrates the changes women experienced from the inner quarter to the modern bedroom. The dressing table further expanded a woman's position in the domestic domain, giving her a specific design for her own use and a space that was marked as hers.

Design motifs are symbolic marks of identity.[40] Flowers and butterflies often depicted on cosmetic cases signified femininity but they were a limited representation of women's imagination of their identities. Chinese landscape was understood even by Europeans to be associated with socially respectable male literati, and its depiction on an ornamental case denoted artistic appreciation and knowledge, as well as cultural refinement (Figure 5.4). Superior craftsmanship and scholarly motifs expressed women's progressive status, derived from better-educated minds and an appreciation of cultural and social surroundings. The automobile *necessaire* expressed mobility, freedom, and technological advancement that were typically associated with masculinity (Figure 5.6). Women who used these designs felt liberated from domestic confines, such as female motorists who became modern spectacles in urban cities. When automobiles became popular in cities in the early twentieth century, women as icons of consumerist modernity transformed cars from dusty machines to urban spectacle, from a masculine modern invention to an everyday necessity utilized by homemakers who desired efficiency in household management. Their fashionable display escalated cars into a cultural commodity. Women motorists became agents of active consumption by denoting better social standing and upward mobility in their stylish demeanours.[41] They accessorized thoughtfully to articulate their new-found identities. Carefully crafted appearances became important markers of redefined female identity and individuality.

Ornamentation enhances the object's functions and expresses a design's unique characteristics. Examples examined in this chapter attest to the fact that ornamentation in modern China was essential as a communicative medium. Modern minimalists regarded ornamentation as merely beautifying, and thus unnecessary because the process of making it consumed time and demanded labour. The elimination of ornamentation in design fell in line with minimalist modernity, and the concepts promoted by Austrian architect and theorist of modern architecture, Adolf Loos (1870–1933). He proclaimed in *Ornament and Crime* (1908), that "The evolution of culture is synonymous with the removal of ornament from objects of daily use", reinforcing modernism's preference for clean lines and austere surfaces in place of ornamentation.[42] Loos regarded ornamentation as deceitful and wasteful. On the other hand, ornamentation generated an experience of the senses when an object and its meanings were appreciated, as American philosopher John Dewey (1859–1952) asserted that a work of art "is recreated every time it is aesthetically experienced"[43], extending the value of ornamentation beyond its surface meaning. At the same time, German art historian and critic, Otto Schulze-Elberfeld (1898–1976), conceded that ornamentation had been misused and had lost its power in the modern age, but nevertheless he highlighted its communicative power like a language, emphasizing interaction between the ornament and the user.[44] Ornamentation was recognized as an essential system of ordering visual phenomena, from which aesthetic pleasure and social meanings were derived. Its role as a transformative agent was most clearly expressed in women's adornment, such as cosmetic cases and dressing tables that embodied the users' identities, tastes, and fantasies.[45] Cosmetic cases provided space for women to read and situate their knowledge in a feminine framework that conveyed the social relevance of women's education (Figure 5.2). Even in an era when their virtue remained largely in the domestic realm as wives and mothers, ornamentation on designed objects offered a means of self-expression. Using a dressing table was ritualistic, involving painting one's face to form a desirable appearance. The daily routine was integral to life's transition such as becoming a woman, getting married, and motherhood. The design was often a gift that marked an important occasion such as a wedding or a birthday. Its usage marked the transition from childhood to adulthood. Whether the dressing table was empty or the user imagined it with the products and tools needed to beautify the appearance, dressing up conveyed femininity and self-fashioning. The ritual connected life's transitional moments, the social ideal of femininity, and respectable appearance. Increasingly elaborate cosmetic cases, dressing tables, and modern motifs such as automobiles symbolized the experiences of self-aware and liberated women, transforming how they regarded their domestic and social status and ultimately their identities. These designs offered them the pleasure of their own spaces where they could adorn themselves while ornamental designs signified their improved status. Using such objects eased women from domesticity to the modern urban environment.

In the early twentieth century, a new generation of Chinese women demanded to be taken seriously. Urban Chinese women participated in the reforming fashion movement, freeing them from authoritarian traditions and reclaiming autonomy in the process. Adorning the body was crucial in redefining gender and mediating identities during unprecedented historical conditions. Young stylish urban women were portrayed in photographs and popular journals, which attracted a readership of young and progressively educated city dwellers. A woman's appearance was not simply a trendy look, it also reinforced self-perception and affirmed identity through the designs and commodities used in their daily lives. It was the first time women in China had access to a larger domain of fashion styles through public media. The redefinition of the female gender became a metaphor for cultural metamorphoses, in which liberation from traditional roles ensured that women's bodies became the site of unending debates on how women could be best dressed and what their functions were. Debates surrounding the adornment of a woman's body and conflicting regulations were constantly in flux;

demonstrating the complex and unstable battleground of the female body and the challenges women encountered in their navigation of modern society. That alluring female images were popular with the public but were also criticized by officials and the intelligentsia reveals the complex nature of adornment. Women's appearance also served as a vehicle to mediate rapid social change. Through modifications of their appearances, modern Chinese women established their status with the freedom of choice that allowed them to emphasize parts of their bodies and identities that were otherwise concealed under layers of clothing.

Notes

1. Early modern era in China refers to the period between the fifteenth and nineteenth centuries.
2. In this chapter, ornamentations refer to decoration on designs while adornment describes how women enhance their appearance.
3. Cosmetic cases are sometimes referred to as vanity cases in literature and museum label descriptions.
4. There is a large amount of literature on the May Fourth movement, including Kai-wing Chow (ed.), *Beyond the May Fourth Paradigm: In Search of Chinese Modernity* (Lexington Books, 2008) and Vera Schwarcz, *The Chinese Enlightenment: Intellectuals and the Legacy of the May Fourth Movement of 1919* (University of California Press, 1986).
5. For an insightful discussion about calendar posters and advertisements on women's dresses in early twentieth China, see Ellen Johnston Laing, "Visual Evidence for the Evolution of 'Politically Correct' Dress for Women in Early Twentieth Century Shanghai", *Nan Nü* 5, no. 1 (2003): 69–114.
6. Martha Huang, "'A Woman Has So Many Parts to Her Body, Life is Very Hard Indeed'", in Valerie Steele and John S. Major (eds.), *China Chic: East Meet West* (Yale University Press, 1999), 134.
7. Antonia Finnane, *Changing Clothes in China: Fashion, History, Nation* (Columbia University Press, 2008), 174.
8. Francesca Dal Lago, "Crossed Legs in 1930s Shanghai: How 'Modern' The Modern Woman?", *East Asian History* 19 (June 2000): 113–14.
9. Antonia Finnane, "What Should Chinese Women Wear? A National Problem", *Modern China* 22, no. 2 (1996): 117.
10. Finnane, "What Should Chinese Women Wear?", 118–19.
11. Huang, "A Woman Has So Many Parts to Her Body", 137; Xu Dishan, "Women's Dress" (*Nuzi di yifu*) (1920).
12. Huang, "A Woman Has So Many Parts to Her Body", 137.
13. Huang, "A Woman Has So Many Parts to Her Body", 137–38.
14. Fangfang Liu, "Probe into Ancient Make-Up", *Cultural Relics in the Spring and Autumn* 13, no. 1 (2011): 43–50.
15. Patricia Buckley Ebrey, *Inner Quarters: Marriage and the Lives of Chinese Women in the Sung Period* (University of California Press, 1993), 261–72.

16. Liang Lu, "The Origin and Development of Dowry and the Change of Social and Cultural Concept", *Songs Bimonthly* 5 (2021): 121–32.
17. Dorothy Ko, *Teachers of the Inner Chambers: Women and Culture in Seventeenth-Century China* (Stanford University Press, 1995), 7.
18. Ko, *Teachers of the Inner Chambers*, 11. For a thorough discussion on women's cultural and social roles in the High Qing period (1683–39), see Susan Mann, *Precious Records: Women in China's Long Eighteenth Century* (Stanford University Press, 1997).
19. Liu, "Probe into Ancient Make-Up", 43–50.
20. Weirong Cheng, "On Women's Property Inheritance Right in Ancient China", *Political Science and Law* 9, no. 8 (2013): 118–25.
21. Rubie S. Watson and Patricia Buckley Ebrey (eds.), *Marriage and Inequality in Chinese Society* (University of California Press, 1991), 99–113; Sun Zhao, "On the Shape and Structure of Beauty Boxes Design in Ming and Qing Dynasties", *Design Research* 9, no. 5 (2019): 15–21.
22. Xiaotang Wang and Zhihui Wu, "The Influence of Ming Dynasty Scholars on Ming Style Furniture", *Furniture* 39, no. 2 (2018): 79–81.
23. Weiqun Jiang, *A Look at the Furniture of the Republic of China* (Beijing United Publishing Company, 2014), 223; Xuebin Zhang, Yachi Zhang, Guangrui Sun and Zhihui Wu, "Current Situation and Trend of Study for Furniture in the Republic of China", *Furniture and Interior Design* 12 (2018): 102–5.
24. Jiang, *A Look at the Furniture of the Republic of China*, 223; Yan Zuo, Kaiping Zhang and Shuyi Li, "From the Mirror Case to the Table: Study on Cultural Causes and Style Characteristics of the Dressing Tables in the Republic of China", *Architecture & Culture* 7 (2020): 36–39.
25. Huajuan Shan and Yushu Chen, "Study of the Sinicization of Foreign Art Styles in Dressing Table", *Furniture* 38, no. 3 (2017): 68–88.
26. Zeng Li and Hua Liu, "Encoding the Development of Shanghai Wood Furniture", *Furniture & Interior Decoration* 12 (2003): 20–22.
27. Zuo et al., "From the Mirror Case to the Table", 36–39; Yingying Guo, "A Comparative Study on the Modernization of Chinese and Japanese Traditional Furniture", PhD dissertation (Central South University of Forestry and Technology, 2020), 53.
28. Zuo et al., "From the Mirror Case to the Table", 36–39; Guo, "A Comparative Study", 53.
29. Wanting Dong and Ziqian Yang, "Analysis of the Ming and Qing Kunya Furniture – Taking the Yongzheng Twelve Beauties as an Example", *Design* 23 (2021): 61–63.
30. Shan and Chen, "Study of the Sinicization of Foreign Art Styles in Dressing Table", 68–88.
31. Sarah Hue-Williams and Peter Edwards, *A Kind of Magic: Art Deco Vanity Cases* (Unicorn Press, 2017), 183.
32. Haiyang Song, *Contrast and Harmony: Selected Vanity Cases and Chinese Furniture of Liang Yi Museum* (Forbidden City Publishing House, 2011), 108.
33. Luxury designs such as *necessaire* were used by privileged Chinese women. A vanity case with a clock designed for Soong May-Ling (1897–2003) featured her married surname "MLC" (May-Ling Chiang). The case was presented at an exhibition that explored the lives of the Soong sisters in Shanghai in 2016.
34. Agnes Rocamora, "Pierre Bourdieu: The Field of Fashion," in Agnes Rocamora and Anneke Smelik (eds.), *Thinking through Fashion: A Guide to Key Theorists* (Bloomsbury, 2019), 241, 242.

35. Tomoko Tamari, "Rise of the Department Store and the Aestheticization of Everyday Life in Early 20th Century Japan", *International Journal of Japanese Sociology* 15, no. 1 (November 2006): 105.
36. It is impossible to determine the number of urban women who drove in the early twentieth century. They were certainly passengers who were driven around by chauffeurs or male companions. The fantasy of freedom associated with driving was reinforced by a significant number of photographs featuring women with automobiles published in popular magazines such as *Ling Long* discussed in this chapter.
37. Louise Edwards, "The Shanghai Modern Woman's American Dreams: Imagining America's Depravity to Produce China's 'Moderate Modernity'", *Pacific Historical Review* 81, no. 4 (November 2012): 567–601. The author suggests that *Ling Long*'s editorial used decadent American images and news to encourage a moderate form of modernity for its Chinese readers.
38. *Ling Long* women's magazine is accessible via Columbia University Libraries online collection: https://exhibitions.library.columbia.edu/exhibits/show/linglong.
39. VESTOJ, "Chinese Life and Fashion by Eileen Chang".
40. Martin J. Powers, *Pattern and Person: Ornament, Society, and Self in Classical China* (Harvard University Press, 2006), 4.
41. Eva Chen, "Pretty Women Don't Drive: Early Women Motorists and the Taming of the Motor-Car", *Women's Studies* 49, no. 2 (2020): 152, 165, 171.
42. Christopher Long, "The Origin and Context of Adolf Loos's 'Ornament and Crime'", *Journal of the Society of Architectural Historians* 68, no. 2 (June 2009): 203. See also Adolf Loos, *Ornament and Crime* (Penguin Random House, 2019).
43. Vlad Glăveanu, "The Function of Ornaments: A Cultural Psychological Exploration", *Culture and Psychology* 20, no.1 (2014): 94.
44. Long, "The Origin and Context of Adolf Loos's 'Ornament and Crime'", 210–11. Otto Schulze-Elberfeld's original statement is "Genuine ornament is like a language".
45. Sarah Frater, "Furniture, Femininity, and Self-fashioning: The Dressing Table in Mid-Twentieth Century Britain", Master's dissertation (Royal College of Art and Victoria & Albert Museum, 2012).

References

Chen, Eva. "Pretty Women Don't Drive: Early Women Motorists and the Taming of the Motor-Car", *Women's Studies* 49, no.2 (2020): 149–79.
Cheng, Weirong. "On Women's Property Inheritance Right in Ancient China", *Political Science and Law* 9, no. 8 (2013): 118–25.
Chow, Kai-wing (ed.). *Beyond the May Fourth Paradigm: In Search of Chinese Modernity*, Lexington Books, 2008.
Dal Lago, Francesca. "Crossed Legs in 1930s Shanghai: How 'Modern' The Modern Woman?", *East Asian History* 19 (June 2000): 103–44.
Dishan, Xu. "Women's Dress" (*Nuzi di yifu*) (1920).
Dong, Wanting and Ziqian Yang. "Analysis of the Ming and Qing Kunya Furniture –Taking the Yongzheng Twelve Beauties as an Example", *Design* 23 (2021): 61- 63.
Ebrey, Patricia Buckley. *Inner Quarters: Marriage and the Lives of Chinese Women in the Sung Period*, University of California Press, 1993.

Edwards, Louise. "The Shanghai Modern Woman's American Dreams: Imagining America's Depravity to Produce China's 'Moderate Modernity'", *Pacific Historical Review* 81, no. 4 (November 2012): 567–601.

Finnane, Antonia. "What Should Chinese Women Wear? A National Problem", *Modern China* 22, no. 2 (1996): 99–131.

Finnane, Antonia. *Changing Clothes in China: Fashion, History, Nation*, Columbia University Press, 2008.

Frater, Sarah. "Furniture, Femininity, and Self-fashioning: The Dressing Table in Mid-Twentieth Century Britain", Master's dissertation, Royal College of Art and Victoria & Albert Museum, 2012.

Glăveanu, Vlad. "The Function of Ornaments: A Cultural Psychological Exploration", *Culture and Psychology* 20, no.1 (2014): 82–101.

Guo, Yingying. "A Comparative Study on the Modernization of Chinese and Japanese Traditional Furniture", PhD dissertation, Central South University of Forestry and Technology, 2020.

Huang, Martha. "'A Woman Has So Many Parts to Her Body, Life is very Hard Indeed'", in Valerie Steele and John S. Major (eds.), *China Chic: East Meet West*, Yale University Press, 1999.

Hue-Williams, Sarah and Peter Edwards. *A Kind of Magic: Art Deco Vanity Cases*, Unicorn Press, 2017.

Jiang, Weiqun. *A Look at the Furniture of the Republic of China*, Beijing United Publishing Company, 2014.

Johnston Laing, Ellen. "Visual Evidence for the Evolution of 'Politically Correct' Dress for Women in Early Twentieth Century Shanghai", *Nan Nü* 5, no. 1 (2003): 69–114.

Ko, Dorothy. *Teachers of the Inner Chambers: Women and Culture in Seventeenth-Century China*, Stanford University Press, 1995.

Li, Zeng and Hua Liu. "Encoding the Development of Shanghai Wood Furniture", *Furniture & Interior Decoration* 12 (2003): 20–22.

Liu, Fangfang. "Probe into Ancient Make-Up", *Cultural Relics in the Spring and Autumn* 13, no. 1 (2011): 43–50.

Long, Christopher. "The Origin and Context of Adolf Loos's 'Ornament and Crime'", *Journal of the Society of Architectural Historians* 68, no. 2 (June 2009): 200–23.

Loos, Adolf. *Ornament and Crime*, Penguin Random House, 2019.

Lu, Liang. "The Origin and Development of Dowry and the Change of Social and Cultural Concept", *Songs Bimonthly* 5 (2021): 121–32.

Ma, W.D. *A Hundred Boxes, a Thousand Boxes, and Ten Thousand Boxes*, Forbidden City

Mann, Susan. *Precious Records: Women in China's Long Eighteenth Century*, Stanford University Press, 1997.

Powers, Martin J. *Pattern and Person: Ornament, Society, and Self in Classical China*, Harvard University Press, 2006.

Rocamora, Agnes. "Pierre Bourdieu: The Field of Fashion", in Agnes Rocamora and Anneke Smelik (eds.), *Thinking through Fashion: A Guide to Key Theorists*, Bloomsbury, 2019.

Schwarcz, Vera. *The Chinese Enlightenment: Intellectuals and the Legacy of the May Fourth Movement of 1919*, University of California Press, 1986.

Shan, Huajuan and Yushu Chen. "Study of the Sinicization of Foreign Art Styles in Dressing Table", *Furniture* 38, no. 3 (2017): 68–88.

Song, Haiyang. *Contrast and Harmony: Selected Vanity Cases and Chinese Furniture of Liang Yi Museum*, Forbidden City Publishing House, 2011.

Tamari, Tomoko. "Rise of the Department Store and the Aestheticization of Everyday Life in Early 20th Century Japan", *International Journal of Japanese Sociology* 15, no. 1 (November 2006): 99–118.

VESTOJ. "Chinese Life and Fashion by Eileen Chang". http://vestoj.com/chinese-life-and-fashions/ (accessed 24 December 2023).

Wang, Xiaotang and Zhihui Wu. "The Influence of Ming Dynasty Scholars on Ming Style Furniture", *Furniture* 39, no. 2 (2018): 79–81.

Watson, Rubie S. and Patricia Buckley Ebrey (eds.). *Marriage and Inequality in Chinese Society*, University of California Press, 1991.

Yan Zuo, Kaiping Zhang and Shuyi Li. "From the Mirror Case to the Table: Study on Cultural Causes and Style Characteristics of the Dressing Tables in the Republic of China", *Architecture & Culture* 7 (2020): 36–39.

Zhang, Xuebin, Yachi Zhang, Guangrui Sun and Zhihui Wu. "Current Situation and Trend of Study for Furniture in the Republic of China", *Furniture and Interior Design* 12 (2018): 102–5.

Zhao, Sun. "On the Shape and Structure of Beauty Boxes Design in Ming and Qing Dynasties", *Design Research* 9, no. 5 (2019): 15–21.

CHAPTER 6
RELIGIOUS AESTHETICS: COLLECTING CHINESE GODS
Valentina Gamberi

Introduction

This chapter extends the reflection on transcultural objects[1] to include European collections of Chinese religious artefacts, particularly gods' wooden statuary for domestic and temple cults. The chapter aims to understand the museographic and aesthetic implications of material religion in museums as transcultural objects. It focuses on the Chinese gods' pantheon acquired by the Sinologist Jan Jakob Maria de Groot (Schiedam 1854–Berlin 1921) – scattered between the Volkenkundemuseum in Leiden and the Musée des Confluences in Lyon – as a case study. By transcultural objects, I refer to material and ritual knowledge imbued by Chinese sculptors and ritual performers that de Groot's collection retained and were absorbed into his conceptualizations and imaginings about Chinese religion.

De Groot was one of the first Sinologists who turned to ethnography as a method through which to explain features of Chinese culture that had previously been analysed using linguistics and philology. My research focuses on de Groot's Chinese statuary as it represents one of the few yet most systematic attempts to represent Chinese folk religion in European museums. Chinese gods' statuary acted, at the same time, as material guidance for de Groot during and after his fieldwork, as well as a didactic tool for communicating his analysis to a European audience through his publications and an exhibition project he planned.

Here, I consider the ambiguous nature of de Groot's Chinese pantheon in serving scholarly theories while evoking the ethnographic context of a lived Chinese religion as filtered through his perspective and encounter with Chinese ritual performers. The chapter aims to reconstruct the different layers of material knowledge and sensorium embedded in de Groot's Chinese statuary and how these affective traces and embodiments guided him in establishing his scholarship. De Groot's sensorium and affects, however, rarely became apparent in his publications. His Chinese pantheon with its ritual detachment – since its statues are not consecrated for ritual purposes but commissioned by de Groot himself to Xiamen artisans – reflects more his attempt to make Chinese religion understandable and intelligible than as lived and experienced. The encyclopaedic cataloguing of gods according to their spiritual hierarchical power impacted the statues' aesthetics, privileging standardization to local variants. The chapter thus shows that in the case of Asian collections in museums, aesthetics is shaped by curators' attempts to prove their scholarly ideas about Asian religions through material means. It highlights how the latter entails a complex network of historical, political, and epistemological dynamics seldom described in museum labels, where Asian artefacts displayed are taken for granted as representative of Asian cultures outside museum walls. Instead, the chapter incorporates contemporary usages of Chinese folk statuaries as experienced in my ethnographic fieldwork in Taiwan (2017–20) to complexify the narrative of Chinese folk religion as offered by museum labels and reported in de Groot's books.[2]

For a transcultural corpothetics

This chapter in part resounds with the scholarship related to "religious aesthetics",[3] "living religion",[4] the material turn of religious studies and anthropology,[5] as well as literature at the nexus of cultural heritage and religion.[6] According to these perspectives, religion can no longer be approached as a textual corpus, but rather a daily practice that interests worshippers' sensorium and shapes it accordingly. Sharing a common sensorium allows worshippers to feel part of a religious community and differentiate themselves from other religious practices and beliefs. Religious materiality also plays a fundamental role in organizing religious communities' rituals and mediating between them and the supernatural. For example, Chinese statuary is crafted so worshippers can efficaciously manipulate gods' spiritual power. Without material support, spiritual power remains an abstract notion that cannot truly condition reality.[7] In this context, aesthetics is no longer confined to the criterion of beauty and iconographic rigour, but rather, encompasses sensory perception and understanding of the world. In other words, aesthetics is an embodied epistemology connected to a material "repertoire".[8]

Christopher Pinney's notion of *corpothetics*,[9] which aligns with the scholarship mentioned above, is appropriate for this chapter. By corpothetics, Pinney means an analysis of the bodily interactions of beholders with images and material artefacts, as well as the latter's efficacy or, in other words, "what they can do" in the world and how they influence human beholders.[10] This chapter expands on Pinney's work in that it understands corpothetics in a transcultural way. Given that Asian artefacts were sensed, touched, collected, and assembled by European collectors and scholars during colonial times, it is necessary to understand how the latter's perspective "sticks to"[11] the artefacts themselves, and intertwines with Asian corpothetics towards material religion. By using Ahmed's expression "sticking to", I emphasize how emotions, feelings, and sensations leave a material trace on artefacts that is stratified through the passing of time and can be partially sensed by those who come into contact with them in the present. By adopting the term "stick", I also want to emphasize the emotional work at stake with *materia sacra*.[12] Colonial collections stimulated fears and expectations among colonial collectors and colonized subjects. Whilst the former saw collecting as a form of disempowerment of idolatrous spiritual power, the latter perceived – and still perceive – the display of religious items of their religions unattended and unworshipped as dangerous.[13] Following this line of reasoning, I analyse Chinese statuary in Leiden by considering how it is sensed both by their religious communities and by de Groot and try and relate these different sensoria.

Research methodology

This chapter presents the findings of archival research and interviews with curators at the Volkenkundemuseum. To trace the corpothetic layers embedded in de Groot's pantheon, I analyse available archival material related to the statues in Leiden, in particular museum entries and museum guides provided at the time of de Groot, as well as the latter's letters and diaries. This material helped verify whether de Groot transcribed his phenomenological experience of Chinese rituals and the circumstances through which the statues came to Leiden. My intention was also to corroborate archival material with interviews with former and current curators at the Volkenkundemuseum to understand whether and how de Groot's experience of Chinese religion influenced museographic exhibits and narratives on the statues, and the possible legacy that this past museographic corpus might have had on the current exhibition, where the majority of de Groot's pantheon is on display. In so doing, I embrace a biographical and ethnographic method, namely tracing de Groot's fieldwork experience and his informants' sensorium.[14]

Archival research has been particularly challenging since de Groot did not provide a written account of the circumstances of his collecting. As emphasized by Zwi Werblowsky (Martin Buber Professor of Comparative Religion at the Hebrew University of Jerusalem) – who, at the end of the 1990s, conducted meticulous research on de Groot's life and its pantheon, both in Leiden and Lyon – de Groot destroyed most of his diaries, judging them as too personal for scientific scrutiny, and was very selective of the information he considered useful for publication.[15]

Despite this tabula rasa, de Groot recorded some memories within a volume of "memoirs", mentioned in de Visser's obituary (1921) and in possession of de Groot's sister, entitled: *Notizen über mein Leben: Familiestuk*. These *Notizen* were passed to the anthropologist Maurice Freedman during his research on de Groot[16] and then entrusted by Freedman's widow to Werblowsky in the 1990s.[17] Unfortunately, after Werblowsky's death, these *Notizen* were not published. Therefore, I could only rely on Werblowky's publications and notes deposited in the Volkenkundemuseum's archive. My inability to consult primary archival sources is reflected in contemporary museum practices in Leiden. The former curator, Paul van Dongen, who designed the current exhibition of de Groot's material, based his work on Werblowky's research. Van Dongen himself conducted brief ethnographic fieldwork in Xiamen in the 1990s in an attempt to corroborate the information he had about de Groot's collection.

My research is thus in line with other work on museum provenance.[18] It is limited by the lack of personal insights or accounts of de Groot's experiences in China and the fact I could not access any written memories. These limitations resulted in two methodological decisions.

On the one hand, I adopted an inferential analysis of de Groot and his fieldwork informants' corpothetics, consulting his main publications (*Les Fêtes annuellement célébrées à Émoui (Amoy)* (1886) and *The Religious System of China* (1892)), as well as the catalogue on the pantheon published by Brill (1890s).[19] Although de Groot filtered out any personal experience, as stated previously, his publications were structured according to a particular narrative style that reflected his perspectives and stance towards Chinese folk religion rather than being a "neutral" description as such.

On the other hand, I filled de Groot's lack of written memories with other voices and perspectives. By comparing de Groot's statues with Taiwanese ritual and sculptural practices encountered during my fieldwork in Taiwan (2017–20), I suggest how contemporary ethnography on religious practices can enrich the information available in a museum collection, as well as clarify the "working through"[20] that shaped colonial artefacts in such a way as to reflect the collector's point of view. The main interpretations of de Groot's approach to Chinese material religion in this chapter are, therefore, derived from de Groot's scholarly work together with live religious practice as recounted by contemporary anthropologists in the field,[21] including my ethnographic research in Taiwan. The chapter discusses ethnographic accounts of Taiwanese material religion, interrogates secondary sources on de Groot, and investigates the corpothetics of de Groot's encounter with Chinese gods' statuary.

Jan Jakob Maria de Groot as early Dutch Sinologist

In his youth, de Groot had longed to travel and discover the world, leading him first to *Indische Instelling* (Indian Institute) in Delft and then to the Chinese Studies Department at the University of Leiden in 1873, where he was a student of Schlegel from 1873 to 1876. Like his colleagues, he entered colonial service. After one year of training, he was appointed as a Chinese interpreter in the Netherlands Indies and sent to Amoy.[22] After a year in Amoy, he served in Cheribon and Western Borneo, before being granted sick leave for two years in the Netherlands owing to ill health as a result of Cheribon's hot and humid climate. He soon realized (1878) that his genuine aspiration and ambition was to conduct scholarly research on Chinese customs, which had engaged him since his first stay in Amoy in 1877. Despite turning to an academic career during his sick leave in the Netherlands in 1883, he continued working as a colonial civil servant until 1892. He was an active member of the Batavian Society of Arts and Sciences from 1878 to 1883 and from 1886 and 1890. During his second stay in China, he was also requested by the Ministry of Colonies to study and promote Chinese migrant workers to Banka and Sumatra, as attested in twenty-five items in de Groot's *Nachlass* in Berlin Archive.[23] A study of Chinese coolie labourers was requested at that time by the colonial administration, as a result of Dutch and Chinese cohabitation, which sometimes escalated into armed conflict, as in the case of the Batavia massacre of Chinese in 1740.[24]

De Groot's direct involvement in the colonial administration as an interpreter on the one hand, and accumulating knowledge on Chinese customs and law for the colonial government on the other,[25] partly explains his interest in delineating a systemic analysis of Chinese religion and its intertwining with social aspects, as claimed in his introduction to *The Religious System of China* (1892). One of the reasons de Groot succeeded in attracting sponsorship for a second journey to China was because he presented his academic endeavours as beneficial for the colonial administration in understanding Chinese ways of living and mastering them for administration purposes. Because of explicit colonial purpose, de Groot's approach to religion was holistic and in line with the newly developing discipline of anthropology. His new methodology for studying religion, which combined ethnographic fieldwork with textual analysis, also aligns with his initial hybrid career as a colonial interpreter and independent scholar, a perspective that other Chinese religious scholars of the time did not have. Therefore, de Groot's historical and political positionality has a bearing on the meanings of Chinese statuary, as will be made clear in this chapter.

A brief biography of de Groot's statuary

Chinese folk religious statuary was initially collected by de Groot during his stay in Amoy in 1877, along with other material artefacts, including musical instruments and puppets, mainly paid for from his salary. During his first stay in China, some of the artefacts he collected were donated to the Museum of Ethnology in Leiden. Upon de Groot's return to the Netherlands, he collaborated again with the museum by thoroughly elaborating on each item based on his ethnographic knowledge. Unfortunately, de Groot did not receive an official mandate to collect further items from the museum's director, Lindor Serrurier (in service from 1881 to 1896), despite him promising de Groot 500 guilders yet not respecting his offer. As a result of his experience with Serrurier, de Groot met the directors of the publishing firm Brill (van Vord and de Stoppelaar), which also collected Orientalia and he was invited to acquire items for them.

The collaboration between de Groot and Brill was akin to that of him as collector and Émile Guimet as museum director, whom he met in Leiden during a conference in which he presented a piece on Chinese burial practices and, subsequently, in Paris, before he departed for China. As pointed out by Werblowky,[26] de Groot's ethnographic methods attracted the interest of Guimet, who conveyed in his museum a sense of living religious traditions through performance, most of the time not by Chinese or Asians but rather by "exotic" performers such as Mata Hari (at that time, Mme. MacLeod).[27]

Guimet's interest in evoking Asian lived religion in his museum is in line with other museum exhibits and designs of colonial times, where visitors were able to experience reconstructions of altars and shrines through the guidance of collectors' museum guides and catalogues fashioned according to a travelogue-like narrative.[28] As argued by Clark,[29] reconstructions of religious spaces usually conveyed curators and collectors' stereotypical views of the "natives", resulting in the freezing of the latter's religious activities within an ethnographic present[30] that was divorced from living practices, both then and at the time of collection. Those reconstructions conveyed the didactic goal of materially demonstrating how Chinese or other religious "systems" work. From archival and secondary material, it is unclear how Guimet intended to use de Groot's pantheon within his exhibits. In addition, de Groot, as will be shown below, did not intend to evoke a ritual atmosphere through material means. What must be highlighted, however, is Guimet and de Groot's shared interest in exhaustively portraying Asian religions to a European audience.

While in Paris, de Groot tried, again, to convince Serrurier to sponsor his collecting, but without success.[31] Interestingly, though, the Museum of Ethnology acquired de Groot's collection, which Brill sold in the early 1890s[32] and is still visible in the permanent display of the museum. Later, Serrurier accused de Groot of breaking an agreement with him and making a deal with Guimet instead, which the Ministry of Colonies judged not to be tenable.[33] The museum entries attached to each statue must be considered an amalgamation of de Groot's written notes elaborated in the 1870s/1880s and his catalogues for Brill and the Musée Guimet. To understand the significance of de Groot's collecting and its transcultural nature, we must observe how Chinese material religion has been lived by its practitioners and to what extent de Groot's encounter with it moulded it, *stuck to* it differently.

Taiwanese material religion: an overview

How worshippers and gods interact in Chinese folk religion has been the realm of anthropologists and Sinologists since the 1970s, who have mainly conducted fieldwork in Taiwan.[34] Without reconstructing the scholarly position on the Chinese folk religious concept of sacred power,[35] as it is beyond the scope of this chapter, I will look at how we can define Chinese folk religion using a corpothetic approach.

Gods and ancestors protect the ordinary world. Whilst ancestors' intervention into the living world is confined to the sphere of their descendants,[36] gods – though deceased, do not have descendants to look after them for funerary and ancestor cults – control a collectivity of families that share a common area. Gods' power exerted on a community represents a mutual obligation between gods and worshippers: gods agree to be confined within a territorial space rather than wandering around, whilst worshippers agree to worship gods to maintain the latter's presence in their community. As argued by Lin, this mutual obligation cannot be possible without a material "support",[37] namely, gods' wooden statues. As exemplified by a sculptor I interviewed during my fieldwork: "The function of sculpture would help to memorize the ancestors and make them immortal in people's mind".[38]

Significantly, gods higher up the Chinese folk religious hierarchy, such as the Jade Emperor, usually do not have statues, seldom enter villages to offer help, and worshippers interact with them with their backs turned to the main altar, facing the outside. Similarly, ancestors do not have statues, but instead have a tablet. In the context where their power is requested to help someone from outside the family, they must be invited to do so through a statue, since this material support will help attest their efficacious, magical power or *ling* (靈), thus enabling miracles, which, in turn, "win" ancestors-gods' "common recognition".[39] Gods' miracles for worshippers also cement the latter's unity, history, and identity. There are several oral narratives that connect the history of settlement formation with certain families' attachment to a deity. For instance, a god may be too heavy to carry, and so the worshippers of that god decide to settle in a specific place to worship it.[40] A god can also assume a distinctive iconography and narrative as long as it settles in a territory.[41]

Carving a statue represents a mediation between sculptors' skills, deities' willingness to be represented in a certain way, and formal obligations between gods, worshippers, and their territory. Lin argues that sculptors receive gods' revelation in dreams, thus stimulating their imagination about gods. In the carving process, the latter reveal their willingness to enter their statues and be portrayed in such a way by carvers. Each sculpture has a specific aesthetic and design due to its god's characteristics and history, but it may also differ from another statue of the same god.[42]

In my fieldwork in Taiwan, Lin's ethnographic account is somehow relativized. A sculptor I met in 2020 in the district of Xinzhuang (New Taipei City) declared that he sometimes dreamt about a deity to sculpt. Still, he relied mainly on reference images and the experience accumulated from his family members and his work. We can, therefore, say that some iconographic traits distinguish a god from others, but gods' iconography generally presents variety, thus requiring of viewers, temple goers, as well as museum curators, the careful contextualization of each statue.

Before god's spirit enters the statue, thus activating it, sculptors introduce specific *materia sacra* within the statue's inner body. According to a woodcarver I interviewed in 2020, this *materia sacra* must be inserted at the level of the statue's heart since this material represents gods' vital organs. This material consists of incense ashes, five or seven precious materials (such as gold, silver, bronze, iron, and tin), grains and beans (such as rice, wheat, and sesame), and five-colour threads (red, yellow, blue, black, and white).[43] Lin also includes a live wasp, although some temple committee members in Xinzhuang declared that inserting live animals within gods' statues may, in some circumstances, be associated with the sculptor or owner's intention to manipulate gods' power for his or her good, thereby activating a bad power or bad *ling*. In the opinion of the Xinzhuang's sculptor, the precious metals represent gods' digestive organs, while grains and beans portray harvesting, thereby granting rich crops to worshippers. If we compare Lin's report,[44] we can see that interpretations of the *materia sacra*'s meaning may vary according to different subjects' experiences.

Crucially, among *materia sacra*, there are five-colour threads and, as pointed out by Lin, amulets or the ashes from incense burners taken from temples.[45] These two elements explain how a god attaches to a territory and is part of a hierarchical relationship with other statues of the same god located elsewhere. As argued by Lin,[46] the five-colour threads represent five spirit soldiers' camps (*wuying*, 五營兵), associated with the five directions in which a territory can be subdivided, namely: the centre, the north, the south, the west, and the east. These five soldiers may also represent ethnic armies mentioned in fourth-century Daoist scriptures in Southern China and can be associated with numerological cosmology. Spirit soldiers' camps originated from deceased souls and are trained by gods to ward off evil spirits from their territory. This territory includes the community's borders and each of the households that comprise the worshippers' community. Inserting the five threads within a statue's inner body allows its god to control the spirit soldiers and, consequently, control its territory.

Regarding the presence of ashes from temple incense burners, let us first refer to the central role played by incense in Chinese folk rituals:[47] lighting an incense stick is the means by which worshippers communicate with gods, who are attracted by the smell of the incense. Each god, then, has its own incense burner. Whether some of a god's worshippers leave that god's territory, or neighbouring villages start to worship that god because of its efficacious power, a new temple dedicated to the god can be inaugurated in another place if the ceremony of the "division of fire" (*fen xiang huo*, 分香火) is performed: part of the incense of the main temple's incense burner is transferred to the new temple by inserting it both in the copy of the god's statue and the new incense burner. The new temple, therefore, is considered a descendant of the main temple, thus using parenthood and ancestry terminology, while distinguishing it from the other "siblings" and "parents", usually through toponyms related to the locality they control.[48]

Gods' extensions are also produced within the same temple to respond to the intimate interactions between a god and its worshippers. In other words, temples' main gods cannot leave the temple space, for the entire equilibrium between gods, territory, and worshippers would otherwise be broken. They can, however, still intervene within worshippers' private houses or patrol the streets of their settlements on special occasions through their copies or extensions. The latter can live with their worshippers for a certain period, established by the nature of the household's problem and on a rotating basis. As emphasized by Baity, gods' extensions may have design and individual traits that distinguish them from other extensions: "in certain cases where the individual statue is particularly popular, it may be named after some particular individual trait as in the case of the 'Falling Nose Tsu-shih' of Tanshui".[49] As I witnessed during my fieldwork in Taiwan, the rotational distribution of gods' extensions can follow the historical evolution of the temple. Initially, the god's statue may have protected and controlled a few households; these families hosted the god in their domestic shrine on a rotating basis each year. Once the god earned a reputation for its miracles, the households would erect a temple, thereby creating god's extensions that could serve each household's possible emergencies.

Temples' gods, though, are not worshipped singularly. They are part of an assemblage of various gods, worshipped equally and in a dynamic relationship with one another. As I noted in my fieldwork: "The main god suggests to temple managers which gods must be put in its temple and how they must be displayed".[50] As already noted, the disposition of different gods within the same shrine follows the hierarchy between gods (the higher the god, the fewer material traces are visible, and the higher the god, the less it intervenes in issues), regarding both the specific function of the temple and its network of affiliations with others. Gods' disposition in shrines is also arranged in a sensical manner to ensure that gods are worshipped respectfully and, as such, do not leave their statues to worship elsewhere. For instance, during a visit to a temple in Xinzhuang, a member of the temple committee explained that the deity Mazu, which must be higher than the deity Guanyin, was located on the right and Guanyin to the front because of the latter's height, which would have obstructed the other deities' faces if placed elsewhere and, consequently, their proper ritual.

It is clear how gods' dispositions and interactions with each other in temple spaces may differ considerably and depend on worshippers' personal interpretations of gods' power. When I showed some pictures of shrines in Xinzhuang temples to a woodcarver, for instance, he noticed some dispositions that were not in accord with his knowledge of standard temple practice. For example, in a picture of a shrine dedicated to the god Baoyi, its extension – a table – appeared on the right-hand side instead of in the middle. Guanggong, which has a higher rank, was placed to the left, a location that is usually reserved for gods of lower rank: "Mazu is higher in rank than Baoyi, but since the main deity is Baoyi (and the tablet could be its extension), Mazu cannot be put in place of the main deity, because she is a guest and cannot occupy the place of the main deity".[51]

To conclude this brief discussion on Chinese folk material religion in Taiwan, the aesthetics and design of gods' statues are intimately shaped by the cultic interaction worshippers established with gods. Whilst gods agree or disagree on how they are sculpted and arranged within a shrine, worshippers materially forge gods' appearances based on their imagination and the detailed history that the god has in a territory. Consequently, Chinese statuary's aesthetics may vary markedly and must be understood within a corpothetic logic.

Explanatory statuary: de Groot's Chinese pantheon and its relationship with de Groot's scholarship

Although de Groot judged Chinese folk religion as "idolatrous" worship, he grasped the dynamics that justifies the need to carve wooden statues in the shapes of gods, as seen in Lin's reflection.[52] According to de Groot, the statues "keep alive the conviction that these are present by continuously arousing the thought of the dead. Such intense association is, in fact, the very backbone of China's inveterate idolatry and fetish-worship and, accordingly, a phenomenon of paramount importance in her Religious System".[53]

Given the importance of Chinese gods' statues in regulating the "Chinese system" – namely, the intertwining of Chinese moral and social structure – de Groot undertook visual training to study Chinese religion. For instance, during his second expedition to China, de Groot trained himself in photography, taking pictures of what he witnessed in the field.[54] Visual and material documentation were accompanied by detailed classification and identification of each god or ethnographic specimen, usually at the end of de Groot's fieldwork. When he shipped material to his clients (Guimet, as well as Brill), de Groot gave each statue a label with the name of the god at its base (Figures 6.1 and 6.2) and corroborated this nomenclature with typological descriptions contained in the catalogues that accompanied the shipment.[55]

De Groot's visual training in Chinese gods' statuary and ritual practices is more meaningful if we consider that he did not acquire Chinese statuaries from temples or Chinese private collectors or art dealers,[56] but instead commissioned deconsecrated gods' statues from Xiamen artisans. As Moore argues, elaborating on Werblowsky, commissioning Chinese statuary was part of "standard ethnological practice in the field" adopted by other collectors for European museums.[57] On the one hand, as argued by Moore,[58] when collaborating with European museums, Chinese artisans disenfranchised

The Dynamics of Modern Asian Design

Figure 6.1 De Groot's water official (水官), one of the three emperor-officials subordinated to the Jade Emperor, who control each person's fate in the afterlife. Collection National Museum van Wereldculturen.

Figure 6.2 De Groot's annotation on the base of the god of water. Collection National Museum van Wereldculturen.

themselves from ritual expectations and were thus able to express their artistic authorship more freely. De Groot's statuary, then, conveys artisans' aesthetic drives as detached from ritual corpothetics, efficacy, and functionality. On the other hand, commissioning gods' statues reflected the needs and requirements of the commissioner, in this case those of de Groot, which were in line with his broader scholarly endeavour.

We can argue that de Groot's commissioned statues conveyed a synthesis of his visual training, memories, and sensorial observations, and his preconceptions, objectives, and needs, rather than being an exact replica of temple statuary. Given the paucity of information on de Groot's phenomenological interaction with Xiamen temples, we cannot infer for definite how his preconceptions and ethnographic sensorium impacted the shape of his pantheon and the level of his understanding of Chinese lived religion. Certainly, his belief in the objectivity of fieldwork and its capacity to reflect with precision Chinese lived religion must be deconstructed.[59] As seen above, de Groot considered Chinese religion as idolatrous, thus reflecting his Christian background. Considering de Groot's bias is advantageous for understanding why he overlooked regional variants: he saw uniformity between social and religious traits in China to the extent that any locality would represent a part of the whole and "local deviations [would] not seriously diminish the value of a picture drawn from such a type".[60] His bias and disregard of regional variants, which contrasts with the rich local variants of gods' iconography observed in Taiwan, are significant in shaping the aesthetics and functionality of his pantheon, serving his intellectual endeavours rather than immersing museum visitors in lived Chinese religion.

The impression that de Groot's pantheon responded to an intellectual and logical representation of Chinese religion, in which everything was structurally dependent on other Chinese social and cultural features – a part of a whole – is offered by both de Groot's guide to his pantheon and his scholarly writing. Brill's catalogue shows that de Groot wanted to share a complete description of Chinese material religion: from the linguistic terms used to indicate specific components of the shrines, to the meaning of particular designs according to religious practice and ritual gestures, such as making a hole in the glass protecting the deities' altars for facilitating the passage of gods' spirits.[61]

If we look at de Groot's scholarly production, we find that each publication on Chinese gods' mythology and ritual worship was accompanied by photos of religious statuaries as exemplars and mapping of Chinese folk gods. It is not coincidental that de Groot assembled his pantheon while writing his first monograph, *Les Fêtes* (1886). De Groot explicitly mentions his monograph in Brill's catalogue, as if he wanted to establish a meaningful connection between his collections and writings.[62] The material specimen had indeed a dual function: to make theoretical arguments compelling, whilst presenting the "Chinese system" in an encyclopaedic fashion, dissecting the whole system whilst showing the connection between the parts and the whole, thus orientating the publication's structure.

For instance, in *Les Fêtes*, each annual festival coincides with the worship of a certain god occupying a certain rank within the pantheon, which the function of the festival itself can explain. Chinese New Year would mark the beginning of a new cycle and, as such, implied the worship of the highest gods in the hierarchy, before descending the pantheon's scale to reach gods of lower status, such as hearth and stove gods. The Chinese year, in de Groot's work, is thus subdivided into: *Le printemps* (spring), involving Chinese New Year ceremonies, celebration of the god sky (*dieu du ciel*), the birth and fecundity of heart, as well of the gods of letters and Mazu; *L'été* (summer), involving the baptism of Buddha, the Dragon Festival, and the god of war; *L'automne* (autumn), which was coincident with the celebration of the dead and the god of the stove; and *L'hiver* (winter), still with the cult of the stove god and those of the municipal gods.

In examining gods' hierarchy and functions in correspondence with each festival, de Groot wanted to prove that Chinese folk religion was a "system" comprising a variety of "religious stages", as formulated by other scholars of his time, such as Frazer and Weber. Animism – considered the most primitive form of religion – and bureaucratic religion – the most "civilized" and "rational" – cohabit in Chinese folk religion, with gods embodying natural forces as well as Buddhist, Confucian, and city gods interacting in the same ritual system. Although scholarship on de Groot has emphasized how he distinguished himself from other Sinologists in understanding Chinese rituals from an emic perspective and not hindered by prejudice,[63] his "system" clearly reflects his positionality within the academic debate of the nineteenth and twentieth centuries.

The encyclopaedic flavour of de Groot's pantheon reflects other Dutch collections of Orientalia during colonial times. Based on a pragmatic need to understand, from an empirical point of view, Chinese culture and linguistics to better serve the Dutch colonial administration's goals,[64] Chinese religious artefacts, along with other material artefacts, were collected in the Netherlands to facilitate Chinese culture and language learning. A clear example of Dutch collectors is provided by Jean Theodore Royer (1737–1807), who acquired disparate Chinese artefacts (from fine arts to utensils) to investigate, from a material angle, the origin and development of Chinese characters.[65] Unlike de Groot, Royer never visited China but tried to gain a sense of the context of the artefacts through the help of VOC officers, as well as Chinese assistants. Artefacts helped him not only understand characters' etymology and Chinese mythology – observing how a certain iconography was recurrent in disparate material items and how it might explain some Chinese cultural traits and their historical development – but also advanced his knowledge of Chinese vocabulary. Chinese assistants who visited Royer's collection helped him record the exact name of each item in Chinese characters and in transliteration, as well as decipher the characters that some items had on their surfaces, leaving written annotations alongside the artefacts displayed.[66] Naming each collection's item and ordering artefacts within an intelligible archive was functional to the ordering needs of Dutch colonizers.[67] De Groot followed Dutch collecting methods by naming each collection's item with Chinese characters and their Latin transcription.

Based on this contextualization of de Groot's writing and Dutch colonial collections, we can infer that his Chinese pantheon reflected his analytical understanding of Chinese religion, thus intertwining a formal, sculptural canon inflated by carvers' mastery with de Groot's mental ordering of an alleged "Chinese cosmos". Each Chinese god commissioned summons common characteristics that de Groot observed in diverse statues of the same god in various temples and are functional to each god's role in maintaining a cosmic and social equilibrium. The standardization of de Groot's experience is further strengthened by the synthetic nomenclature for each god contained in Brill's catalogue, where just gods' names and general functions are listed, rather than any concrete, historical examples of gods' interventions among Xiamen's communities.

What de Groot built was an explanatory pantheon that might be applied to an ideal-typical Chinese religion, thus following the holistic, positivist, and pragmatic goals of Dutch Sinology and colonial administration. Each god was commissioned in sequence, following the pantheon's hierarchy and with no consideration of how they were ritualistically and heterogeneously combined in Chinese altars for reflecting worshippers' interactions with gods, from the local, community level to the family, private one. It is not the case that de Groot's writing described and explained god-human relationships within the yearly cycle of festivities for regulating ghosts' menace and harvest; it did not mention gods' domestic visits to single households regarding family affairs either.

De Groot's statues were not simply carved for corpothetic reasons. Although de Groot was scrupulous in dissecting Chinese religion in all its particulars, collecting and describing the usual assemblage for a domestic altar – from the incense burner to the lateral lights – what can be sensed in Brill's catalogue is the lack of an evoking atmosphere. We do not read a ritual, ethnographic account summoned by his experience in Xiamen temples; instead, we have a logical description of each collected item and how it is inserted within the broader "puzzle" of the altar. De Groot probably did not intend to immerse the audience and beholders in an imaginary ritual setting but instead take them on an intellectual journey. De Groot's statues served as *intellectual models*, things good to think with, probably addressed to museumgoers that coincided with de Groot's readers rather than a wider audience. It is not coincidental that the contemporary museum display has a video shot by Paul van Dongen in the 1990s among Xiamen temples, as curatorial practice infuses evocative experiences and life into something that was not intended for a contemporary immersive museum experience.

Conclusions

Revisiting colonial collections through the lens of corpothetics and transculturality signals a loss of sensorium during the organizing of these collections. It is obvious that de Groot, whilst on fieldwork, experienced Chinese material religion: his *Notizen* alluded to his experiential journey. Despite his bias, the Dutch Sinologist understood the significance of wooden statues' mediation in Chinese religion. However, the experiential and phenomenological development that led him from fieldwork to his painstaking reconstruction of gods' hierarchy and his detached, analytic pantheon cannot be recollected, since everything de Groot experienced, and wrote in his notebooks, was destroyed or intellectualized.

The complex interactions between worshippers and gods de Groot observed in fieldwork were fractionated into semantic units or classifications, rather than portrayed as such. De Groot did not commission the exact copy of a god's local variant attached to the history of a specific Xiamen temple but an ideal-typical iconography that could embrace the *whole* Chinese religion as the fruit of a homogeneous doctrine, practice, and history. In other words, he reduced the complexity of what he certainly experienced in the field to a specimen, a token. Consequently, de Groot's Chinese folk religious pantheon resulted from the encounter between de Groot's reduction and Xiamen artisans' aesthetic mastery. This research thus expands Ahmed's notion of "sticking to" by showing how museum artefacts also absorb the filtering of emotions in a transcultural context, leaving an experiential gap that Hicks would define as "necropolitics".[68]

Research on colonial collections opens the space to reflect upon how European, ethnocentric, and scientific scholarship has shaped a homogeneous aesthetic of non-European material culture, forcing it into restricted categories and reducing its multivocality and complexity. De Groot and other early Sinologists' museography resounds with an "aesthetic of fragmentation",[69] where the destruction, decontextualization, fragmentation, and deformation of religious icons in colonized countries was reframed as aesthetically or intellectually appealing to Europeans – a contemporary example of this is reproducing and collecting Buddha heads as if Buddha icons were bodiless. Studying European collections and their representation of the "colonized" from a transcultural perspective – thus deconstructing the process of aestheticization of material culture that removes it from its local sensorium – remains an ethical question for researchers.

Acknowledgements

This research was made possible by the Junior Fellowship of the Research Centre for Material Culture. I thank the contemporary and former China Curators, Willemijn van Noord and Paul van Dongen, for their guidance. Thanks also go to Sandy Ng, who patiently waited for this chapter to form amidst my precarious post-doctoral life, and Megha Rajguru, for her painstaking revisions and comments.

Notes

1. A. Grasskamp and M. Juneja (eds.), *Eurasian Matters: China, Europe and the Transcultural Object 1600–1800* (Springer, 2018); A. Grasskamp, "The Matter of Cultural Exchange: China, Europe, and Early Modern Material Connections", in L.A. De Cunzo and C. Dann Roeber (eds.), *The Cambridge Handbook of Material Culture Studies* (Cambridge University Press, 2022), 269–302.
2. Although ethnographic material comes from Taiwan, the statuary and rituals performed on the island are similar to what de Groot witnessed in mainland China and, thus, can be used for the sake of the chapter's main argumentation. The latter does not focus on a regional variety but on Chinese folk religion, which is present in each Asian country with a Han ethnic community.

3. A.K. Grieser and J. Johnston (eds.), *Aesthetics of Religion: A Connective Concept* (De Gruyter, 2017); E. Baffelli and J. Caple, "Religious Authority in East Asia: Materiality, Media, and Aesthetics", *Asian Ethnology* 78, no. 2 (2019): 3–23; E. Baffelli, J. Caple, L. McLaughlin and Frederik Schröer, "The Aesthetics and Emotions of Religious Belonging: Examples from the Buddhist World", *Numen* 68 (2021): 421–35.
4. K. Knibbe and H. Kupari, "Theorizing Lived Religion: An Introduction", *Journal of Contemporary Religion* 35, no. 2 (2020): 157–76.
5. B. Meyer (ed.), *Aesthetic Formations: Media, Religion and the Senses* (Palgrave, 2009); D. Morgan, "Art, Material Culture, and Lived Religion", in F.B. Brown (ed.), *The Oxford Handbook of Religion and the Arts* (Oxford University Press, 2014), 480–97.
6. C. Isnart and N. Cerezales (eds.), *The Religious Heritage Complex: Legacy, Conservation and Christianity* (Bloomsbury Publishing, 2020).
7. W.-P. Lin, "Conceptualizing Gods through Statues: A Study of Personification and Localization in Taiwan", *Comparative Studies in Society and History* 50, no. 2 (2008): 461 and Lin, *Materializing Magic Power: Chinese Popular Religion in Villages and Cities* (Harvard University Press, 2015), 32.
8. Grieser and Johnston, *Aesthetics of Religion*, 16.
9. C. Pinney, *"Photos of the Gods": The Printed Image and Political Struggle in India* (Reaktion Books, 2004).
10. Pinney, *"Photos of the Gods"*, 194.
11. S. Ahmed, *The Cultural Politics of Emotion*, 2nd edition (Edinburgh University Press, 2014).
12. By this term, I mean any material used during consecration rituals believed to enliven gods' statues and make them gods' embodiments.
13. B. Meyer, "Legba-figures and dzokawo: Unpacking a Missionary Collection from the Übersee-Museum Bremen", *Boasblog*, 7 September 2021; R. Corbey and F.K. Weener, "Collecting while Converting: Missionaries and Ethnographics", *Journal of Art Historiography* 12 (2015): 1–14.
14. In certain respects, Paul Katz anticipated this idea of integrating art methodologies with religious studies and ethnographic fieldwork. Katz, *Images of the Immortal: The Cult of Lü Dongbin and the Palace of Eternal Joy* (University of Hawaii Press, 1999).
15. R.J.Z. Werblowsky, *The Beaten Track of Science: The Life and Work of Jan Jakob Maria de Groot* (Harrassowitz, 2002), 34.
16. M. Freedman, "Sinology and the Social Sciences: Some Reflections on the Social Anthropology of China", *Ethnos: Journal of Anthropology* 40, nos. 1–4 (1975): 194–211.
17. Werblowsky, *The Beaten Track of Science*, 34; see also Werblowsky, "The Western Perception of China 1700–1900: From Leibniz to de Groot", Archives of the Wereldmuseum, Leiden, n.d.
18. M. von Oswald, *Working through Colonial Collections: An Ethnography of the Ethnological Museum in Berlin* (Leuven University Press, 2022).
19. *Catalouge de différentes Collections Ethnographiques provenant de la Chine et appartenant à la Maison E.J. Brill à Leide*, Archives of the Wereldmuseum, Leiden, 5.
20. M. von Oswald and J. Tinius (eds.), *Across Anthropology. Troubling Colonial Legacies, Museums, and the Curatorial* (Leuven University Press, 2020).
21. In particular, Lin, "Conceptualizing Gods through Statues" and Lin, *Materializing Magic Power*.

22. K. Kuiper, *The Early Dutch Sinologists (1854–1900): Training in Holland and China, Functions in the Netherlands Indies*, Brill, 2017), 1001–2.
23. See Werblowsky, *The Beaten Track of Science*, 38, note 1.
24. W.L. Idema, "Chinese Studies in the Netherlands", in W.L. Idema (ed.), *Chinese Studies in the Netherlands: Past, Present and Future* (Brill, 2014), 3.
25. Cf. Kuiper, *The Early Dutch Sinologists*, 1004 and Idema, "Chinese Studies in the Netherlands", 15.
26. Werblowsky, *The Beaten Track of Science*, 72–74.
27. See Guimet quoted in Werblowsky, *The Beaten Track of Science*, 74.
28. An example of a ritual reconstruction in a museum gallery is the Buddhist Temple in Penn Museum, established by Maxwell Sommerville (1829–1904) in 1899. The temple was an assemblage of material from various temples and monasteries in Japan. Sommerville thought the temple could serve as a pan-Buddhist temple for Philadelphia's Chinese community, and he wore a Buddhist ritual garment while chanting sutras during museum opening hours. See V. Gamberi, *Experiencing Materiality: Museum Perspectives* (Berghahn Books, 2021), 80–88.
29. I. Clark, "Exhibiting the Exotic, Simulating the Sacred: Tibetan Shrines at British and American Museums", *Ateliers d'Anthropologie* 43 (2016).
30. J. Fabian, *Time and the Other: How Anthropology Makes Its Object* (Columbia University Press, [1983] 2014).
31. Werblowsky, *The Beaten Track of Science*, 57.
32. Werblowsky, *The Beaten Track of Science*, 58.
33. See Werblowsky, *The Beaten Track of Science*, 63–66.
34. D.K. Jordan, *Gods, Ghosts and Ancestors: Folk Religion in a Taiwanese Village* (Caves Books, 1972); P.C. Baity, *Religion in a Chinese Town* (The Orient Cultural Service, 1975) and Baity, "The Ranking of Gods in Chinese Folk Religion", *Asian Folklore Studies* 35 (1977): 75–84; H. Chang, "Incense-Offering and Obtaining the Magical Power of Qi: The Mazu (Heavenly Mother) Pilgrimage in Taiwan", PhD dissertation (University of California, Berkeley, 1993); S. Sangren, *History and Magical Power in a Chinese Community* (Stanford University Press, 1987) and Sangren, *Chinese Sociologics: An Anthropological Account of the Role of Alienation in Social Production* (Athlone Press, 2000); Lin, "Conceptualizing Gods through Statues" and Lin, *Materializing Magic Power*.
35. Cf. Sangren, *History and Magical Power*, Chang, "Incense-Offering and Obtaining the Magical Power of Qi", and Lin, *Materializing Magic Power*.
36. Baity, "The Ranking of Gods in Chinese Folk Religion", 75.
37. Lin, "Conceptualizing Gods through Statues", 459.
38. Informal conversation, 21 April 2020; cf. Lin, *Materializing Magic Power*.
39. Lin, "Conceptualizing Gods through Statues", 462.
40. Cf. Lin, "Conceptualizing Gods through Statues", 459; Sangren, *History and Magical Power* and Sangren, *Chinese Sociologics*.
41. Lin, "Conceptualizing Gods through Statues", 472.
42. Lin, "Conceptualizing Gods through Statues", 464.
43. Cf. Lin, "Conceptualizing Gods through Statues", 464.
44. Lin, "Conceptualizing Gods through Statues", 465.

45. Lin, "Conceptualizing Gods through Statues", 464.
46. Lin, "Conceptualizing Gods through Statues", 465, 466–68.
47. S. Habkirk and H. Chang, "Scents, Community, and Incense in Traditional Chinese Religion", *Material Religion* 13, no. 2 (2017): 156–74.
48. Cf. Baity, "The Ranking of Gods in Chinese Folk Religion".
49. Baity, "The Ranking of Gods in Chinese Folk Religion", 82.
50. Informal conversation, 21 April 2020.
51. Informal conversation, 29 May 2020.
52. Lin, "Conceptualizing Gods through Statues" and Lin, *Materializing Magic Power*.
53. J.J.M. De Groot, *The Religious System of China. Its Ancient Forms, Evolution, History and Present Aspect, Manners, Customs and Social Institutions Connected Therewith, vol. IV, book II: On the Soul and Ancestral Worship. Part I, The Soul in Philosophy and Folk-Conception* (Brill, 1901), 340.
54. O. Moore, "China's Art and Material Culture", in W.L. Idema (ed.), *Chinese Studies in the Netherlands: Past, Present and Future*, Brill, 2014, 226.
55. Werblowsky, *The Beaten Track of Science*, 67.
56. Other European collections of Chinese folk religious statuary, such as that of Patrice Fava, were realized through the acquisition of consecrated statues that had been subsequently purchased for the art market. See P. Fava, *Aux portes du ciel. La statuaire taoïste du Hunan. Art et anthropologie de la Chine* (Les Belles Lettres École Française d'Extréme-Orient, 2013) and A. Arrault, *A History of Cultic Images in China: The Domestic Statuary of Hunan* (Chinese University of Hong Kong Press, 2020).
57. Moore, "China's Art and Material Culture", 225; Werblowsky, *The Beaten Track of Science*, 68.
58. Moore, "China's Art and Material Culture", 226.
59. See, for instance, J.J.M. De Groot, *Les Fêtes annuellement célébrées à Émoui (Amoy). Étude concernant la religion populaire des Chinois*, Ernest Leroux, 1886, IX.
60. J.J.M. De Groot, J.J.M. *The Religious System of China: Its Ancient Forms, Evolution, History and Present Aspect, Manners, Customs and Social Institutions Connected Therewith, vol. I, book I: On the Disposal of the Dead. Part I, Funeral Rites, Part II, the Idea of Resurrection*, Brill, 1892, IX.
61. *Catalouge de différentes Collections Ethnographiques provenant de la Chine et appartenant à la Maison E.J. Brill à Leide*, Archives of the Wereldmuseum, Leiden, 5.
62. *Catalouge de différentes Collections*, 14–15.
63. Werblowsky, "The Western Perception of China 1700–1900".
64. Idema, "Chinese Studies in the Netherlands", 5, 10.
65. See Moore, "China's Art and Material Culture", 216; J. van Campen, *Collecting China: Jean Theodore Royer (1737–1807) Collections and Chinese Studies* (Verloren, 2021), 99.
66. van Campen, *Collecting China: Jean Theodore Royer*, 91–94.
67. For a nexus between archives and power, see J. Derrida, *Archive Fever: A Freudian Impression* (Cambridge University Press, 1996).
68. D. Hicks, *The Brutish Museums: The Benin Bronzes, Colonial Violence and Cultural Restitution* (Pluto Press, 2021).
69. A. Grasskamp and A. Loeseke, "Asia in Your Window Frame: Museum Displays, Window Curators and Dutch-Asian Material Culture", *World Art* 5, no. 2 (2015), 230.

References

Ahmed, S. *The Cultural Politics of Emotion*, 2nd edition, Edinburgh University Press, 2014.
Arrault, A. *A History of Cultic Images in China: The Domestic Statuary of Hunan*, Chinese University of Hong Kong Press, 2020.
Baffelli, E. and J. Caple. "Religious Authority in East Asia: Materiality, Media, and Aesthetics", *Asian Ethnology* 78, no. 2 (2019): 3–23.
Baffelli, E., J. Caple, L. McLaughlin and Frederik Schröer. "The Aesthetics and Emotions of Religious Belonging: Examples from the Buddhist World", *Numen* 68 (2021): 421–35.
Baity, P.C. *Religion in a Chinese Town*, The Orient Cultural Service, 1975.
Baity, P.C. "The Ranking of Gods in Chinese Folk Religion", *Asian Folklore Studies* 35 (1977): 75–84.
Chang, H. "Incense-Offering and Obtaining the Magical Power of Qi: The Mazu (Heavenly Mother) Pilgrimage in Taiwan", PhD dissertation, University of California, Berkeley, 1993.
Clark, I. "Exhibiting the Exotic, Simulating the Sacred: Tibetan Shrines at British and American Museums", *Ateliers d'Anthropologie* 43 (2016): https://doi.org/10.4000/ateliers.10300.
Corbey, R. and F.K. Weener. "Collecting while Converting: Missionaries and Ethnographics", *Journal of Art Historiography* 12 (2015): 1–14.
De Groot, J.J.M. *Les Fêtes annuellement célébrées à Émoui (Amoy). Étude concernant la religion populaire des Chinois*, Ernest Leroux, 1886.
De Groot, J.J.M. *The Religious System of China: Its Ancient Forms, Evolution, History and Present Aspect, Manners, Customs and Social Institutions Connected Therewith, vol. I, book I: On the Disposal of the Dead. Part I, Funeral Rites, Part II, the Idea of Resurrection*, Brill, 1892.
De Groot, J.J.M. *The Religious System of China. Its Ancient Forms, Evolution, History and Present Aspect, Manners, Customs and Social Institutions Connected Therewith, vol. IV, book II: On the Soul and Ancestral Worship. Part I, The Soul in Philosophy and Folk-Conception*, Brill, 1901.
Derrida, J. *Archive Fever: A Freudian Impression*, Cambridge University Press, 1996.
Fabian, J. *Time and the Other: How Anthropology Makes Its Object*, Columbia University Press, [1983] 2014.
Fava, P. *Aux portes du ciel. La statuaire taoïste du Hunan. Art et anthropologie de la Chine*, Les Belles Lettres École Française d'Extréme-Orient, 2013.
Freedman, M. "Sinology and the Social Sciences: Some Reflections on the Social Anthropology of China", *Ethnos: Journal of Anthropology* 40, nos. 1–4 (1975): 194–211.
Gamberi, V. *Experiencing Materiality: Museum Perspectives*, Berghahn Books, 2021.
Grasskamp, A. "The Matter of Cultural Exchange: China, Europe, and Early Modern Material Connections", in L.A. De Cunzo and C. Dann Roeber (eds.), *The Cambridge Handbook of Material Culture Studies*, Cambridge University Press, 2022, 269–302.
Grasskamp, A. and M. Juneja (eds.). *Eurasian Matters: China, Europe and the Transcultural Object 1600–1800*, Springer, 2018.
Grasskamp, A. and A. Loeseke. "Asia in Your Window Frame: Museum Displays, Window Curators and Dutch-Asian Material Culture", *World Art* 5, no. 2 (2015): 223–48.
Grieser, A.K. and J. Johnston (eds.). *Aesthetics of Religion: A Connective Concept*, De Gruyter, 2017.
Habkirk, S. and H. Chang. "Scents, Community, and Incense in Traditional Chinese Religion", *Material Religion* 13, no. 2 (2017): 156–74.
Hicks, D. *The Brutish Museums: The Benin Bronzes, Colonial Violence and Cultural Restitution*, Pluto Press, 2021.
Idema, W.L. "Chinese Studies in the Netherlands", in W.L. Idema (ed.), *Chinese Studies in the Netherlands: Past, Present and Future*, Brill, 2014, 1–25.
Isnart, C. and N. Cerezales (eds.). *The Religious Heritage Complex: Legacy, Conservation and Christianity*, Bloomsbury Publishing, 2020.

Jordan, D.K. *Gods, Ghosts and Ancestors: Folk Religion in a Taiwanese Village*, Caves Books, 1972.

Katz, P. *Images of the Immortal: The Cult of Lü Dongbin and the Palace of Eternal Joy*, University of Hawaii Press, 1999.

Knibbe, K. and H. Kupari. "Theorizing Lived Religion: An Introduction", *Journal of Contemporary Religion* 35, no. 2 (2020): 157–76.

Kuiper, K. *The Early Dutch Sinologists (1854–1900): Training in Holland and China, Functions in the Netherlands Indies*, Brill, 2017.

Lin, W.-P. "Conceptualizing Gods through Statues: A Study of Personification and Localization in Taiwan", *Comparative Studies in Society and History* 50, no. 2 (2008): 454–77.

Lin, W.-P. *Materializing Magic Power: Chinese Popular Religion in Villages and Cities*, Harvard University Press, 2015.

Meyer, B. (ed.). *Aesthetic Formations: Media, Religion and the Senses*, Palgrave, 2009.

Meyer, B. "Legba-figures and dzokawo: Unpacking a Missionary Collection from the Übersee-Museum Bremen", *Boasblog*, 7 September 2021. https://boasblogs.org/dcntr/legba-figures-and-dzokawo/ (accessed 1 February 2023).

Moore, O. "China's Art and Material Culture", in W.L. Idema (ed.), *Chinese Studies in the Netherlands: Past, Present and Future*, Brill, 2014, 211–50.

Morgan, D. "Art, Material Culture, and Lived Religion", in F.B. Brown (ed.), *The Oxford Handbook of Religion and the Arts*, Oxford University Press, 2014, 480–97.

Pinney, C. *"Photos of the Gods": The Printed Image and Political Struggle in India*, Reaktion Books, 2004.

Sangren, S. *History and Magical Power in a Chinese Community*, Stanford University Press, 1987.

Sangren, S. *Chinese Sociologics: An Anthropological Account of the Role of Alienation in Social Production*, Athlone Press, 2000.

Van Campen, J. *Collecting China: Jean Theodore Royer (1737–1807) Collections and Chinese Studies*, Verloren, 2021.

von Oswald, M. *Working through Colonial Collections: An Ethnography of the Ethnological Museum in Berlin*, Leuven University Press, 2022.

von Oswald, M. and J. Tinius (eds.). *Across Anthropology. Troubling Colonial Legacies, Museums, and the Curatorial*, Leuven University Press, 2020.

Werblowsky, R.J.Z. *The Beaten Track of Science: The Life and Work of Jan Jakob Maria de Groot*, Harrassowitz, 2002.

Archival material

Werblowsky, R.J. Z. "The Western Perception of China 1700–1900: From Leibniz to de Groot", Archives of the Wereldmuseum, Leiden.

Catalouge de différentes Collections Ethnographiques provenant de la Chine et appartenant à la Maison E.J. Brill à Leide, Archives of the Wereldmuseum, Leiden, 1890s.

PART III
THE BIOGRAPHY OF DESIGN

CHAPTER 7
THE AESTHETICS OF CONCRETE WATCHTOWERS: THE HYBRID AND CONTEXTUAL ARCHITECTURE OF KAIPING

Kwok-wah Tung

Introduction

Concrete watchtowers (*diaolou*) flourished in Kaiping city, Guangdong province and helped characterize the built and natural environments there. Their widespread construction in the early twentieth century was primarily a result of the region's emigrant workers, who brought the reinforced concrete construction method and foreign architectural styles that they had encountered abroad to their hometowns. Clusters of Kaiping concrete watchtowers were designated as World Heritage sites by the United Nations Educational, Scientific, and Cultural Organization (UNESCO) in 2007 due to their outstanding architectural and cultural value. While aesthetics plays an essential role in this designation, the aesthetic significance of their hybrid composition, and the relationship between their composition and the local natural context, have not been fully explored either in the UNESCO documents or in major architectural studies of concrete watchtowers. This chapter, therefore, aims to fill this gap by analysing the aesthetics of Kaiping concrete watchtowers, followed by a phenomenological study that focuses on their local context. I argue that instead of being simply for its own sake (as disinterested fine art) or too superfluous to be stripped away (as in the modernist treatment), the ornamental aspect of these watchtowers contributes to the naturalization of concrete, by virtue of which the very functional watchtowers become simultaneously a manifestation of locals' cultural views on nature. Finally, I highlight the fact that Kaiping concrete watchtowers belong to a kind of contextual architecture that is characterized by a harmonious relationship with nature and the cultivation of a tranquil lifestyle.

Culture of Kaiping

Kaiping shares the key characteristics of Lingnan culture. The geographical features of the Lingnan region played a decisive role in its cultural development. On the one hand, the Five Ranges to the north defined the region geographically and contributed to a sense of identity constituting a blend of vernacular culture and Han culture from the central plains of China. On the other hand, the South China Sea to the south had resulted in its participation in global trade since the Qin dynasty, through which it encountered external cultures that helped form its wider worldview.[1] These two seemingly opposing features led the region to establish a conservative yet open attitude towards the outside world. This has resulted in the cultural process of glocalization,[2] which, as Roland Robertson explains it, involves "a complex interaction of global and local elements characterized by cultural borrowing".[3] The cultural development of the region, including Kaiping, accordingly underwent a process of hybridization in which the absorption of external cultures was both conscious and selective, while retaining local cultural characteristics. The architecture of Kaiping watchtowers, as one of the key cultural products of the region, was largely shaped by the critical adoption of imported modern concrete construction and foreign stylistic expression.

The function and structure of concrete watchtowers

As a result of complex social and economic circumstances, the crime rate in Guangdong province rose significantly from the beginning of the eighteenth century. Kidnappings and the theft of property and crops were widespread in the core regions near the Pearl River Delta.[4] According to data from the *Three Palace Memorials*, Guangzhou prefecture (which was considered a major part of the Pearl River Delta) had the highest number of prosecuted cases; for example, the prefecture is recorded as successfully prosecuting more than half of the total 3,032 cases of banditry in the country between 1837 and 1839.[5] The region's crime rate continued to rise from the late eighteenth through the early twentieth century. From 1921 to 1930, at least 71 serious cases of banditry took place in Kaiping, as a result of which more than 100 people were killed, 210 working animals were stolen, and numerous properties were robbed.[6]

According to Robert J. Antony, since bandits were widespread throughout the mountainous area of Kaiping during the Ming and Qing dynasties, two- and three-storey stone or brick vernacular watchtowers were constructed as a safeguarding measure.[7] At the turn of the twentieth century, (reinforced) concrete watchtowers began to be built by locals to help protect villages and their agricultural produce from roving gangs comprising a few to several hundred individuals.[8] The concrete watchtowers are similar to the organically formed vernacular buildings in rural areas in terms of their response to locals' basic needs in that they connect functionally with the local communities and "the landscape they occupy and help form".[9] In other words, the concrete watchtowers, like vernacular buildings, form a "functional fit" with their environment, resulting in a functional unity that is analogous to interlocking ecosystems in nature.[10] From this perspective, an appreciation of the concrete watchtowers depends largely on their functional contribution to the establishment and survival of the villages.[11] This sheds light on the region's traditional saying that "no village can be formed without a watchtower".

The vernacular watchtowers in Kaiping (the predecessor to concrete watchtowers) adopted a system of load-bearing walls (constructed with bricks, rammed earth, or stones) under Chinese fir beams that support a tiled pitched roof.[12] The vernacular watchtower type is exemplified by Yinglong Tower at Sanmenli, Kaiping built in the

Figure 7.1 Yinglong Tower. Photo by the author.

sixteenth century (Figure 7.1).[13] To meet its defensive aims, the walls of this vernacular watchtower type were customarily made thick to an extent that was beyond their load-bearing function; in the case of Yinglong Tower, the walls are approximately 0.9 m thick.[14] Moreover, the openings were relatively small and guarded by iron lattices and panels in most cases.

Kaiping has 1,833 watchtowers, of which 1,474 are made of (reinforced) concrete.[15] In particular, due to their "Outstanding Universal Value",[16] three clusters of Kaiping concrete watchtowers (including their corresponding sites) were designated as the World Heritage sites by UNESCO in 2007.[17] The existing watchtowers can be categorized into three main types according to their use: 62% were private residential watchtowers built by rich families to protect themselves against banditry, typhoons, and floods; 26% were communal watchtowers for providing refuge to villagers during times of danger; and 12% were towers of relatively simple structure built at strategic locations around villages to act as lookouts and for raising alarms.[18] The construction of concrete watchtowers was at its peak in the region from 1910 into the 1930s.[19] The cost of construction was met primarily by contributions from clan members working abroad who, based on their allegiance to their hometowns, wished to improve the defence of their families against bandits.[20] The materials used to construct the concrete watchtowers in Kaiping, including cement, iron bars, steel plates and rebars, were mostly imported from Hong Kong,

Macau, and Europe before 1940. Cement produced in Guangzhou only became available in Kaiping after the peak period of the watchtowers' construction.[21]

Those well-formed concrete watchtowers of Kaiping represented the pinnacle of the development of local defensive structures since the Ming dynasty.[22] In line with the structural system of the region's vernacular watchtowers, Kaiping's concrete watchtowers often included load-bearing walls, but they were made of reinforced concrete instead of bricks, rammed earth, or stones. The construction of the foundations for the concrete watchtowers differed significantly from present-day practices primarily due to a lack of machinery. One common practice was described in detail by the elderly local builder He Dean in an interview conducted by Zhang Guoxiong in June 2006.[23] The building of a concrete watchtower's foundations involved the hammering of long pine trunks into the earth as piles by workers. Concrete ground beams connecting the trunks were then cast to serve as the base upon which concrete walls, beams, and slabs of the upper floors were moulded (in some cases, timber beams were used instead).[24]

The concrete construction not only enhanced the watchtowers' defensive capabilities, but also enabled them to exceed the height of vernacular watchtowers, up to nine storeys at times.[25] With the exception of some inclined watchtowers caused by insufficient foundations, and wear and tear resulting from natural forces, most existing concrete watchtowers remain durable.[26] The use of reinforced concrete construction for the Kaiping watchtowers began in the late nineteenth century, which was contemporary with, if not earlier than, the Chinese reinforced concrete projects overseen by pioneering international architects like Henry K. Murphy.[27] All in all, the Kaiping watchtowers realized an unexpected advanced technical development and ground-breaking adoption of modern materials in this rural area of China.[28]

Analytic study of concrete watchtowers' aesthetics

Although most concrete watchtowers were designed and built by local builders, their patrons often had an input. For example, sketches or drawings were sometimes made by owners and their clan members to communicate design ideas,[29] leading to a design process that was in fact a collaborative endeavour. The drawings of concrete watchtowers had no standard format and their quality varied. Some were very brief single-line drawings so that the aesthetic modelling of the architectural parts largely depended on the on-site execution of experienced builders or craftsmen. Postcards portraying European and eclectic-style architecture sent by overseas clan members may not have been intended for design purposes, but they were often used as a design reference by local builders and patrons of watchtowers.[30] In addition, some local builders had been involved in the construction of colonial buildings since the nineteenth century (including the warehouses with neo-classical façades in the Thirteen Factories in Guangzhou and the European-style buildings in Shamian) and had acquired knowledge of their design. Local builders then adapted these architectural patterns, modifying them for later projects, which resulted in innovative styles of architecture in the region.

The Aesthetics of Concrete Watchtowers

Kaiping concrete watchtowers are composed of two principal parts: the main core and the upper part. The upper part can be further divided into the cantilevered portion and the roof (Figure 7.2). Most concrete watchtowers were more than four storeys high. Generally, the main core was more or less square (with sides of 4–10 m), and usually adopted the common "three-bay, two-chamber" layout of local residences, with the living area in the middle and a bedroom either side.[31] Following the fenestration of Kaiping vernacular watchtowers, the window openings of concrete watchtowers were predominantly relatively small and furnished with iron lattices and panels. Similarly, doors were usually reinforced by iron cages and panels. Moreover, the walls of concrete watchtowers were normally made relatively thick (approximately 0.3 m) to resist attacks from bandits, in addition to their load-bearing function. Cantilevered colonnades, corner platforms ("swallows nests"), and/or turrets (with "o"-, "T"-, or "⊥"-shaped holes to allow weapons to be fired) were often included in the cantilevered portions to further increase the defensive capacity of the concrete watchtowers.[32] It should be noted that a building type called a concrete villa (*lo*), which looks very similar to a concrete

Figure 7.2 The typical composition of a concrete watchtower, as exemplified by Ruishi Tower. Photo by the author.

watchtower, was also very common in the region. Concrete villas were primarily residential and defensive in nature, and were often built next to concrete residential watchtowers, as in Zili Village in Kaiping. These villas have sometimes been confused with watchtowers in terms of their overall form and material. Based on an on-site interview with Huang Yaoji (the great grandson of the owner of Ruishi Tower) conducted by the author in February 2019, the key differentiating feature is the cantilevered defensive structure (e.g. cantilevered colonnades, corner platforms, and turrets), which is a necessary component of concrete watchtowers, but is absent from concrete villas.

Except for some ornamentation at the main entrance, such as classical columns and pediments, the articulation of the exterior of a concrete watchtower's main core, like that of the region's vernacular watchtowers, was generally meagre (e.g. thin mouldings of window frames and pilasters), mainly as a result of the functional consideration that flat exteriors were more likely to deter bandits from climbing up to gain access to the upper parts.[33] As informed by this functional consideration, the artistic aspirations of the builders and patrons only found their full expression further up the watchtower, where delicately ornamented architectural parts were incorporated. This resulted in the distinctive combination of a relatively plain core and a highly ornamented upper part. Concrete watchtowers, therefore, illustrate well Roger Scruton's characterization that "architecture represents an almost indescribable synthesis of" functional and aesthetic considerations,[34] as well as Leon Battista Alberti's architectural principle that the notion of *utilitas* "acquires an influence over aesthetic criteria of *venustas*, but the latter are not absorbed in the former".[35]

The elaborate upper parts of concrete watchtowers usually adopted architectural elements from diverse styles, including ancient Greek, Roman, Byzantine, Gothic, Renaissance, Baroque, and Islamic traditions. This reference to diverse architectural styles contributed to the symbolic meaning of concrete watchtowers, in that they are the "index"[36] of the broad knowledge of the owners and clan members since their designs were usually associated with the owners' and clan members' exposure to overseas architecture, of which the local residents were proud.[37] Moreover, concrete watchtowers involved a significant fusion of foreign architectural styles and local practice, which, as the International Council on Monuments and Sites (ICOMOS) describes it, reflects "an important interchange of human values".[38] However, this fusion was far from straightforward. As previously indicated, the local process of cultural hybridization rejected a total acceptance of exterior elements. It meant that the adoption of foreign classical architectural elements in the watchtowers was mostly conscious and involved a stylistic departure driven by the locals' innovative input, through which local characteristics could be expressed.

According to Scruton, "architects have always been motivated by a search for rule, they have discovered rules only to depart from them".[39] As motivated by the innovative endeavours of architects and builders, departures from established architectural rules via transformations of styles have characterized the history of architecture.[40] This was especially prominent in Western traditions, as illustrated, for example, by the effective departure from "the succession of historical revivals" by Art Nouveau via its adoption of new materials, such as cast iron, and its aesthetically sound compositional transformation of previous classical styles.[41] This kind of departure and transformation was not at all common in what was relatively stable traditional Chinese architectural practice –[42] Kaiping concrete watchtowers were the first exception in the modern period.[43] The aforementioned local process of cultural hybridization did indeed reinforce Kaiping builders' and owners' desire for architectural flexibility in a way that would bypass some of the rigid standardized architectural rules of foreigners as recorded in classical pattern books, and hence establish their own innovative ways of making, modifying, and recombining various stylistic parts for their creative and hybrid watchtower architecture.[44] This highly individualistic approach led to tailored juxtapositions of stylistic parts for concrete watchtowers – or, as Zhang describes them, "a thousand Kaiping watchtowers actually have a thousand different appearances".[45]

Furthermore, due to the aesthetic senses of local builders, many of the tailored juxtapositions of stylistic parts became meticulous configurations characterized by a harmonious relationship among echoing and fitting stylistic parts. This allowed the stylistically hybrid concrete watchtowers to become pieces of aesthetically remarkable architecture, and hence serve as an attractive visual focus within each of their villages. This aesthetic accomplishment is best exemplified by the Ruishi Tower situated in Jinjiangli Village.

Case study of the Ruishi Tower

Jinjiangli Village was founded during the Guangxu regime of the Qing dynasty (1875–1908).[46] With the financial support of clan members working abroad, Jinjiang Tower, Shengfeng Tower, and Ruishi Tower (Figure 7.3) were constructed one after the other at the rear of the village to offer protection from natural disasters and attacks from bandits, who would often travel along the Jinjiang River to the village by boat. It would seem that these three watchtowers served their purpose because, after their completion, no banditry of the village was recorded.[47] The five-storey communal concrete Jinjiang Tower was constructed in 1918 to offer only basic protection to the villagers.[48] It is thus relatively plain, with a little ornamentation only that includes scrolled corbels (which articulate the cantilever portion), Lingnan and Western floral stucco reliefs, and orb-like finials (which decorate the parapet walls). Shengfeng Tower, a six-storey private residential concrete watchtower built in 1919 and located to the right of Jinjiang Tower, is much more ornamented – the cantilever portion that occupied its third and fourth floors consists of ornamented colonnades; the turrets for firing weapons at the four corners of the cantilever portion are well defined by Baroque domes; and the "three joint columnsets" of colossal columns are punctuated by sophisticated Roman composite capitals.[49]

Ruishi Tower, located to the left of Jinjiang Tower, was a private residential watchtower built by Huang Bixiu (a businessman in Hong Kong) in 1923. Its construction materials were imported and cost approximately 30,000 Hong Kong dollars. According to an on-site interview with one of the great great granddaughters of the owner conducted by the

Figure 7.3 Shengfeng Tower (left), Jinjiang Tower (middle), and Ruishi Tower (right). Photo by the author.

author in October 2017, cement was imported from Germany and rebars from the Netherlands. The construction was carried out by builders from Guangdong province: the bricklayers, ironworkers, and construction site workers were from Cangcheng, Enping, and Kaiping respectively.[50] The watchtower was not designed by a professional architect; instead, the owner's nephew and local builders worked on the design together.[51]

The plans of the core and cantilevered portion of Ruishi Tower are square, with dimensions of about 9 × 9 m and 11 × 11 m, respectively.[52] The core part (the ground floor to the fourth floor) and the fifth floor (which is part of the cantilevered portion) were residential. Similar to a traditional Chinese courtyard complex, the watchtower offered living space to the owner's extended family members; for example, Huang Yaoji's family lived on the third floor. Except for the ground floor, which only had one bedroom and hence a bigger living room, the residential floors adopted the common "three-bay, two-chamber" layout (the bedrooms to the sides of the living area formed the east and west wings of the watchtower) (Figure 7.4). Each residential floor was usually inhabited by one household and was intended to be self-sufficient, as reflected by the private toilet and kitchen on each residential floor. Besides offering space for keeping watch and repelling invaders, the cantilevered colonnades (including the corner platforms) that surrounded the watchtower's fifth floor provided circulation and a shaded outdoor space for its inhabitants to enjoy during ordinary peaceful days (Figure 7.5). In this way, the cantilevered colonnades were somewhat similar to the colonnades erected between the houses and the inner courtyard of a traditional Chinese courtyard complex. The hall on the sixth floor, which served as the shrine for ancestral worship, corresponded to the central/main hall of a traditional Chinese courtyard complex. The colonnades and open platform on the sixth floor, and the open platforms on the seventh floor, acted as a space

The Aesthetics of Concrete Watchtowers

Figure 7.4 The living room on the fourth floor of Ruishi Tower (the doors of the east wing are to the left-hand side). Photo by the author.

for leisure and viewing the surrounding scenery, comparable to the inner courtyard of a traditional Chinese courtyard complex.[53] Nevertheless, the spatial order of the watchtower was not horizontal, as in a traditional Chinese courtyard complex, but vertical. In other words, the traditional pattern of life embodied in a traditional Chinese courtyard complex was transposed onto the vertical spatial layout of the concrete watchtower.

Due to the aforementioned defensive considerations, Ruishi Tower possessed relatively thick concrete walls (approximately 0.25 m). Most of its small window openings incorporated several defensive layers, such as outer swing iron panels, an iron lattice, and inner sliding iron/wooden panels. The exterior of the core part was relatively plain, but significant articulation through subtle ornamentation, which contributed to its aesthetic quality, is still visible; for example, string courses wrap around and divide the façades of the core part into intelligible parts at each level (Figure 7.6). Moreover, probably in reference to the Baroque style, the string courses run continuously round the corners, overlapping with the implied corner pilasters and acting as their capitals, and hence contribute to the significant vertical transition from floor to floor. This kind of fitting/

Figure 7.5 The fifth-floor cantilevered colonnade of Ruishi Tower. Photo by the author.

correspondence of parts based on detail illustrates the concept that architecture is "an art of the ensemble".[54] In this case, details such as string courses and pilasters play an indispensable role in our aesthetic appreciation of the whole composition that is the watchtower. As Scruton describes it, "It is through the reading of details that we may come to see one feature of a building as providing an adequate visual reason for another feature" so that we can appreciate the parts forming a fitting whole.[55] It is noteworthy that a similar aesthetic treatment with string courses and pilasters can be found on the front and side façades of the arcade building, Rain Pavilion Villa built in 1925 in Chikan old town, Kaiping.[56] This could be explained by Howard Davis's observation concerning building culture that executions of similar details in buildings were probably the result of the spread of building knowledge that occurred "through the movement of craftsmen from one place to another" or the "interrelationships between craftsmen".[57] Thus, the craftsmen responsible for the modelling of Ruishi Tower may have later been involved in the construction of Rain Pavilion Villa, or may have had a working relationship with those who built the villa.

The upper part of Ruishi Tower (from the fifth to the eighth floors) was well ornamented. Most concrete ornamented parts, such as the column capitals and

The Aesthetics of Concrete Watchtowers

Figure 7.6 The main core of Ruishi Tower. Photo by the author.

pediments, were moulded on site and assembled onto the main structure.[58] The cantilevered colonnades on the fifth floor (approximately 0.8 m wide and 3.6 m tall[59]), produced to resemble Renaissance architecture, reveal a hybrid but fitting composition which mainly consists of round Ionic columns (without the entasis and flute), Norman triangular arches, Roman semi-circular arches, and Caernarvon/shouldered arches. The Ionic diagonal capitals (the capitals composed of angled volutes) on the fifth floor are not direct copies of the typical composition of Roman or Scamozzi's Iconic order,[60] rather they are a transformation of them – a fitting composition of modified elements, including an enlarged Ionic curved abacus, reduced Ionic diagonal volutes (with an egg-and-dart moulding at the ovolos between volutes), and an elongated Doric necking (Figure 7.5). The colonnades on the sixth floor (approximately 0.6 m wide and 3.3 m tall[61]) are similarly composed of round Ionic columns (without entasis, flute, and base), Roman semi-circular arches and elongated Caernarvon/shouldered arches. Similar to the capitals of the fifth floor, the Ionic-like diagonal capitals of the sixth floor comprise a synthesis of elements, including an enlarged Ionic square abacus, Ionic diagonal volutes (without any egg-and-dart moulding), and a Doric necking (Figure 7.7). A similar transformation can also be found in the synthesis of a relatively thick Doric square

The Dynamics of Modern Asian Design

Figure 7.7 The colonnades of the hall on the sixth floor of Ruishi Tower. Photo by the author.

Figure 7.8 Composite columns on the fourth floor of Shengfeng Tower. Photo by the author.

abacus and a Composite capital (with volutes and leaves pattern) adopted on the columns on the fourth floor of Shengfeng Tower (Figure 7.8). These modified compositions were innovative, and could not have been achieved without significant departures from the standard patterns driven by the aesthetic sense of the local craftsmen.

The transformed composition of the colonnades on the sixth floor further illustrates the concept of architecture as "an art of ensemble'" (Figure 7.7). The semi-circular arches at the corner, which are well articulated by a semi-circular moulding, provide an adequate visual reason for the making of the enlarged abaci of the Ionic columns, upon which the arches sit firmly and hence fittingly. The composition of the seventh-floor parapet walls and the sixth-floor colonnades is comparable to that of a typical Renaissance pulpit, but the height of the parapet walls here was limited (just around 70 cm tall) to the extent that they were barely able to perform their function of preventing people from falling outside of it (they seem quite low when compared with the upper parapet walls of the Renaissance model). This departure seems to be driven by an aesthetic consideration that the shorter parapet walls are more in proportion with the arches and columns below. The corners of the parapet walls are highlighted by the two joint short pilasters, which correspond vertically to the Ionic corner columns below. In addition to articulating the top of the parapet walls, the top cornices, like the aforementioned string courses of the core part of the watchtower, also act as the capitals of the short pilasters at the corners to offer an apt visual conclusion to the vertical transition, contributing to the fitting relationship between parts in the colonnades.

Ruishi Tower is the region's tallest watchtower, at approximately 29.8 m.[62] The pavilion on the seventh floor is enclosed by concrete walls and round Ionic pilasters (without flute and bases)[63] and capped by a dome, which includes a cupola lantern. The composition of the dome of the pavilion references the Renaissance or Baroque lantern-dome construction, but the size of the cupola lantern is bigger than that of the typical Renaissance or Baroque model.[64] According to Huang Yaoji, the enlargement of the cupola lantern was based primarily on a Chinese geomantic (*feng shui*) principle – odd numbers refer to yang (positive) and even numbers refer to yin (negative). To make the watchtower a "positive" place to live, the cupola lantern was enlarged to enclose a usable interior space, which is counted as the eighth floor, so that Ruishi Tower would have an odd (positive) number of storeys: nine instead of eight. This enlargement of the cupola lantern does not appear odd aesthetically since, through the overall configuration achieved by the builders, the four Renaissance/Baroque cupolas at the corner turrets of the sixth floor echo the enlarged cupola of the cupola lantern in terms of form and proportion, resulting in a formal correspondence in the upper part of the watchtower (Figure 7.3).

All in all, these fitting compositions contributed essentially to the aesthetic quality of Ruishi Tower, by virtue of which it is considered the finest watchtower in Kaiping. From an analytic point of view, the aesthetic significance of this kind of concrete watchtower lies in the fittingness and echoes of transformed parts, a "part-answering-part" relation, from which a sense of "visual validity" can be grasped through our daily contemplation.[65] This sense of "visual validity" is of paramount importance to us because, as Scruton explains, it answers the fundamental aesthetic aspiration of humans as intellectual beings and is thus responsible for our feeling of aesthetic pleasure, thereby constituting an indispensable part of our daily lives.[66]

Phenomenological understanding of concrete watchtowers

The meaningful relationship between the concrete residential watchtowers' aesthetics and people's daily lives can also be elaborated upon through a phenomenological understanding of such watchtowers. As John Haldane rightly points out, works of architecture are cultural products in that they do not only involve "a mere quantity of matter having a certain shape", but more importantly serve as embodiments of values of human life – values of human life mediated through the spatial, formal, ornamental, and material features of architecture.[67] In view of this, the architectural elements are not to be arranged in a mere art-for-art's-sake manner, but structured and articulated according to the cultural values that shape and enhance life.[68] In this sense, the aesthetic experience of architecture should not be entirely the same as that of fine art, but instead has to be conditioned by a deeper understanding of architecture as "a setting for life".[69] Kaiping concrete residential watchtowers, in being constructed and articulated as a particular kind of setting for life in the region, epitomize this phenomenological interpretation of architecture.

The culture of the rice-farming societies in the region is strongly shaped by the values of Taoism and geomancy that propose the ideal of a harmonious relationship between nature and humans – a conviction similar to the ecocentric worldview in which human beings are considered a member of nature instead of its master.[70] The indigenous culture of the region has thereby been characterized by local affection for nature,[71] which played a key role in the spatial organization of concrete residential watchtowers. The core parts of the watchtowers were solid – their interior living spaces were enclosed by thick concrete walls with small openings – as a means of effective defence. In contrast, their upper parts, which consisted of outdoor platforms and open structures (e.g. colonnades), were designed as key void spaces to allow proximity to nature – a panorama of the surrounding natural landscape, in which one is literally surrounded by, or even merged with, the natural environment with little or no obstruction. The upper voids, therefore, introduced an essential naturalistic dimension to the otherwise almost isolated daily life of the mostly enclosed living places of the core parts. Via the upper voids, life in concrete watchtowers was enhanced due to the proximity to, and harmony with, nature. The particular solid-and-void spatial arrangement of Kaiping concrete residential watchtowers is not inconsequential, but rather a result of shaping the concrete watchtowers as "a setting for life" based on both functional and cultural considerations.

Reinforced concrete construction is almost always linked with the Modern Style, which, according to Haldane, holds that "architecture should disclose reality by stripping away the [decorated] 'surface'" and thus attempt to offer a logical order as the stable point of contact for the intellect to grasp in the assumed contingent, irregular, and imperfect physical world.[72] The corresponding process, according to Peter Galison, is to obtain and express, via formal reduction, a "transparent construction" of elementary geometry so as to break away from any reference to the supposed inferior physical world.[73] This results in a rejection of visual representation of, and cultural association with, the ordinary world we inhabit on a daily basis, especially one mediated by ornamentation. This rejection explains why a lot of buildings in the Modern Style are viewed as being unrelated to their environment and cultural context. Furthermore, concrete is an artificial material, and since reinforced concrete, unlike natural materials, can resist natural forces well (e.g. gravity, weather), it thus, as Adrian Forty describes it, "gives us power over nature to a greater degree than most other materials", and hence it gives rise to a sense that "'to concrete over' is to erase all trace of nature".[74] Modern exposed concrete structures, therefore, do not usually fit with their natural environment visually and phenomenologically, and hence seemingly isolate humans from nature.[75]

Unexpectedly, the adoption of reinforced concrete construction in Kaiping in general did not involve the Modern Style or the notion of formal reduction. Early Chinese modern architects introduced Modern-Style concrete projects to China beginning in the first half of the twentieth century, thanks to economic considerations and the expression of "the spirit of the age".[76] In contrast, most locals and local builders of Kaiping preferred ornamental styles that offered them abundant references to ornamented architectural parts for the aesthetic modelling of their residences, including concrete residential watchtowers, concrete villas, and ordinary houses close to the watchtowers. Apart from the aesthetic value of the ornamented parts, the locals' preference for ornamentation over modern abstract forms may be viewed in cultural terms – the ornamentation was probably not treated as meaningless surface decoration to be stripped away but was very likely adopted to mediate the locals' positive vision of and passion for nature. The extensive use of reinforced concrete construction and exposed concrete surfaces should have made the concrete residential watchtowers incoherent with their surrounding natural and semi-natural (i.e. agricultural) landscapes. This would have been undesirable because nature is understood as indispensable to life in the local culture. The delicate ornamentation, therefore, played a decisive role in the design of concrete residential watchtowers since it could naturalize the unfitting appearance of concrete structures.

The adopted ornaments for concrete residential watchtowers, like the classical mouldings they referenced, often involved the minute imitation of natural elements; for example, the composite capitals of Shengfeng Tower consisted of tiers of acanthus leaf patterns (Figure 7.8) and the parapet walls of Ruishi Tower portrayed detailed stucco mouldings of the same such leaves (Figure 7.7). Through such imitation, the non-natural concrete was moderated, and perceptually, the concrete watchtowers matched more closely and hence fit better with the surrounding natural context. Furthermore, as the adopted ornaments usually involved the artistic interpretation of natural forms, they consisted of curvilinear forms that can establish formal correspondences with natural elements. This is particularly evident in Ruishi Tower, where the curvilinear volutes or scrolled brackets (which were derived from natural forms such as shells or spiral ovules) of the adapted

"Iconic" capitals, the "Renaissance" colonnades and the Baroque pediments, and the shell-form mouldings of the cupolas' finials, together with the round Renaissance/Baroque cupolas,[77] echo the undulating forms and contours of the surrounding shrubs, crowns of trees, and hills (Figure 7.3). It should also be noted that the outstanding aesthetic sensibility and crafting skill of the local builders and craftsmen played a crucial role here. It was because most of the ornaments were moulded in concrete, only in the skilful hands of the craftsmen could this artificial material be unexpectedly moulded and carved into the delicate forms and details. These forms and details successfully imitated or reinterpreted natural forms, and became perceptually closer to nature,[78] on the strength of which the naturalization of the concrete residential watchtowers was further enhanced.[79]

As exemplified by Ruishi Tower, many concrete residential watchtowers did not adopt the phenomenologically inappropriate Modern Style that has reduced architecture to a mere demonstration of rational order in the format of formalism. Instead, via their upper void spaces and the naturalization contributed by the manipulation of forms and the adoption and execution of concrete ornaments, the concrete residential watchtowers were structured and articulated in such a way that their form, craftsmanship, and purpose were inseparable from the consideration of their natural context.[80] This has led to a type of contextual architecture that respects the natural order in its own right – nature is equally important, if not superior, to architecture, a man-made product.[81] As a result, the concrete residential watchtowers form with nature "a continuous unity" – a unification of the rational and natural order[82] – that transcends the being of a mere rational man-made object. In the context of concrete residential watchtowers, any attempt to relegate nature as inferior, chaotic, and defective, waiting to be replaced by a human rational order, as proposed by modernists, seems implausible.[83] The daily experience of the harmonious relationship with nature mediated by this contextual architecture contributes to a tranquil lifestyle that has been adopted and cherished by its inhabitants for generations. This explains the locals' long-term engagement with the concrete residential watchtowers. The story of Zhou Qiyou recorded by Zhang in April 2003 provides us with a very relevant case. Zhou has lived in the concrete watchtower Xunzhi Xuan (located in Qixing village, Tangkou town) since childhood.[84] He owned a three-storey Modern-Style mansion in the small town Tanxi in Kaiping but he chose to stay in his less convenient concrete watchtower, partly because of his enjoyment of the tranquil lifestyle mediated by the watchtower.[85] All in all, the concrete residential watchtowers should be considered valuable architectural references, since they embody and preserve the traditional life pattern of bonding with nature that was cultivated before the alienation of humans from natural environments caused by the formal reduction of Modernism.

Conclusion

The construction of concrete watchtowers in Kaiping was one of the first attempts to modernize the region's built environment via the adoption of reinforced concrete construction imported from European nations, including Germany and the Netherlands;

nonetheless, the architecture of Kaiping concrete watchtowers should be distinguished from the mainstream modern reductionistic practice. In the local process of cultural hybridization, foreign stylistic elements were absorbed and transformed as a result of innovative endeavours and the aesthetic sense of the locals and local builders, leading to a kind of aesthetically remarkable hybrid architecture. The aesthetic aim of the Kaiping concrete watchtowers was not and has never been superficial. They are not only works of art for appreciation, but also settings for the local tranquil lifestyle. Through the naturalization achieved by ornamentation, manipulation of forms, and craftsmanship, together with their upper-floor void spaces, the concrete watchtowers blended in with their natural context and have thus become a kind of contextual architecture that is "both in and of the world".[86] They are in stark contrast, therefore, with those abstract and decontextualized Modern-Style concrete buildings and can be considered to offer an alternative "Modernization" – a kind of "Modernization" that can help to preserve the traditional relationship between nature and humans in the region, and hence to mediate in the home villages of the local rice-farming societies a distinctively harmonious and tranquil lifestyle for generations, through which locals can draw value from their places and surroundings, and deepen their sense of belonging.[87]

Notes

1. Lin Lin, *Gang Ao Yu Zhujiang Sanjiaozhou Di Yu Jian Zhu: Guangdong Qi Lou* (Regional Architecture in Hong Kong, Macao and the Pearl River Delta: Guangdong Arcade Building) (Ke Xue Chu Ban She, 2006), 13.
2. "Glocalization" is an interdisciplinary term that emerged in 1990–91 that can be traced to the Japanese concept "global localization" from the 1980s. See Victor N. Roudometof, "Glocalization", *Oxford Bibliographies*, 15 January 2020.
3. Roland Robertson, "Glocalization: Time-Space and Homogeneity-Heterogeneity", in Mike Featherstone, Scott Lash and Roland Robertson (eds.), *Global Modernities* (Sage, 1995), 25–32.
4. Robert J. Antony, *Unruly People: Crime, Community, and State in Late Imperial South China* (Hong Kong University Press, 2016), 56.
5. Antony, *Unruly People*, 59, 168.
6. The State Administration of Cultural Heritage of the People's Republic of China, "Description", chapter 2 in *Kaiping Diaolou and Villages* (December 2005).
7. Antony, *Unruly People*, 80, 85.
8. Antony, *Unruly People*, 105.
9. Allen Carlson, "Reconsidering the Aesthetics of Architecture", *Journal of Aesthetic Education* 20, no. 4 (Winter 1986), 22, 23.
10. Carlson, "Reconsidering the Aesthetics of Architecture", 22, 23.
11. Carlson, "Reconsidering the Aesthetics of Architecture", 22, 23.
12. Cheng Jianjun, *Kaiping diaolou: Zhong xi he bi de qiao xiang wen hua jing guan* (Kaiping Watchtowers: The Cultural Landscape of Chinese and Western Synthesis in Overseas Chinese Hometowns) (Zhongguo Jian Zhu Gong Ye Chu Ban She, 2007), 27.

13. The ground floor and the first floor of the watchtower were built of red brick during the Ming dynasty. The third floor was a later blue-brick addition constructed in 1920. See ICOMOS, "Evaluations of Cultural Properties (2007)", 39.
14. Zhang Guoxiong, *Kaiping diaolou yu cun luo* (Kaiping Diaolou and Villages) (Zhongguo Huaqiao Chu Ban She, 2011), 123.
15. The State Administration of Cultural Heritage of the People's Republic of China, "Description", chapter 2 in *Kaiping Diaolou and Villages*.
16. The discussion of the "Outstanding Universal Value" of the concrete watchtowers was based on criteria ii, iii, and iv of the "Criteria for Selection" of the World Heritage. For a detailed discussion, see ICOMOS, "Evaluations of Cultural Properties", 41, 42.
17. The nominated sites of concrete watchtowers in Kaiping are: (a) Zili Village, which includes Mingshi Tower and eight other concrete watchtowers/villas; (b) Majianlong Village Cluster, which includes seven concrete watchtowers/villas; and (c) Jinjiangli Village, which includes Ruishi Tower, Shengfeng Tower, and Jinjiang Tower. See ICOMOS, "Evaluations of Cultural Properties", 39.
18. The State Administration of Cultural Heritage of the People's Republic of China, "Description", chapter 2 in *Kaiping Diaolou and Villages*.
19. In the late 1930s, the speed of the construction of Kaiping watchtowers and villas was reduced due to the economic downturn of the Great Depression, which saw overseas Kaiping clan members experience a significant drop in income. See The State Administration of Cultural Heritage of the People's Republic of China, "Description", chapter 2 in *Kaiping Diaolou and Villages*.
20. ICOMOS, "Evaluations of Cultural Properties", 41.
21. Zhang, *Kaiping diaolou yu cun luo*, 86.
22. ICOMOS, "Evaluations of Cultural Properties", 45.
23. Zhang, *Kaiping diaolou yu cun luo*, 87, 91.
24. Zhang, *Kaiping diaolou yu cun luo*, 91.
25. Zhang, *Kaiping diaolou yu cun luo*, 60.
26. ICOMOS, "Evaluations of Cultural Properties", 43.
27. Peter G. Rowe and Seng Kuan, *Architectural Encounters with Essence and Form in Modern China* (MIT Press, 2002), 64–65.
28. The State Administration of Cultural Heritage of the People's Republic of China, "Justification for Inscription", chapter 3 in *Kaiping Diaolou and Villages*.
29. Cheng, *Kaiping diaolou*, 118.
30. Cheng, *Kaiping diaolou*, 118, 126.
31. Zhang, *Kaiping diaolou yu cun luo*, 94–95.
32. Zhang, *Kaiping diaolou yu cun luo*, 95.
33. Zhang Guoxiong, "Shi xi kaiping diao lou di gong neng – qiao xiang wen shu yan jiu zhi san (An Analysis of the Functions of Kaiping Watchtowers – Research on Documents of Overseas Chinese Hometown 3)", *Journal of Wuyi University (Social Sciences Edition)* 6, no. 4 (November 2004), 54.
34. Roger Scruton, *The Aesthetics of Architecture* (Princeton University Press, 1979), 6, 223.
35. Hanno-Walter Kruft, *A History of Architectural Theory: From Vitruvius to the Present*, trans. Ronald Taylor, Elsie Callander and Antony Wood (Princeton Architectural Press, 1994), 45.

36. According to C.S. Peirce, an "index" is "a sign with a direct existential connection with its object". See John Fiske, "Communication, Meaning, and Signs", in *Introduction to Communication Studies*, 2nd edition (Routledge, 1990), 47.
37. Zhang, *Kaiping diaolou yu cun luo*, 75.
38. ICOMOS, "Evaluations of Cultural Properties", 45.
39. Scruton, *The Aesthetics of Architecture*, 172.
40. Scruton, *The Aesthetics of Architecture*, 172.
41. Hugh Honour and John Fleming, *A World History of Art* (Laurence King Publishing, 2009), 725.
42. Nancy S. Steinhardt, "Chinese Architecture on the Eve of the Beaux-Arts", in Jeffery W. Cody, Nancy S. Steinhardt and Tony Atkin (eds.), *Chinese Architecture and the Beaux-Arts* (Hong Kong University Press, 2011), 4–5.
43. The projects designed by foreign architects, such as the Ginling College Recitation Building by Henry K. Murphy (built 1924–27), primarily involved the faithful imitation and realization of Chinese architectural form and features (e.g. uplifted roof eaves) by concrete construction. They thus did not engage the innovative departure and transformation found in the concrete watchtowers. See Jeffery W. Cody, *Building in China: Henry K. Murphy's "Adaptive Architecture," 1914–1935* (Chinese University of Hong Kong Press, 2001), 113.
44. Kwok-wah Tung, "Chikan's Arcade Buildings: The Hybrid and Civil Architecture of Lingnan", *Architecture and Culture* 6, no. 2 (December 2018), 335.
45. My translation. Zhang, *Kaiping diaolou yu cun luo*, 122.
46. The State Administration of Cultural Heritage of the People's Republic of China, "Description", chapter 2 in *Kaiping Diaolou and Villages*.
47. The State Administration of Cultural Heritage of the People's Republic of China, "Description", chapter 2 in *Kaiping Diaolou and Villages*.
48. The State Administration of Cultural Heritage of the People's Republic of China, "Description", chapter 2 in *Kaiping Diaolou and Villages*.
49. The State Administration of Cultural Heritage of the People's Republic of China, "Description", chapter 2 in *Kaiping Diaolou and Villages*.
50. Urban Planning and Design Center of Peking University, *Protection and Management Plan on Kaiping Diaolou and Villages (Extracts)* (December 2001), 8.
51. Urban Planning and Design Center of Peking University, *Protection and Management Plan*.
52. These measurements were taken by the author on site.
53. Their main difference is that for the inner courtyard of a typical traditional Chinese courtyard complex, the view is towards the internal artificial garden, while for the open spaces of the concrete watchtowers, the view is towards the external natural environment.
54. Scruton, *The Aesthetics of Architecture*, 11.
55. Scruton, *The Aesthetics of Architecture*, 219.
56. Tung, "Chikan's Arcade Buildings", 338–39.
57. Howard Davis, *The Culture of Building* (Oxford University, 2006), 132.
58. Zhang, *Kaiping diaolou yu cun luo*, 87.
59. These measurements were taken by the author on site.
60. The diagonal volutes were made smaller than the typical Iconic ones, so that their proportion is closer to that of the volutes of the Corinthian order.

61. These measurements were taken by the author on site.
62. The technical measurement was given by Huang Yaoji during the site visit in February 2019.
63. The pilasters were measured at approximately 3.1 m tall by the author on site.
64. Some would propose that the uppermost cupola imitates a Byzantine dome; however, this proposal seems less convincing in structural terms because this cupola sits on a drum instead of a larger dome structure.
65. Scruton, *The Aesthetics of Architecture*, 206, 211, 219, 240.
66. Scruton, *The Aesthetics of Architecture*, 240.
67. John Haldane, "Aesthetic Naturalism and the Decline of Architecture, Part 1: Architecture and Aesthetic Perception", *International Journal of Moral and Social Studies* 2 (1987), 217, 220–21.
68. Haldane, "Aesthetic Naturalism and the Decline of Architecture, Part 1", 221–22.
69. Haldane, "Aesthetic Naturalism and the Decline of Architecture, Part 1", 217, 220–21.
70. John A. Fisher, "Environmental Aesthetics", in Jerrold Levinson (ed.), *The Oxford Handbook of Aesthetics* (Oxford University Press, 2003), 667.
71. The State Administration of Cultural Heritage of the People's Republic of China, "Justification for Inscription," chap. 3 in *Kaiping Diaolou and Villages*.
72. John Haldane, "Aesthetic Naturalism and the Decline of Architecture, Part 2: Form, Matter and Understanding", *International Journal of Moral and Social Studies* 3 (1988), 181.
73. According to Peter Galison, the "transparent construction" is "a manifest building up from simple elements to all higher forms that would by virtue of the systematic constructional program itself, guarantee the exclusion of the decorative, mystical, or metaphysical". See Peter Galison, "Aufbau/Bauhaus: Logical Positivism and Architectural Modernism", *Critical Inquiry* 16, no. 4 (Summer 1990), 710.
74. Adrian Forty, *Concrete and Culture: A Material History* (Reaktion Books, 2012), 43.
75. Forty, *Concrete and Culture*, 43.
76. Rowe et. al., *Architectural Encounters with Essence and Form*, 105.
77. The cupolas of the turrets and their well-articulated apexes reflected an influence from Islamic architecture.
78. According to Adrian Forty, other attempts of naturalizing modern concrete buildings have been made – "generally by making it [concrete] look like either stone or wood" or "leaving the imprint of wooden formwork on the surface of the finished concrete: all are ways of connecting to the natural world a substance perceived as 'unnatural'": see Forty, *Concrete and Culture*, 44.
79. John Ruskin's discussion of the merit of old buildings may also be applied here that the ageing of concrete watchtowers can contribute to the naturalization process, since for architecture, "the rents, or fractures, or stains, or vegetation" may assimilate it "with the work of Nature". See John Ruskin, *The Seven Lamps of Architecture* (Dover Publications, 1989), 193.
80. Haldane, "Aesthetic Naturalism and the Decline of Architecture, Part 2", 185, 186.
81. Fisher, "Environmental Aesthetics", 667.
82. Haldane, "Aesthetic Naturalism and the Decline of Architecture, Part 2", 173, 186.
83. Haldane, "Aesthetic Naturalism and the Decline of Architecture, Part 2", 186.
84. Zhang, *Kaiping diaolou yu cun luo*, 144–45.

85. Zhang, *Kaiping diaolou yu cun luo*, 148–49, 151.
86. Haldane, "Aesthetic Naturalism and the Decline of Architecture, Part 2", 185, 186.
87. Haldane, "Aesthetic Naturalism and the Decline of Architecture, Part 2", 183, 187.

References

Antony, Robert J. *Unruly People: Crime, Community, and State in Late Imperial South China*, Hong Kong University Press, 2016.
Carlson, Allen. "Reconsidering the Aesthetics of Architecture", *Journal of Aesthetic Education* 20, no. 4 (Winter 1986): 21–27.
Cheng Jianjun. *Kaiping diaolou: Zhong xi he bi de qiao xiang wen hua jing guan* (Kaiping Watchtowers: The Cultural Landscape of Chinese and Western Synthesis in Overseas Chinese Hometowns), Zhongguo Jian Zhu Gong Ye Chu Ban She, 2007.
Cody, Jeffery W. *Building in China: Henry K. Murphy's "Adaptive Architecture," 1914–1935*, Chinese University of Hong Kong Press, 2001.
Davis, Howard. *The Culture of Building*, Oxford University, 2006.
Fisher, John A. "Environmental Aesthetics", in Jerrold Levinson (ed.), *The Oxford Handbook of Aesthetics*, Oxford University Press, 2003.
Fiske, John. "Communication, Meaning, and Signs", in *Introduction to Communication Studies*, 2nd edition, Routledge, 1990.
Forty, Adrian. *Concrete and Culture: A Material History*, Reaktion Books, 2012.
Galison, Peter. "Aufbau/Bauhaus: Logical Positivism and Architectural Modernism", *Critical Inquiry* 16, no. 4 (Summer 1990): 709–52.
Haldane, John. "Aesthetic Naturalism and the Decline of Architecture, Part 1: Architecture and Aesthetic Perception", *International Journal of Moral and Social Studies* 2 (1987): 210–24.
Haldane, John. "Aesthetic Naturalism and the Decline of Architecture, Part 2: Form, Matter and Understanding", *International Journal of Moral and Social Studies* 3 (1988): 173–90.
Honour, Hugh and John Fleming. *A World History of Art*, Laurence King, 2009.
International Council on Monuments and Sites (ICOMOS). "Evaluations of Cultural Properties (2007)". https://www.icomos.org/en/our-work/evaluation/the-evaluation-process-in-detail-2 (accessed 23 February 2021).
Kruft, Hanno-Walter. *A History of Architectural Theory: From Vitruvius to the Present*, trans. Ronald Taylor, Elsie Callander and Antony Wood, Princeton Architectural Press, 1994.
Kwok-wah Tung. "Chikan's Arcade Buildings: The Hybrid and Civil Architecture of Lingnan", *Architecture and Culture* 6, no. 2 (December 2018): 329–51.
Lin Lin. *Gang Ao Yu Zhujiang Sanjiaozhou Di Yu Jian Zhu: Guangdong Qi Lou* (Regional Architecture in Hong Kong, Macao and the Pearl River Delta: Guangdong Arcade Building), Ke Xue Chu Ban She, 2006.
Robertson, Roland. "Glocalization: Time-Space and Homogeneity-Heterogeneity", in Mike Featherstone, Scott Lash and Roland Robertson (eds.), *Global Modernities*, Sage, 1995.
Roudometof, Victor N. "Glocalization", *Oxford Bibliographies*, 15 January 2020. https://www.oxfordbibliographies.com/display/document/obo-9780199756841/obo-9780199756841-0241.xml (accessed 2 January 2024).
Rowe, Peter G. and Seng Kuan. *Architectural Encounters with Essence and Form in Modern China*, MIT Press, 2002.
Ruskin, John. *The Seven Lamps of Architecture*, Dover Publications, 1989.
Scruton, Roger. *The Aesthetics of Architecture*, Princeton University Press, 1979.

Steinhardt, Nancy S. "Chinese Architecture on the Eve of the Beaux- Arts", in Jeffery W. Cody, Nancy S. Steinhardt and Tony Atkin (eds.), *Chinese Architecture and the Beaux-Arts*, Hong Kong University Press, 2011.

The State Administration of Cultural Heritage of the People's Republic of China. *Kaiping Diaolou and Villages* (December 2005). https://whc.unesco.org/uploads/nominations/1112.pdf (accessed 23 February 2021).

Urban Planning and Design Center of Peking University. *Protection and Management Plan on Kaiping Diaolou and Villages (Extracts)* (December 2001). https://whc.unesco.org/uploads/nominations/1112.pdf (accessed 23 February 2021).

Zhang Guoxiong. "Shi xi kaiping diao lou di gong neng – qiao xiang wen shu yan jiu zhi san (An Analysis of the Functions of Kaiping Watchtowers – Research on Documents of Overseas Chinese Hometown 3)", *Journal of Wuyi University (Social Sciences Edition)* 6, no. 4 (November 2004): 51–56.

Zhang Guoxiong. *Kaiping diaolou yu cun luo* (Kaiping Diaolou and Villages), Zhongguo Huaqiao Chu Ban She, 2011.

CHAPTER 8
THE HOME AND THE STREET: POVERTY, DEVELOPMENT, AND HERITAGE IN HOUSING DESIGN IN INDIA IN THE 1980S
Megha Rajguru

Introduction

In an article published in 1988 in the journal *Mimar*, Babar Mumtaz, an urban planner and development economist, opened his arguments with a reflection on Friedrich Engel's *Housing Question* published in 1872, highlighting the long-standing conundrum of housing workers in the context of urban migration for work.[1] Shortages of land and resources, questions of affordable design, and inequitable distribution of wealth were all points Engels had raised, and Mumtaz examined these to address shortages in housing across the Global South a century on. Mumtaz was critical of nation-states' hostility to fund housing for the people with the lowest or no incomes, arguing for better policy and design, where swathes of populations were left to fend for themselves. Mumtaz was critical of housing experiments in the 1940s and 1950s that couched self-help as an answer to housing problems, stating that they did not consider labour time, skills, and financial flexibility. He argued for a community-led design approach where people had autonomy to create their own homes incrementally through the provision of low-cost building materials, specifically indigenous materials, and building knowledge.

This chapter returns to these ideas, and studies the 1980s as a crucial period in the history of housing in India, when questions of who gets housed where and how, were being asked, and architects were working closely with national and international organizations to make homes for people with less. It looks at two well-known incremental housing projects – Aranya Housing, Indore, in the state of Madhya Pradesh and Artists' Village, also known as Belapur Housing, in Mumbai, in the state of Maharashtra – to understand the meanings of minimal living and how this kind of living was positioned as a form of empowerment by architects Balkrishna Doshi and Charles Correa, respectively. This chapter examines the concept of minimal design as understood and materialized through the perspective of development. Drawing upon archival papers from the World Bank, the architects' own marketing and planning documents, as well as contemporary publications, it asks: in what ways was minimal living imagined in the 1980s in India? How was participation or self-help materialized through the living spaces, including the interiors, and outdoors?

Addressing these questions helps trace the historical trajectories of modern interiors in postcolonial contexts in India, particularly in relation to canonical projects by modernist architects, as these have acted as blueprints for designers. Given extensive designer-produced materials, such as writings, sketches, and photography at the sites, it is possible to focus attention on the ways in which modern or contemporary living within urban contexts for communities classed as low or middle income were materialized through design. I have previously examined the imaginations of modern living by architects through their visual materials.[2] In that article I address concepts and practices of production – the making of homes – and the material choices built into the designs to make these imaginations tangible. These examples and their analyses contribute to the histories of interiors produced by people beyond the upper strata of urban society in India, and shed light on the enmeshing of development ideas with architectural design.

It is important to note here that the two projects were not the only ones designed as incremental during this period. The Sites and Services project at Charkop in Bombay (now Mumbai), funded by the World Bank and developed by Maharashtra Housing and Area Development, and the UN-funded project Madipur Widows Housing colony in Delhi, have helped scholars understand the changes that have taken place over time through community involvement. These studies have addressed the social, economic, and design choices made by residents over time.[3] Beyond India, housing projects in South Asia – in Karachi, Pakistan; Columbo, Sri Lanka; and Singapore – experimented with incrementality to solve the urban housing crises for lower-income working communities. These forays into design for development were perceived as utopian, with the power to solve urban problems of migration and poverty. The two studies here move beyond a focus on incrementality and temporal change, or housing need and policy, and examine the ways in which designs were conceived by the two architects and the infrastructure to accommodate the material culture of everyday living was produced. This approach helps examine the specific geographical, postcolonial Indian developmental context.

In the book *Of Greater Dignity than Riches*, Farhan Karim discusses housing design in India between the 1920s and the 1950s within the context of the discourse of austerity.[4] It also addresses developmental contexts, tracing the involvement of international architects and agencies, as well as the agendas of the Indian Government. The book examines housing prototypes for exhibitions, model villages, and Gandhian philosophy, addressing modernization and modernism embedded in the concept of minimum living. The core thrust of Karim's argument is the elevation of poverty and scarcity as a paradigm of dignity, producing design not without its limitations, but nevertheless negotiated everyday life with forms of national material culture.

This chapter expands upon the concept of austere modernism to address its development beyond the 1960s, visualized and materialized by Indian architects. Where everyday life and national material culture were "squared" within the limitations of design by the international architects before the 1950s, two decades later home-grown architects attempted to focus on those very concepts, but through the lens of tangible and intangible heritages. Vernacular design, local ways of living, and material culture framed their works, for these were valued as forms of heritage carried by communities who had left villages for work. The use of outdoor spaces, the streets, the verandas and balconies, as interfaces with the public, located the designs as part of an urban fabric.

These approaches specifically spoke to the condition and challenges of poverty within processes of modernization, where heritage maintained through local skills, materials, and everyday life was the solution for dignity. This was made possible with international and national fiscal support, promising equity and growth. These communities, for the two Indian architects Correa and Doshi, would be able to make their homes over time and be empowered.

Grace-Lees Maffei and Rebecca Houze have examined disciplinary overlaps between design history and heritage studies, offering insights into ways in which design history has its distinguishing characteristics, primarily a "concern for the process and products of design".[5] They discuss how designed objects, such as buildings, help understand their relevance to shared cultural identities, as well as how design, its use, collecting, preservation, and gifting, connect to broader cultural histories that shape cultural heritage. This chapter engages with heritage studies to draw out the ways in which cultural discourse and design aligned with concepts of development in the 1980s, when participation was regarded as an important method. The notion of participation was not new in the field of design and architecture, with discussions on the user's perspective in urban planning taking place in the United States in the early 1960s, including community design, the development of citizen participation in the planning process through reimagining planning, as well as supporting grassroots neighbourhood planning.[6] These radical ideas were also present in development thinking, albeit less grassroots and much more organization-led, in the 1980s, and a book by Robert Chambers, *Rural Development: Putting the Last First*, critiqued the outsider urban authoritarian view of the rural from the point of view of developing it. Chambers critically discussed participation or community involvement as methods that predicate an outsider to "involve" and enable participation. His argument is that abstaining from helping is also an action and results in prioritizing the needs of the poor, and one way to remedy the power relation is to start their work with the priorities of the poor. He suggests that knowing and following the priorities of the poor will reduce the urban-poor paternalistic relation.[7]

This developmental discourse of participation and self-help is central to both projects' developmental ambition and design method. Therefore, the chapter addresses how these informed the design process and outcome, with heritage practice employed as a mechanism for locating these abstract concepts in the specific geography and culture.

The historical context

Under the slogan of *Garibi Hatao* (eradicate poverty), Prime Minister Indira Gandhi's Congress government rolled out a number of schemes through a Twenty Point Programme, which included clean drinking water, health for all, improvement for slums, and housing for the people.[8] Introduced in 1971, the slogan and its underpinning ideals survived into 1986 despite changes in government. While on the surface these ideals had gained currency since Indian independence in 1947, and improving the lives of the poor was the agenda for many designers, the mechanisms through which poverty could be alleviated attracted much debate. For example, in a 1985 article in *Economic and Political Weekly*, Nilakantha Rath discussed the failures of the Integrated Rural Development Programme, arguing for a multi-pronged approach of wage and employment creation over simply subsidies.[9] While Rath blamed the mechanisms of schemes since the 1970s for the failures, in another article in the same journal, M.L. Dantwala pointed out the very basis for Rath's argument, a structural matter, where systemic inequalities were produced and sustained, had to be called into question.[10] They asked for an alternative vision, one in which the poor could aspire to be producers, and owners of assets, including homes. They had self-generated financial means to sustain livelihoods through owning a *charkha* (hand-spinning wheel) or a loom rather than rely on the benevolence of either their employers or the State. These lively debates took place within a shift towards less-Socialist models of development in India, to partially subsidized and partially market-driven policies, shaping modes of access to markers of modernity and economic growth, including to housing ownership. These concepts formulated housing schemes that supported the production of the homes, aligning with approaches towards housing access employed by international development agencies such as the World Bank and the United Nations. Despite Indira Gandhi's socialist ideals, design and planning for low-income housing during the late 1970s and the 1980s in India were driven by financial growth and self-sufficiency models, enabled through bank loan schemes. For both Aranya Township and Artists' Village, loan schemes were available, involving monthly instalments calculated according to the family incomes.

Arturo Escobar has reflected on the repetition of the international development discourse at local levels across the Global South from the 1970s.[11] He argues that while studies into how this played out at regional levels are only just being conducted, there is strong evidence of the insertion of the language of development and its indicators within local contexts adapted for local relevance, producing hybridized versions. This is clearly evident within the two cases here. In the 1980s, studies on the Indian economy in relation to urban development noted that larger cities such as Bombay, Delhi, Calcutta, and Madras had seen significant amounts of financial growth, and migration of people for work causing rents to increase. This prompted the need for urban expansion, with movement of people away from the centre. Carried out by the World Bank, one such study surveyed Indore (where Aranya is located), as well as Bombay as cities that grew exponentially.[12] With Bombay growing at a rate of 3.2% annually between 1971 and 1981, it had significant manufacturing employment, while Indore, with its production of cloth, chemicals, and medicine, was one of the larger cities in the state of Madhya Pradesh. The study reported the actions of the government of India in controlling city sizes. This involved planning decisions, such as shifting the focus of new employment opportunities, particularly in manufacturing; the prohibition of movement; land use regulations, and housing. Public housing development was withheld from large cities and concentrated on the periphery. The report presents a word of caution, as such controls could cause harm to social mobility, but also reflects on the failure to limit city growth, despite such measures undertaken for approximately three decades since the 1950s.

Aligning with some of these concerns, the World Bank had already conceived urban development projects, called the Sites and Services projects across the Global South, since 1974. In India, the World Bank funded the program across 27 cities. The program's primary premise was to address unplanned squatter housing developed as a result of urban migration and population growth; improve infrastructure and environment for the residents and generate savings and income, as well as boost self-help.[13] The design for the housing projects had to be standardized in each context, but these standards had to be minimal, with a core unit providing water access and electricity, as well as a plot of land. The frameworks and planning had to be set to afford incremental flexibility and low costs. The Sites and Services framework established minimal aesthetic standards. These included the "organization of provision of building materials and technical assistance in self-help" to avoid building excesses and "monotony of standardization of dwellings".[14] Attractive surroundings involving good layouts of streets and location of buildings, as well as planting of trees, were posited as important considerations, and it was crucial that these sites were located well away from "modernizing central business districts".[15] Access to employment opportunities should also be at a low cost, and these would typically involve walking or cycling.

Simultaneous to these urban development ideas being delivered at an international scale, in India, in the city of Bombay, major planning for the development of a satellite city, New Bombay, was taking place in the 1970s. Led by architects and planners Charles Correa, Pravina Doshi, and Shirish Patel, the central concept of the project was to manage the growth of the city, and shift the nodal point from South Bombay across the creek to the east. The plans saw a radical percentage of the housing planned for communities with lower incomes and the new city was described as being designed for 'the common man'. A project similar in scale and ambition, it has been compared with the Garden City concept, produced on new land with radical ambitions of greenbelts, easy access to employment, and improved housing. The designers of the new city went as far as comparing New Bombay plans to towns in Great Britain. A number of housing projects in this new city were funded by City and Development Corporation (CIDCO), as well as other private enterprises, but also the World Bank under the Sites and Services program.

Amid these historic contexts, the materialization of the concepts of housing access and urban planning, shaped by architects, planners, development specialists, and bankers, show the processes of design that were also implicitly employing the language of development and wherein the individual – the common person – sharing cultural identities with others within communities in postcolonial India, had agency.

Minimal housing in Indore and Bombay

The Aranya Township and Artists' Village projects in Indore and Bombay respectively were produced as low-rise cluster homes employing a "'classic' architectural approach to large-scale, low-cost dwellings for the poor"[16] (Figures 8.1 and 8.2). In both cases, the

Figure 8.1 Cluster housing, Aranya Township. © Aga Khan Trust for Culture/Yatin Pandya.

Figure 8.2 Homes in close proximity to one another. Photo by the author.

clients were the urban development agencies and were either funded entirely by the World Bank (Aranya as a Sites and Services Project) or partly by the public body City and Industrial Development Corporation of Maharashtra (Artists' Village), and some areas in the vicinity. Aranya was conceived in 1982 and comprised 7,000 housing units across income categories, but a majority of the homes were to be for people from economically weaker sections of society. The ambition of the project was the creation, through effective design, of a community of people, who could expand their homes over time. Vastu Shilpa, Balkrishna Doshi's architecture firm, argued for a sustainable ecosystem of finance, material banks, and training centres to support self-building. Altogether, 6,500 plots were allocated, for 40,000 people, with a growth of population of up to 65,000.[17] Those earmarked for the lower-income residents contained a core unit, a toilet, bathroom, and one room forming the critical infrastructure for life to develop. Alongside these, town planning approaches involved the marking of streets for access.

Similarly, Artists Village (1983) was shaped around the basic amenities model.[18] The toilet, washroom, and one room were to form the primary core of each unit, with opportunities to expand the space. The Village was designed to house 550 families. When fully expanded, the houses would be clustered, with courtyards into which the main doors opened. Inner walkways leading from one cluster to another became part of the infrastructure of the village. Similar to Aranya, Artists' Village was imagined to accommodate differences, described as plural, and equitable, to enable a level of financial sustainability and a quality of life. In both cases, the architects used concrete to lay down the foundation, and bricks to make the homes (Figure 8.3). Beyond construction – the production of additional rooms – the design of the township would only become clear upon maximum expansion, the painting of the walls, the exterior decorative elements, and the growth of vegetation.

The concept of minimal living here consisted of the production of shelter that could grow upon the availability of finance, ultimately creating an asset and a mechanism to alleviate poverty across generations. The provision of plumbing and wash facilities as the service core of each house, as well as access to electricity, was deeply rooted in the

Figure 8.3 Urbanization and self-building, Artists' Village. Charles Correa Foundation.

developmental model of dignified housing, where the lack of wash facilities and effective sanitation systems, would be a major hurdle for communities to thrive. Given the cost implications of creating effective water and sanitation systems, both projects aligned minimal living with basic needs. These projects are, therefore, widely praised for their ingenious design.

Further to this important attention to basic humanitarian access to living spaces, the projects departed from high-rise tenement-style housing, to low-rise, human-scale, architectural formation. The material fabric of each would facilitate human-scale activity and forms of mobility over modernist town planning, which considered the motor car as a primary method for travel. These would be facilitated by narrow streets that would connect each cluster of homes, or short streets with cul-de-sacs (Figure 8.4).[19] The narrowest streets would allow access to emergency vehicles, but they would also act as outdoor spaces to the houses. Both Correa and Doshi imagined the outdoor spaces to serve as sites for domestic and commercial activity, making the village or town a flexible site. Doshi described the architectural features of each house and those of the streets to accommodate gatherings, similar to a *mohalla* (in Mughal towns) or a *pol* (in Ahmedabad). The inner courtyard and/or a terrace, would act as tranquil semi-private areas, while the doorstep, the front-facing balcony, and the external courtyard would facilitate households' interactions with communities, and host gatherings. The narrow streets would lead to wider vehicular streets, formulating private public areas of various levels. These streets would ultimately accommodate play, repose, and sociability and form the material fabric for daily interactions (Figure 8.5).

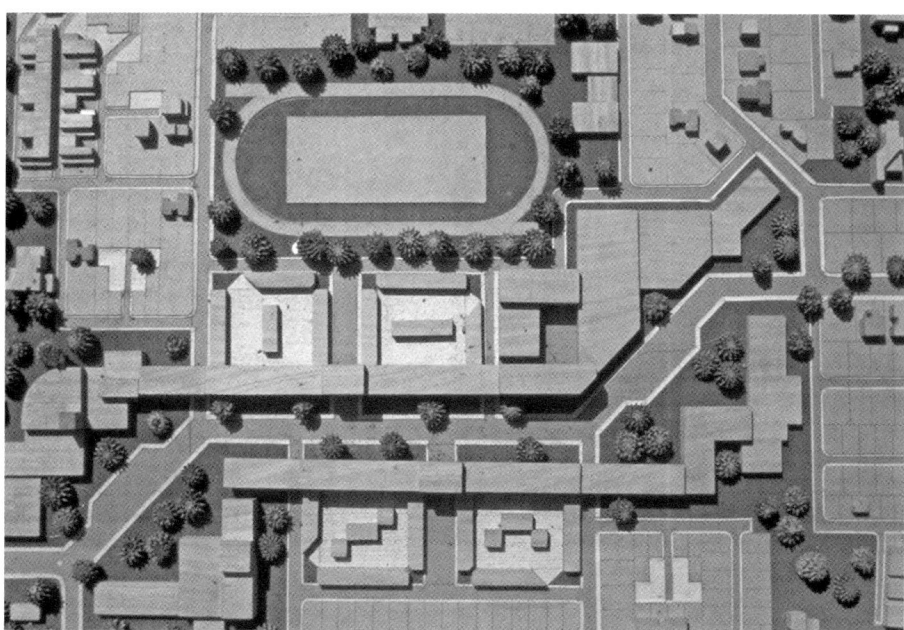

Figure 8.4 Street layouts. © Aga Khan Trust for Culture/Yatin Pandya.

The Home and the Street

Figure 8.5 Design for sociability. © Aga Khan Trust for Culture/Yatin Pandya.

Material culture and heritage

Doshi's architectural practice draws inspiration from what he describes as "traditional" ways of life, but also forms of indigenous architecture, and the material culture of everyday life in India. He argues that the success of historical forms of Indian architecture (such as temples) and towns (such as Jaipur) is in the accommodation of the ways of life of the people, and their ability to accommodate change. He compares this with another form of design, the *sari*:

> The sari that the Indian woman wears is only a six yard long piece of cloth, but when worn, looks very different on each woman despite its standardised production. This suggests that when the elements provide inherent flexibility, a personalised combination and individual identity can emerge.[20]

Like the sari, the interior was a flexible space noted Doshi: ". . . formed as compartments, the rooms get used for different things depending on the attitude of the users and the occasion. Therefore, the character of the space is only established through the functions that take place".[21] This flexible approach to design afforded change and could be manipulated by the users to embed their identities into their homes. Furthermore, the analogy of the sari applied to Indian towns and buildings locate design within the framework of heritage, where use and identity align with the material designs of each.

Like Doshi, Charles Correa has argued that in order to facilitate wellbeing and equity, Indian lifestyles and age-old values must be preserved through architecture. These values producing a blueprint for ideal forms of architecture, and specifically housing, underscore the ways in which housing for the poor had to be produced for ways of living particular to India, which meant in response to its climate, as well as cultural traditions. For both architects, outdoor spaces held the promise of an ideal home for communities, and therefore, not exclusively offered by the four walls or interior spaces. While the interior functioned as shelter, and contained aspects of daily life, outdoor spaces held currency. They enabled connection between neighbours and extended networks of the community. These spaces were where shared cultural practices and identities were expressed. What was inside the enclosed "box" and outside of it were not mutually exclusive, but connected. Correa, critical of the influence of the "West" on the built environment in India, stated:

> Overly influenced by the architects of the West, we have been caught in the intricacies of their game ... the box, and those signs/symbols which can be communicated (i.e. tattooed on) through surface-patterning. Because of... everyday experiences, people in tropical countries have developed totally different attitudes to build form. Thus while the symbol for education in North America is the little red schoolhouse, In India – as in most of Asia – it is a guru sitting under a tree.[22]

Following a period when design in India had lost its identity, for Correa, ancient practices of living had to be reflected in modern India. The materialization of these concepts emerged in the ways in which the outdoor spaces were constructed. At Artists' Village, the open-to-sky spaces were produced through the organization of the core interior structures, the washing spaces and a room, and were structured to enable expansion driven by the individual household's flexible use. By organizing space, a form of order was to be imposed, prompting ways of living that required privacy, semi-privacy, or total sociability. Today, Artists' Village has grown into a shape where these outdoor spaces almost act like living rooms for social engagement or containing domestic activities (see Figures 8.2 and 8.6).

Correa and Doshi both wrote about traditional ways of life in India, which their architecture would help preserve. Through participation in the production of their homes, these traditional ways of life would be embedded in the very formulation of the homes. They would create a kind of "plurality" but within the plot and its defined boundaries. This form of modern design – of controlling space and facilitating the production of the built environment through some levels of standardization but with individual taste and choice – formed the ultimate combination of sustaining heritage through the provision of homes. Here, the forms of heritage were multiple: everyday life rituals that were passed down the generations, mechanisms of commerce and sociability, where the vegetable and fruit cart would arrive at the doorstep, and children could play. As Doshi described his intention:

> I have also attempted to recreate the spatial experiences of traditional towns and cities while reinterpreting the traditional social values, which are still valid and cherished by inhabitants in contemporary times.[23]

Figure 8.6 Outdoor spaces for domestic activities. Photo by the author.

Beyond the functional relevance of design, where heritage marked the formulation of space, the use of terracotta exterior paint in the first few model homes in Aranya, and the elements of light and shade were aestheticized, and as Doshi said, "provided continuity and visual conformity of elements". In the model homes, which were inhabited by families, staircases, porches, balconies, and rooftop terraces create the building shapes that were repeated and standardized to produce a small cluster of homes (Figure 8.7). These elements reproduce what Doshi viewed as long-lasting examples of Indian architecture that accommodated the lives of Indians over centuries.

In both housing projects, Artists' Village as well as Aranya, the emphasis on pedestrianized streets over motorized roads to create arteries for movement, is noteworthy of living taking place at the scale of a village (Figures 8.8 and 8.9). Not only did a village produce a safe and peaceful setting, in historic and heritage terms, it would depart from another historic urban project, viewed by both Correa and Doshi as a Western experiment for urban planning in postcolonial India: Chandigarh, designed by Le Corbusier in the 1950s. In an article for the *MARG Magazine*, Le Corbusier described his research in 1950, at UNESCO's request, as seven types of roads called "The 7 V Rule"

Figure 8.7 External architectural features. © Aga Khan Trust for Culture/Yatin Pandya.

for "the man of the mechanical civilization". All seven roads involved the use of motorized vehicles or walking. He proceeded to discuss the challenge to this rule:

> But the "7 V Rule" was to be the object of an assault: the onrush of bicycles in different countries. The "V8" was subsequently created, the "V8" independent of the others. Effectively, the "two-wheels" have customs, which are antagonistic to those of the "four wheels". At Chandigarh, the "V8" were created a little later on. The matter was then honestly formulated: "The Rule of the 7 Vs . . . which are 8". This gives you something to think over, and it is not so bad![24]

Correa offered criticism of these roads in his 1987 article "Chandigarh: A View from Benares", describing these as non-contemporaneous to contemporary life in 1950s Punjab, but akin to planning from the "British Raj" with large plots of land and a public transport system unviable for "hapless Indians" who in the "middle of a scorchingly hot afternoon" have to plod along "on foot or bicycle down mercilessly long straight roads, between brick walls, to infinity".[25] Furthermore, the designs of the building, both exteriors and interiors, were impractical for everyday occupation. Rather than "old-fashioned verandas", which were useful to regulate the temperature in the houses during summer, Corbusier used sun-breakers at the Capitol, which absorbed heat and radiated it back to the building at night. He also criticized the lack of understanding of the users, referring to the cafeteria on the roof at the Secretariat building, with an exposed concrete counter,

The Home and the Street

Figure 8.8 Pedestrianized streets, Artists' Village. Photo by the author.

Figure 8.9 Pedestrianized streets, Aranya Township. © Aga Khan Trust for Culture/Yatin Pandya.

that even an animal would not eat from, and the food is kept on the floor. And finally, he described the loss of the traditional Indian relationship between the client and the architect as eroded, where the architect acts alone and does not share the same aesthetics and values as the client.

The human scale of architecture, or the village model, was seen by Correa and Doshi as meeting the needs of their clients. Artists' Village and Aranya Township would allow for communities to thrive where social networks would aid in small-scale cottage industry and entrepreneurial efforts. These ideas aligned perfectly with the Gandhian ideology of developmental self-sufficiency, and the pedestrian-friendly streets offered the space and context for public interactions.

The material culture of the homes, from the buildings and their architectural components to their outdoor spaces, experiments in materializing intangible heritage, could be argued as heritage practice. Laurajane Smith has described fishing by senior Aboriginal Waanyi women in far northern Queensland as heritage.

> Heritage wasn't only about the past – though it was that too – it also wasn't just about material things – though it was that as well – heritage was a process of engagement, an act of communication and an act of making meaning in and for the present.[26]

The processes of engagement with the past and making meaning in the present in the design process marks the two examples of housing as heritage, even though these were not formally conceived as such or defined as heritage by the architects in the early 1980s. Smith highlights that material heritage or the "physical reality" of heritage, or "any knowledge of it can only be understood within the discourse we construct about it".[27] Correa and Doshi were instrumental in establishing a discourse around housing and urban planning relevant for postcolonial India. In examining histories of housing and domestic living in historic towns and villages, they engaged with tangible and intangible heritages, as well as the identities of the residents. The daily rituals of commuting to school or work, leaving the bicycle at a specific place, practices of resting outdoors in the evening, and hanging out washing to dry, the architects produced core spaces from which these activities could lead to the configuration of space with the relevant material objects that would facilitate this living.

While the tangible and the intangible are useful terms to understand process, the binary opposition of these concepts, argues Smith, is unhelpful as it isolates a formalized notion of the physical object of heritage. If all heritage is understood as intangible, despite the construction and existence of a physical space and place, the focus on the affect of heritage – here, the architects' engagement with these forms of living – means that the physical can be seen as part of the embodiment of thought, emotion, and cultural practice. Smith engages with heritage sites in her writing, but also addresses the various actors in the process of heritage conservation. This includes architects. By conserving architecture, through preservation of forms, rebuilt or maintained, architects are not simply acting as custodians of history, they monumentalize the historic buildings, and construct meanings that have cultural resonance. Both Charles Correa and Balkrishna Doshi were engaged in understanding the architectural histories of India. They participated in an exhibition titled *Vistara: The Architecture of India* in 1986 in Bombay as part of the Festival of India celebrations. Correa, as the chief organizer of the exhibition, along with a team of designers and researchers, constructed a timeline of the architecture of India, focusing on classical and ancient forms of architecture such as temples, and the historic urban sites of Jaisalmer, Sanchi, and Nalanda, as well as minimal forms of housing, sheltering indigenous life in villages, or the lives of the poor living in self-constructed homes in cities.[28] Based on photographs, objects, and installations, the exhibition traced architectural heritage that would help understand contemporary architecture.

Correa and Doshi were also attentive to vernacular forms of making homes produced locally using local materials, with their designs responding to the local climate. They have both argued in their writing that local conditions (climate, as well occupations, social groupings, and social interactions) were responsive to the designs of the built environment and vice versa. Doshi writes about Jaipur (founded in the eighteenth century) and Ahmedabad (built in the fifteenth century), two cities that have accommodated modern life owing to their flexibility:

> Jaipur combines the formal peripheral streets carrying all of the infrastructure and fast moving traffic along with the village like inner fabric with a variety of clusters, courtyards and meandering pedestrian paths. Streets of Ahmedabad are similar except the clusters. They have porches to enter private streets. The quietness and leisure are the same.
>
> The spaces in traditional buildings incorporate flexibility.
>
> All the activities including the open to sky sleeping take place on these streets where house becomes the true extension of the street. The streets get further animated with interactive building elements such as porches, ottas, verandas, courts, jharokhas, balconies and terraces. Reintroduction of these elements has helped modulate adverse climate conditions while becoming comfortable spaces.[29]

Through this process of identifying the "things and places that can be given meaning and value as 'heritage', [and] reflecting contemporary cultural and social values, debates and aspirations",[30] the work of the architect forms part of heritage discourse. Correa and Doshi reconstructed and negotiated identities and practices – social, domestic, and architectural – in their present. They studied, interpreted, and conserved these in ways that embodied "acts of remembrance and commemoration while negotiating and constructing a sense of place, belonging and understanding in the present". The designs of Artists' Village and Aranya Township were produced through a reworking of the past in the architects' present.

Two objects represented domestic life in the new housing projects in the photographs produced after the construction of the homes: the bicycle and water container. The bicycle featured in almost every Aranya photograph as a readily available mode of transport for the residents. As a minimal form of transport, it indicates the simplicity of village or town life, but also the residents' financial status as earners of incomes, with a distinct need to travel for activities. It indicates mobility, but at a human scale. The proportion of the bicycles makes apparent the spatial characteristics, such as the scale and use of the streets or buildings. Their movement on the roads, their storage in a niche within the building, or ready availability outside the home, all expose the material object's possibilities for movement, and therefore potential for local employment or other social uses. The bicycle becomes a sign of empowerment.

In contrast, the water containers carried by the women on their heads indicated yet another domestic object, a form of design that was the source of all life and activities in the village (Figure 8.10). Water containers have featured in art and design extensively in India. The *lota* as an ideal form of design proposed by Charles and Ray Eames in India, which became the foundation of the India Report of 1954 is one example.[31] In *Vistara: The Architecture of India* exhibition, a photograph of women carrying water containers on their heads outside a sixteenth-century Kund-vav, a subterranean step well, is accompanied by a caption that describes the process of filling water and keeping it on the landing of the step well from where it is transferred to their heads.[32] Kangra paintings of the mid-nineteenth century featuring Lord Krisha and his *gopis* regularly depicted scenes where the *gopis* carried water containers on their heads when they chanced upon Krishna.[33] Artists' Village was designed to provide running water to all residents, making this representation of the women a visual sign of domestic activity, rural practices, and

Figure 8.10 Women carrying water containers. Charles Correa Foundation.

Indian myths, rather than an actuality. The water containers being transported to the houses on the heads of the women showed the purpose and scale of the streets. It accommodated the age-old activity of collecting water and clearly referenced cultural associations.

Both the bicycle and the water container represented a complex set of meanings that are culturally specific but also easily readable and distinctly Indian. Amid the houses and the streets, with the *gulmohar* trees and the vibrancy of the bright colours on the exteriors of the houses, the bicycle and the water container showed human activities that were positive and empowering – the availability of water and transport, two elements that would sustain the communities.'

Conclusion

This chapter has examined the ways in which minimal living was organized by the architects through active engagement with developmental ideas as well as heritage. The World Bank-promoted Sites and Services program and the state-led drive towards housing for poverty alleviation as outlined in the Sixth Five Year Plan,[34] proposed a need for self-sustainability through availability of local resources, including building materials. The localized element of the brief and a requirement to supply basic shelter at low cost offered design possibilities to Correa and Doshi that would prompt a turning to existing examples, both historic and contemporary, of functional and long-lasting design.

In this context, the architects argued that people in India had already been participating in home-making, either through close collaborative working with architects (as suggested by Correa) or as a result of the need for shelter arising from precarity. Their perspective that more needed to be done to provide improved living conditions for the majority (evident in their professional practice) could be attributed to the wider frameworks of debate of the time, as well as their professional responsibility. As architects concerned with urban planning, they believed that urban squatter communities who migrated from rural areas could be better housed through their own participation deploying existing skills and materials found within the local areas. The paternalism discussed by Robert Chambers is certainly an aspect that prompts questioning around the participatory nature of development. Where communities' priorities were drawn from developmental reports and set strategies, as well as inspired by tangible and intangible heritages, the work of these architects clearly indicate the priorities of the projects as multi-directional. For them, improvement in modern housing could happen if the basic needs of the people were served, such as access to running water and electricity, as well as to local employment opportunities. Water from the communal well or the communal water tap would be replaced by individualized access in the housing projects, where plots for homes offered people access to land and future houses in the cities. This would help create equity and growth, a fundamental shift from austere modern housing to the flexible minimal.

While the flexible minimal interior in these cases involved spaces created through basic structures with architectural features such as walls, windows, and a roof, the exterior of these buildings, their materials and colour, as well as the material culture of daily life outdoors, were the indicators of modern living. These were represented in the photographs produced for housing commissioners and professional dissemination. The street with its intermediaries of the veranda and the courtyard would become a crucial extension of the interior as the semi-private/semi-public space. This became the space for empowerment supporting authentic ways of living. After this historical moment, social housing and a concern for producing housing for the poor that was empowering and dignified through carefully considered design, started to wane, replaced by wholesale slum rehabilitation plans in cities such as Mumbai, that were disconnected from the realities of the communities' ways of life.

Notes

1. Babar Khan Mumtaz, "The Housing Question", in Hasan-Uddin Khan (ed.), *Mimar 28: Architecture in Development* (Concept Media, 1988), 18.
2. Megha Rajguru, "Visions of Modernity: Architectural Vignettes and Modern Living in India 1975–1990", *Journal of Design History* 31, no 1 (February 2017): 83–101.
3. Andrea Testi, "Exploring the Relation Between 'Sites and Services' Projects and Urban Adaptability: A Case Study of Charkop (Mumbai)", *Habitat International* 139 (2023): 102901; Ayona Datta, "Architecture of Low-Income Widow Housing: 'Spatial Opportunities' in Madipur, West Delhi", *Cultural Geographies* 15, no. 2 (2008): 231–53.
4. Farhan Karim, Farhan. *Of Greater Dignity than Riches: Austerity & Housing Design in India* (University of Pittsburgh Press, 2019).
5. Grace Lees-Maffei and Rebecca Houze, *Design and Heritage: The Construction of Identity and Belonging* (Routledge, 2022), 7.
6. Mary C. Comerio, "Community Design: Idealism and Entrepreneurship", *Journal of Architectural and Planning Research* 1, no. 4 (1984): 227–43.
7. Robert Chambers, *Putting the Last First* (Routledge, 1983).
8. See Indira Gandhi Memorial Trust, "The Garibi Hatao Programme".
9. Nilakantha Rath, "'Garibi Hatao': Can IRDP Do It?", *Economic and Political Weekly* 20, no. 6 (1985): 238–46.
10. M.L. Dantwala, "'Garibi Hatao': Strategy Options", *Economic and Political Weekly* 20, no. 11 (1985): 475–76.
11. Arturo Escobar, *Encountering Development: The Making and Unmaking of the Third World* (Princeton University Press, 2011), 94–97.
12. World Bank, "Studies in Urban Development, Water Supply and Urban Development Research Material – Indian Urban Development – Koichi Mera – Vibhooti Shukla – Edwin S. Mill – Charles Becker – December 1985 – December 1986, 30253682", WB IBRD/IDA URB-563S, 02/01/1981-12/31/1986, World Bank Group Archives, Washington DC.
13. World Bank, "Sites and Services Projects: A World Bank Paper", Working Paper 77777, 1974/04/01, World Bank Group, Washington, DC.
14. World Bank, "Sites and Services Projects", 11.
15. World Bank, "Sites and Services Projects", 12.

16. Balkrishna V. Doshi, "Aranya Township", in Hasan-Uddin Khan (ed.), *Mimar 28: Architecture in Development* (Concept Media, 1988).
17. Aga Khan Development Network. "Aranya Community Housing".
18. Hasan-Uddin Khan, "Belapur Housing", in *Charles Correa* (Concept Media, 1987), 70–75.
19. Balkrishna V. Doshi, *"Living Environments": Housing Designs by Balkrishna Doshi* (Vastu Shilpa Foundation, 1991).
20. Doshi, *"Living Environments"*.
21. Doshi, *"Living Environments"*.
22. Charles Correa, , "The Public, the Private, and the Sacred", *Daedalus* 118, no. 4 (Fall 1989), 95.
23. Doshi, *"Living Environments"*.
24. Le Corbusier, "The Master Plan", *Marg: A Magazine of the Arts* 15, no. 1 (December 1961), 5–19.
25. Charles Correa, "Chandigarh: The View from Benares", *Architecture + Design* 3, no. 6 (September 1987), 74.
26. Laurajane Smith, *Uses of Heritage* (Routledge, 2006), 1.
27. Smith, *Uses of Heritage*, 54.
28. Carmen Kagal (ed.), *Vistara: The Architecture of India* (Tata Press, 1986).
29. Doshi, *"Living Environments"*.
30. Smith, *Uses of Heritage*, 4.
31. Saloni Mathur, "Charles and Ray Eames in India", *Art Journal* 70, no. 1 (March 2011), 34-53.
32. Kagal (ed.), *Vistara*, 82.
33. See the image in the Victoria & Albert Museum collection: *Radha and Krishna*, 1847. https://collections.vam.ac.uk/item/O68934/radha-and-krishna-painting-inknown/ (accessed 30 April 2024).
34. Government of India. "Five Year Plans", Planning Commission.

References

Aga Khan Development Network. "Aranya Community Housing". https://the.akdn/en/how-we-work/our-agencies/aga-khan-trust-culture/akaa/aranya-community-housing (accessed 30 April 2024).
Chambers Robert. *Putting the Last First*, Routledge, 1983.
Comerio, Mary C. "Community Design: Idealism and Entrepreneurship", *Journal of Architectural and Planning Research* 1, no. 4 (1984): 227–43.
Correa, Charles. "Chandigarh: The View from Benares", *Architecture + Design* 3, no. 6 (September 1987): 73–75.
Correa, Charles. "The Public, the Private, and the Sacred", *Daedalus* 118, no. 4 (Fall 1989): 95.
Dantwala, M.L. "'Garibi Hatao': Strategy Options", *Economic and Political Weekly* 20, no. 11 (1985): 475–76.
Datta, Ayona. "Architecture of Low-Income Widow Housing: 'Spatial Opportunities' in Madipur, West Delhi", *Cultural Geographies* 15, no. 2 (2008): 231–53.
Doshi, Balkrishna V. "Aranya Township", in Hasan-Uddin Khan (ed.), *Mimar 28: Architecture in Development*, Concept Media, 1988.
Doshi, Balkrishna V. *"Living Environments": Housing Designs by Balkrishna Doshi*, Vastu Shilpa Foundation, 1991.

Escobar, Arturo. *Encountering Development: The Making and Unmaking of the Third World*, Princeton University Press, 2011.
Government of India. "Five Year Plans", Planning Commission. https://www.india.gov.in/five-year-plans-planning-commission (accessed 30 April 2024).
Indira Gandhi Memorial Trust. "The Garibi Hatao Programme". https://indiragandhi.in/en/timeline/index/garibi-hatao-timeline (accessed 30 April 2024).
Kagal, Carmen (ed.). *Vistara: The Architecture of India*, Tata Press, 1986.
Karim, Farhan. *Of Greater Dignity than Riches: Austerity & Housing Design in India*, University of Pittsburgh Press, 2019.
Khan, Hasan-Uddin. "Belapur Housing", in *Charles Correa*, Concept Media, 1987.
Le Corbusier, "The Master Plan", *Marg: A Magazine of the Arts* 15, no. 1 (December 1961), 5–19.
Lees-Maffei, Grace and Rebecca Houze. *Design and Heritage: The Construction of Identity and Belonging*, Routledge, 2022.
Mathur, Saloni. "Charles and Ray Eames in India", *Art Journal* 70, no. 1 (March 2011): 34–53.
Mumtaz, Babar Khan. "The Housing Question", in Hasan-Uddin Khan (ed.), *Mimar 28: Architecture in Development*, Concept Media, 1988.
Rajguru, Megha. "Visions of Modernity: Architectural Vignettes and Modern Living in India 1975–1990", *Journal of Design History* 31, no 1 (February 2017): 83–101.
Rath, Nilakantha. "'Garibi Hatao': Can IRDP Do It?", *Economic and Political Weekly* 20, no. 6 (1985): 238–46.
Smith, Laurajane. *Uses of Heritage*, Routledge, 2006.
Testi, Andrea. "Exploring the Relation Between 'Sites and Services' Projects and Urban Adaptability: A Case Study of Charkop (Mumbai)", *Habitat International* 139 (2023): 102901. https://doi.org/10.1016/j.habitatint.2023.102901.
World Bank. "Sites and Services Projects: A World Bank Paper", Working Paper 77777, 1974/04/01, World Bank Group, Washington, DC. http://documents.worldbank.org/curated/en/148991468330876502/Sites-and-services-projects-a-World-Bank-paper (accessed 30 April 2024).
World Bank. "Studies in Urban Development, Water Supply and Urban Development Research Material – Indian Urban Development – Koichi Mera – Vibhooti Shukla – Edwin S. Mill – Charles Becker – December 1985 – December 1986, 30253682", WB IBRD/IDA URB-563S, 02/01/1981-12/31/1986, World Bank Group Archives, Washington DC.

CHAPTER 9
THE WEFT OF NATIONS: CIRCULATING IMAGERY OF CHINESE TEXTILE TECHNOLOGY ON THE EVE OF BRITAIN'S INDUSTRIAL REVOLUTION[1]

Roslyn Lee Hammers

Historians have defined the Industrial Revolution as a period, roughly from the 1750s to the 1850s, in which mechanized manufacturing processes developed into capitalist modes of commodity production.[2] They have investigated diverse aspects of the developments of this era as it intersects with the formation of discourses on science, technology, and nationalism in national and global arenas.[3] This chapter supplements research by introducing aspects of material culture through images in publications. By examining the representations of Chinese textile technology approximately a century earlier than were published in Britain, I offer a concise history of Chinese technological imagery to explore its roles in the dissemination of technological knowledge in Britain. In addition, this chapter situates printed representations of the Chinese fabric workers in their historical context by analysing depictions of them in earlier publications in Europe and in China. Through this, it evaluates the spectrum of associations they brought to understandings of Chinese technology. In reclaiming the transfer of information from sources external to Britain, it challenges the overarching nationalist narratives of the Industrial Revolution. In this chapter, China is a heuristic term that refers to the history of various dynasties and polities, encompassing shifts in identities and territory in areas that may now comprise the People's Republic of China. It was in use during the eighteenth century and later, although at times authors may have used the term Tartar or Tartary to indicate the Manchu identity of the Qing (1644–1911) court.

Publishers incorporated imagery from the *Pictures of Tilling and Weaving* (*Gengzhi Tu* 耕織圖), a type of imagery that was initiated in the twelfth century in Song-dynasty China (960–1279) to represent Chinese workers in the sixteenth and seventeenth centuries. Imagery from this genre depicted women producing silk fabric and men cultivating rice and was combined with poetry that gave voice to the plight of the farming families.[4] The production of silk fabric was represented in a sequence of twenty-four steps, starting with the hatching of silkworms and concluding with the storage of silk fabric. In China, the *Pictures of Tilling and Weaving* inspired later officials or scholars of agronomy to design agricultural treatises which drew upon their representations while expanding the range of labour and commodities addressed in text and image. One such text, the magisterial *Nong Zheng Quan Shu* 農政全書 (*Complete Book of the Administration of Agriculture* by Xu Guangqi 徐光 (1562–1633) published posthumously in 1639 was available in France and presumably consulted by book publishers. It was an invaluable source for the depictions of Chinese farming families working with various kinds of textile equipment. French and then British representations of weavers, based on these Chinese prints, were situated with commentary designed to encourage the readers to harness the technologically superior techniques of China. A consideration of the circulation of the imagery associated with Chinese textile production in Britain enables a narrative which posits that the British Industrial Revolution was developed, in part, as a response to representations of Chinese technology.

Depicting Chinese weavers at work in Europe and in Britain

Some of the earliest representations of Chinese textile labourers in Europe, women textile artisans who work with silk, appear in the insignia marginalia found on maps of China in books. For example, in Jesuit Martino Martini's (1614–1661) *Novus atlas Sinensis* (*New Atlas of China*), a volume dating to 1655 published in Amsterdam by Joan Blaeu (1596–1673), women reel silk from cocoons around the label of the map for Zhejiang (transcribed as Chekiang), a province known in China for its production of excellent silk fabric (Figure 9.1).

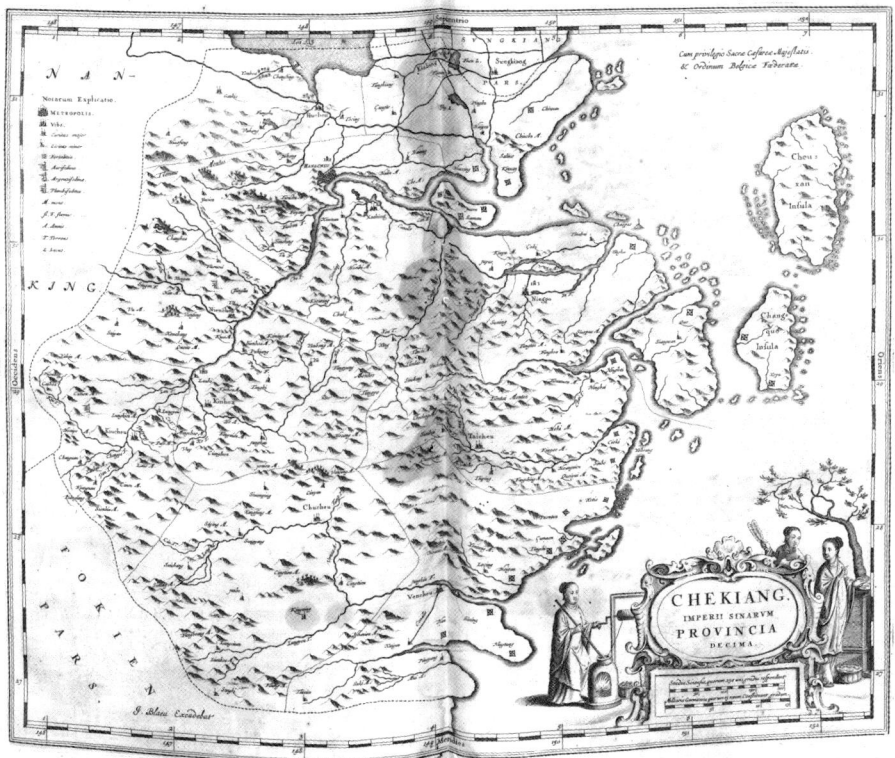

Figure 9.1 "Chekiang" (Zhejiang). From *Novus atlas Sinensis* (New Atlas of China), 1655, engraving. Courtesy of Special Collections, The University Libraries of Hong Kong.

Figure 9.2 Detail from "Chekiang" (Zhejiang). From *Novus atlas Sinensis* (New Atlas of China), 1655, engraving. Courtesy of Special Collections, The University Libraries of Hong Kong.

The woman to the viewer's left boils silk cocoons in a pan over a fire and turns a crank to wind the threads onto a swift, a device with four rails or more that form a large open spool. In the Zhejiang print, the swift is positioned horizontally (Figure 9.2). The central figure holds two leaves to fan the fire while the woman to the right has her hand placed on a tray of cocoons with another container of them at her feet. When China as a geographical entity was beginning to be defined in maps, aspects of the commodities that China produced were included.

Eighteenth-century commentators attest to the prized status Chinese silk enjoyed in Europe, and with its visibility on the map, it served to remind readers of the material wealth and technological sophistication of the country. The production of silk fabric required specialized techniques that China had brought to near perfection through its many centuries of manufacturing experience. The number of scenes in the *Pictures of Tilling and Weaving* indicates that the production of silk fabric requires many procedures, including activities such as the raising of silkworms, harvesting of cocoons, reeling of silk filaments from the cocoons, the arranging of the warp threads, the preparing of the loom, to weaving fabric.[5]

By the eighteenth century, Jean-Batiste du Halde (1674–1743), a Jesuit, discussed silk manufacturing in an edited compilation of letters on the subject of China, mostly written by Jesuits, with other writings, and included images in a four-tome publication. Entitled *Description géographique, historique, chronologique, politique, et physique de l'empire de la Chine et de la Tartarie chinoise, enrichie des cartes générales et particulieres de ces pays, de la carte générale et des cartes particulieres du Thibet, & de la Corée; & ornée d'un grand nombre de figures & de vignettes gravées en tailledouce* (hereafter *Description géographique*), the books were published in France starting in 1736. The tomes were translated and reproduced in English as a serial starting in 1738 and ending in 1742 as *A Description of the Empire of China and Chinese-Tartary: together with the kingdoms of Korea, and Tibet: Containing the geography and history (natural as well as civil) of those countries. Enrich'd with general and particular maps, and adorned with a great number of cuts* (hereafter *Description of the Empire of China*) by Edward Cave (1691–1754). As the titles suggest, these volumes served as an encyclopaedic repository of knowledge on China as described by Jesuits who, unlike du Halde and Cave, worked and served the mission in China.

A plate of imagery by the engraver Jean-Baptiste Haussard (1679/80–1752) depicting Chinese procedures for fabric production is inserted in the French 1935 edition (Figure 9.3).[6] In the 1738 English version, a similar plate engraved by Isaac Basire (1704–1768) represents the same procedures and equipment, with minor amendments (Figure 9.4).[7] Focusing on the English edition, its label reads in part as "This Plate representing the Silk Manufacture is gratefully inscribed to Sr. Nathanael Curzon" (hereafter "Silk Manufacture"). Eleven activities are depicted, enclosed within a rectangular frame aligned in four horizontal registers. The scenes are thrown together randomly with little

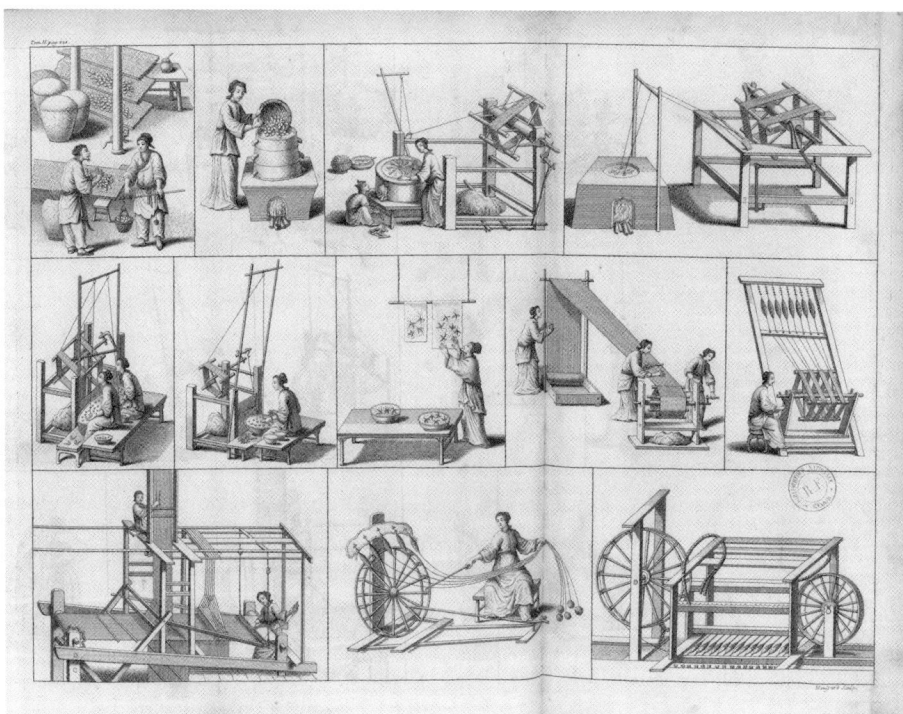

Figure 9.3 Plate of "Textile Manufacturing". From *Description géographique*, 1736, engraving by Jean-Baptiste Haussard (1679/80–1752), 1736. Courtesy of the Bibliothèque nationale de France, Paris.

The Weft of Nations

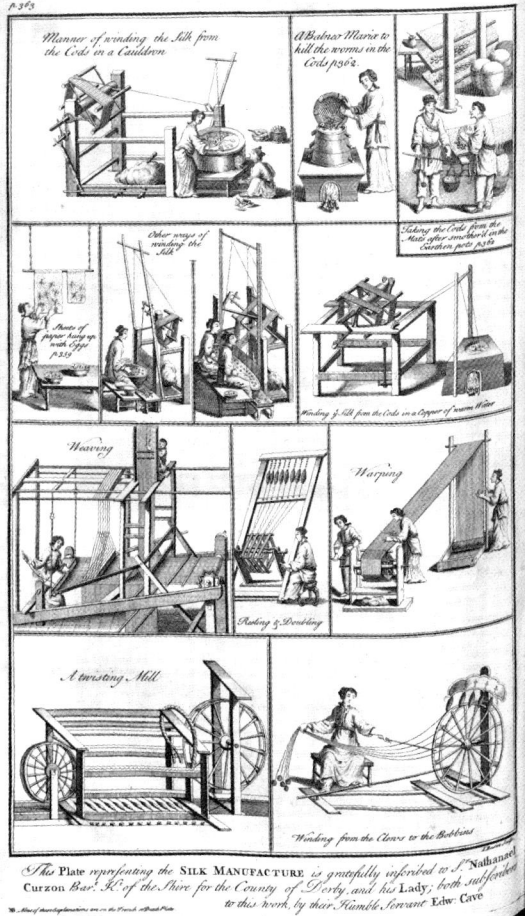

Figure 9.4 Plate of "Silk Manufacture". From *Description of the Empire of China*, 1738, engraving by Isaac Basire (1704–1768). Courtesy of Special Collections, The University Libraries of Hong Kong.

effort to narrate a sequence of the procedures. Moreover, readers might assume that the imagery, as labelled, represents processes specific to the manufacturing of silk, but if we consider the commentary associated with the imagery in its original context, we can recognize that this is not the case. Some of the tasks or equipment depicted are devoted to the production of hemp or cotton. Chinese agronomists did not regard the use of some of the devices represented in the plate as appropriate for silk.

A study of the page helps take an account of the scenes so that we can identify the technology that was represented in the *Description of the Empire of China*. Starting at the top left in the first register, the steps are labelled "Manner of winding the Silk from the Cods in a Cauldron", "A Balneo Mariae to kill the worms in the Cods", and "Taking the Cods from the Mats after smother'd in the Earthen pots". Cods here refer to the cocoons the maturing silkworms spun as they prepared to metamorphosize into adult moths. In this plate, we see depictions of the specific methods Chinese used for destroying the pupa or chrysalids before reeling the silk from cocoons. This allowed for a longer period to reel the silk off the cocoons. With the pupa dead, the workers did not have to worry that the moths would emerge from the cocoon and shred the silk into bits. The chrysalids were either steamed to death in a double boiler or smothered in large urns sealed with mud.

The scenes of the next register from left to right are entitled, "Sheets of paper hung up with Eggs", "Other ways of winding the Silk", and "Winding of Silk from the Cods in a Copper of warm Water". Every year, farmers reserved some of the pupa to reach adulthood and emerge from the cocoons in order to procreate and generate the eggs for the next year's harvest. Moths laid eggs on the paper that would later hatch into silkworms. Cocoons were boiled in water to dissolve the sericin or glue that enabled the cocoons to form. The ends of the filaments were then drawn up into a swift and wound onto bobbins.

The third row consists of the scenes "Weaving", " Reeling & Doubling", and "Warping". These procedures are undertaken in the manufacturing of fabric. In traditional weaving practices, parallel strands of thread, known as the warp, are attached to the loom. They provide the structure into which the weft threads are woven. Typically, the weft threads are doubled, that is, two strands of thread are twisted together to make thicker yarns. Once spun, they are the strands of material that the weavers pass into the warp to produce fabric. The lowest register depicts "A twisting Mill" and "Winding from the Clews to the Bobbins". These two procedures are not used in the production of silk fabric. The mill was a device used to process hemp fibre, and the winding of skeins or clews was a technique for the production of cotton, rather than silk.

Historian Isabelle Landry-Deron has identified the source of the textile imagery included in the French publication and reiterated in the English volume. By comparing the European scenes with those located in Chinese publications of the seventeenth century, she has determined that du Halde's iconography is derived from original prints produced in China from Xu Guangqi's *Complete Book of the Administration of Agriculture*.[8] Du Halde himself comments on the origins of his manuscript's material. In the 1738 English volume, the text states,

> An author of reputation, who lived in a Province abounding with Silk Manufactories, under the Dynasty of the Ming, wrote a pretty large Treatise on this Subject. Father Dentrecolles sent me an Extract of it, from which I have taken all the Directions I thought necessary for the managing, with success, so fine a Manufacture; concluding, that the new Lights given by the Chinese on so profitable a Work, that employs so many Ships, will not be altogether useless.[9]

Landry-Deron has posited that Father François Xavier d'Entrecolles (1664–1741), a Jesuit in China, was referring to Xu Guangqi as the reputed author during the Ming dynasty (1368–1644). Xu Guangqi had converted to Christianity and was in close contact with other Jesuits in China, including Matteo Ricci (1552–1610), the renowned Italian missionary. The *Complete Book of the Administration of Agriculture* was in Paris before 1716 in the library of Arcadio Huang (1679–1716), a convert to Christianity whose Chinese name was Huang

Jialüe 黄嘉略. The Society of Foreign Missions brought Huang to Paris to teach the Chinese language.[10] As Landry-Deron has reasoned, in all likelihood du Halde frequented Huang's library to conduct research for *Description géographique*.

Chinese textile labour in mid-eighteenth-century Europe

The representations in the publications were crucial to convey knowledge about the superior technology used in Chinese fabric production. Du Halde explicitly mentions the merit of the representations of Chinese textile technology and labour when explaining his motivations to include imagery. It was not simply to illustrate the text. In the English version, the passage reads,

> The Chinese have very simple Instruments for this [textile] Work: But 'tis hardly possible from Words to form a just Idea of Things, which the Eye is the proper Judge of. The Figures on the opposite Plate represent the various utensils that serve in managing the Worms, with the several Tools and Instruments by which they work, to such Perfection, those fine and beautiful Pieces they send us.[11]

Du Halde hoped that careful scrutiny of the machines might enable the devices to be reconstructed in France. In my reading of the passage, he admires the ability of humble tools to produce the excellent quality of silk that Europe imports. In contrast, Michael Adas, historian of science and technology, has described du Halde as ambivalent in his appraisal of Chinese technology: the Jesuit appreciated the skills the Chinese brought to the manufacturing of porcelain and silk, but he disparaged their tools as "simple".[12] While the tools are described as simple, the task of representing them, as the earlier quote indicates, was to enable emulation to benefit the domestic European economy.

For du Halde, the "Eye" was privileged over "Words", although the images, especially that of "A twisting Mill", greatly dimmed the "new Lights given by the Chinese" that were to elucidate the superiority of their technology. At the time of the publication of the 1736 *Description géographique*, print media in Europe and China did not wholly embrace precision and accuracy in the representation of machines. As historian John R. Pannabecker has argued, the *Encyclopédie* with eminent philosopher Denis Diderot (1713–1784) as its editor that was inaugurated in 1750 instigated a great paradigmatic shift in understanding the roles of systematic writing and pictorial representation of technology to deliver insight into the knowledge artisans possessed in their minds.[13] The imagery in du Halde's book (as well as that of Xu Guangqi) does not provide the necessary visual information to reproduce a functioning spinning wheel.

A comparison of the device called "A twisting Mill" in du Halde's *Description of the Empire of China* (Figure 9.5) with its parallel, the "Fang che" 紡車 (Spinning wheel) in Xu Guangqi's *Complete Book of the Administration of Agriculture* (Figure 9.6) is particularly illuminating for a discussion of cotton production and spinning yarn in England. The similarities these two images share may serve as representatives to

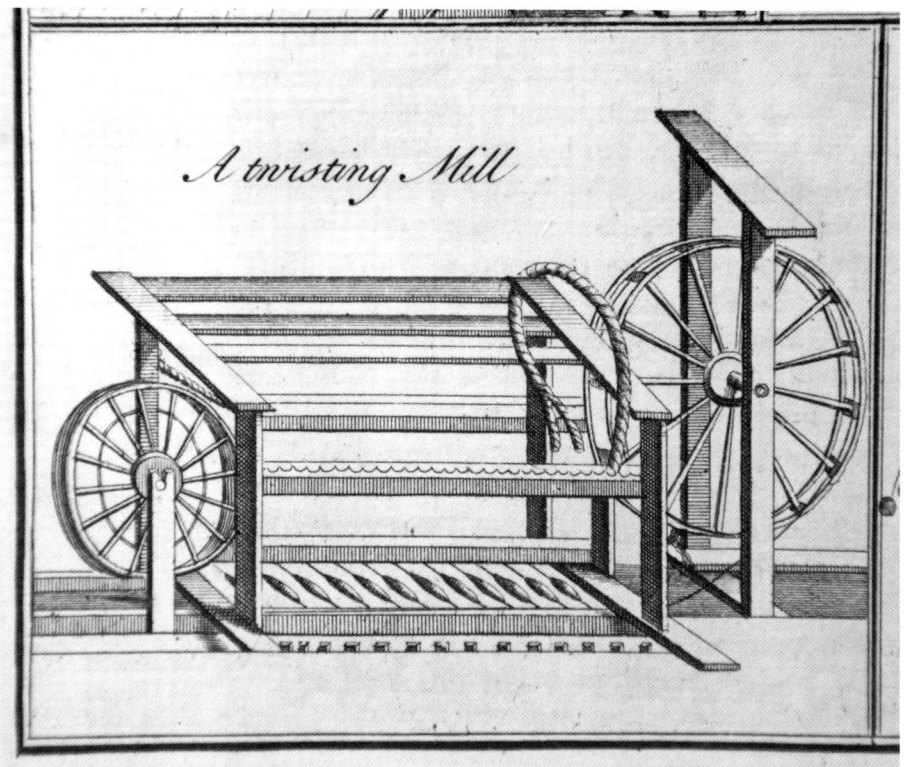

Figure 9.5 "A Twisting Mill", from the plate "Silk Manufacture". From *Description of the Empire of China*, 1738, engraving by Isaac Basire (1704–1768). Courtesy of Special Collections, The University Libraries of Hong Kong.

demonstrate the close resemblance that all the depictions on the page "Silk Manufacture" have with Xu Guangqi's book. The British image is modified by European visual modes of the engravers. "A twisting Mill" is shown in an axonometric view, without the use of linear perspective. It has modest shading to give it an illusion of three-dimensionality.

Xu Guangqi, however, was not the first Chinese agronomist to represent textile equipment in technological treatises. He drew upon earlier representations including the *Book of Agriculture* (*Nong Shu* 農書) by Wang Zhen 王禎 (fl. 1290–1333) that has a preface dated to 1313. Xu Guangqi quoted material from the *Book of Agriculture* and recreated imagery from it. The fourteenth-century edition is lost, but an edition dated to 1530 includes an image entitled "Da fang che" 大紡車 (Large spinning wheel) (Figure 9.7). As historian of science and technology Francesca Bray has pointed out, in China, contemporaneous readers of technological books, including Wang Zhen's *Book of Agriculture*, were directed to show the imagery to carpenters who would understand how to create the objects.[14] During the eighteenth century, the desire for imagery to display accurate information was developing, yet the Chinese images and the European versions are not sufficiently clear to recreate "A twisting Mill"/"Large spinning wheel".[15]

The Weft of Nations

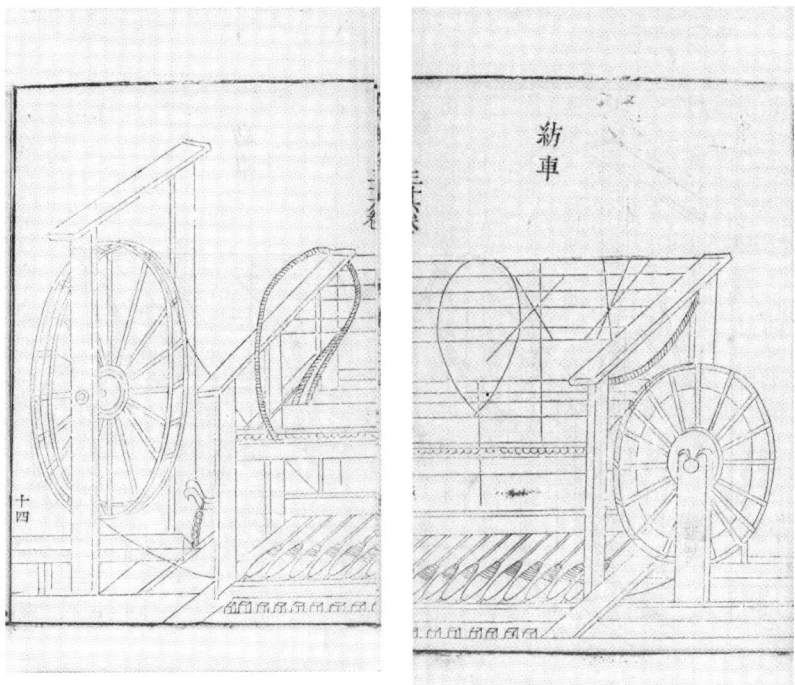

Figure 9.6 "Fang che" (Spinning wheel). From the *Complete Book of the Administration of Agriculture*, 1636. Courtesy of Harvard University Library, Cambridge, MA.

Figure 9.7 "Da fang che" (Large spinning wheel). From the *Book of Agriculture*, 1530. Courtesy of Harvard University Library, Cambridge, MA.

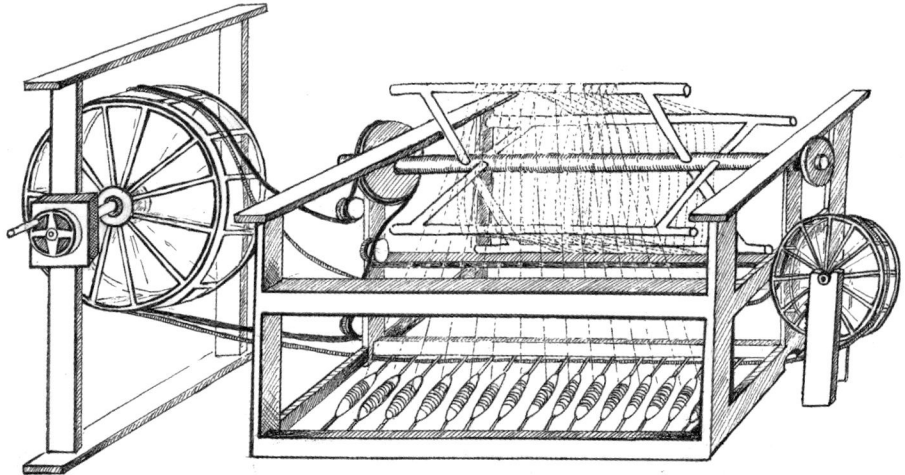

Figure 9.8 Model reconstruction of "Da fang che" (Large spinning wheel). Courtesy of Nicole Fung.

As reconstructed from a modern model (Figure 9.8), the central part of the spinning apparatus includes a large swift, the rotating spool, a structure included in the silk processing scene of the Zhejiang map (Figure 9.2).[16]

Chinese textile workers of the eighteenth century (and earlier) lined up skeins of hemp thread on the "spinning wheels" or "twisting mills". Threads were then spun tightly before they were gathered on the bobbins below. The swift structure is represented by the crossed x-shaped lines that seem to be suspended in the device in both Chinese prints, but do not appear in "A twisting Mill" from the plate "Silk Manufacture". The belt that rotates the mechanism is simply drawn as the loop of rope that encircles the swift (the device upon which the yarn is reeled) and its supporting beams. The images provide further evidence of Bray's observation that accuracy was not a motivating principle for the rendering of technological equipment as the readers were expected to consult with knowledgeable artisans who would understand the generalized representation.

Spinning machines in Britain in the mid- to late eighteenth century and Chinese technology

In 1738, when the English volume of *Description of the Empire of China* was produced, knowledge of the technology for "A twisting Mill" or a machine to effectively spin multiple threads with numerous spindles was on the cusp of discovery in Britain, but it had not yet achieved efficient application, according to Edward Baines (1800–1890), one of the first historians who authored an account of cotton manufacturing in Britain.[17] Writing in 1835, the author addresses the early history of cotton and its introduction to

England to arrive at the "era of invention" that was kicked off in 1738 with John Kay's (1704–1779) creation of the flying shuttle, a device that enabled thread to move swiftly across the length of the fabric when weaving that allowed for the reduction of the number of weavers attending a loom. This was followed in approximately 1740 with John Wyatt's (1700–1766) and the Frenchman Lewis Paul's (d. 1759) efforts to create a machine to spin thread into yarn.[18]

According to Baine's research, it was only in 1769 that Sir Richard Arkwright (1732–1792) was able to patent a practical "Spinning Machine", and while James Hargreave may have invented his "spinning jenny", an apparatus that spun eleven strands of thread in around 1764, he waited until 1770 to apply for a patent.[19] Arkwright, unlike Hargreave, became fabulously wealthy for his improvements of a number of pieces of textile machinery. The equipment he developed, including carding machines and water-frames – the latter a device that employed water to spin thread – could not be incorporated into cottage settings. As a consequence, Arkwright is credited with the formation of the factory system in Britain,[20] a development crucial for the emergence of the Industrial Revolution.

This historical context suggests strongly that the representation of "A twisting Mill" of 1738 (or in the French edition of 1736) may have provided visual clues for the technological developments in British textile production. Consumers of the imagery in du Halde's publication in England were interested in the representation of textile machinery. Returning to the plate "Silk Manufacture" in the English 1738 edition, the printer Edward Cave provided a label that connects the representation of textile technology to wealthy members of British society. The complete caption for the plate "Silk Manufacture" reads,

> This Plate representing the Silk Manufacture is gratefully inscribed to Sr. [Sir] Nathanael Curzon Bart. [Baronet]. Kt [Knight] of the Shire for the County of Derby, and his Lady; both subscribers to this work, by their Humble Servant Edw: [Edward] Cave.[21]

Sir Baronet and Knight Curzon (1726–1804) and his Lady (Mary Assheton, 1695–1776) patronized one engraving in Cave's publications on China. This flowery text uses the largest size font in the entire publication for a label. This is the only plate in the *Description of the Empire of China* in which Edward Cave signed off as "Humble Servant". It appears that Cave sought to flatter Curzon with his inscription. For other plates he pens shorter and less prominently placed dedicatory inscriptions referring to himself as "the editor" with his name added at times or not. Derbyshire, the county that Curzon represented as a Member of Parliament, is the location of the first silk mill in England. The mill doubled silk thread through the use of large water wheels for power. With such an expansive caption, it appears that the manufacturing of silk and knowledge of textile technology was highly valued by Curzon.

Moreover, the printer Edward Cave himself invested in cotton manufacturing.[22] Within a few years of the publication, in 1740 or so, Cave founded Marvell's (also

Marvel's) textile mill with Lewis Paul, an inventor associated with creating a machine to spin thread.[23] In 1738, the year Cave published this print featuring Chinese textile technology, Lewis Paul applied for a patent for a spinning machine. I am not suggesting that Cave's publication of *Description of the Empire of China* provided the spark for this English invention; the dates do not allow me. Paul and Wyatt had a device that successfully spun cotton thread in 1733. However, I am suggesting that Cave was an astute businessman and saw financial opportunities in textile technology and knowledge of it. Like Curzon, Cave, who had become wealthy with his publications, understood the financial gains that textile technology could confer. In England, the advances in weaving introduced by the flying shuttle necessitated the production of greater amounts of spun thread. Cave saw possibilities in Paul's machine, and by 1740 he invested in a mill with him. Then in 1742 the publisher copied the silk factory in Curzon's Derbyshire to build the first water-powered cotton mill in England that turned his partner's spinning machines.

Owing to lack of evidence, while it is difficult to claim that Chinese technology contributed to Cave's textile ventures, it is clear that Cave, similar to Curzon, sought financial benefits. In view of Cave's investment in textile mills, the images in "Silk Manufacture" must have been intriguing to him and others, such as Curzon. As great as the invention of spinning machines that Cave's partner Lewis Paul helped to invent, the device still needed further developments to become economically viable. Richard Arkwright, the inventor who patented a "Spinning machine" in 1769, managed to improve the apparatus and gained great profits.

While this evidence for British application of representations of Chinese technological knowledge is elusive, the images invited many to study them for informative clues. One last image from the "Silk Manufacture" plate, the "Winding from the Clews to the Bobbins" (Figure 9.9), allows a focus on the sophistication of Chinese textile technology compared with contemporary British practices of the eighteenth century. As modern historian Chao Kang has discussed, Europeans would not have understood the multi-spindle device in this image.[24] The woman with the clews (skeins) appears to be able to spin five cotton rovings with one hand. Chinese spinners could place one strand of yarn between each finger (and perhaps one in her closed palm), close the hand tightly, holding the slivers while spinning them. Five strands of yarn were simultaneously spun tightly into thread. This was a difficult feat for even the most skilled spinners in China. At the time Cave's print was published, one woman spun one length of yarn per wheel into thread in Britain.

Imagery plays an important role in material culture studies as it assists in studying engagements with objects, as well as the communication of material information. In 1764, James Hargreaves (*c*. 1720–1778) invented the spinning jenny, a multi-spindle spinning device depicted in Baines' *History of the Cotton Manufacture* (Figure 9.10). As highlighted by Chao Kang, Hargreaves needed to reproduce in his device the controlling action of the fingers that clamp the strands tightly to spin them and then also the act of releasing the threads which are then gathered on the bobbins. This aspect is illustrated in "Winding from the Clews to the Bobbins", showing the importance of the clamping action of the fingers and hands that hold multiple strands that are twisted into thread.

The Weft of Nations

Figure 9.9 "Winding from the Clews to the Bobbins". From *Description of the Empire of China*, 1738, engraving by Isaac Basire (1704–1768). Courtesy of Special Collections, The University Libraries of Hong Kong.

Figure 9.10 "The Spinning Jenny". From *History of the Cotton Manufacture*, 1835, engraving by Thomas Edward Nicholson (act. 1830s–1850s). Image in private collection, Arlington, VA.

This action and skill to make thread in "A twisting Mill" with its swift, misunderstood as wooden slats and incorporating a drawbar, appears imaginatively, replacing the hand with a mechanical system in a straight length of wood or a rod that like the fingers clamp down on multiple strands and holds them in place for twisting.

The image for "A twisting Mill" and that for Hargreaves' spinning jenny as reproduced by Baines share many formal similarities and were constructed as functionally identical. Hargreaves' spinning jenny's drawbar accomplished the clamping action that the spinning woman's hand performs holding the rovings. Based on imagery, the functional and formal similarities between Hargreaves' spinning jenny as reproduced in Baines' publication and in Cave's "A twisting Mill" are hard to ignore. Baines writes that Hargreaves was "poor", "humble and illiterate", and this suggests he may not have had access to publications. With some investors' interest in spinning thread and its profitability, as well as reproduced images for observation, it is not unlikely that Hargreaves could have seen or heard of alternative techniques for spinning. It seems reasonable to speculate that he may have been aware of images related to Chinese textile technology.

Motivations for imagery dedicated to the production of fabric in China during the eighteenth century

Commentary in Europe surrounding the publication of Chinese images associated with textile manufacturing demonstrate that the desire for profit was a guiding principle for the exploration of their technology. As quoted above, du Halde connected the fine quality of Chinese silk fabrics with profit and suggested that the extract of Xu Guangqi's treatise on their production could be useful. I have already mentioned that the alliance between Curzon and Cave that is evident in their shared interest in textile technology imagery was emboldened by potential financial gains. In the Chinese context, however, in theory, the dissemination of knowledge associated with the production of commodities was designed to "nourish the people" or "*yang min* 養民". In imperial China, a responsible monarch devises policies to ensure that all members of society enjoy an adequate standard of living.[25] Modern scholars such as R. Bin Wong, Pierre-Étienne Will, and Francesca Bray have explored how officials and governments alike have engaged with such concepts that were often combined with "the promotion of agriculture" (*quan nong* 勸農).[26] As Francesca Bray, historian of science and technology, has argued, the interest in promoting economics was consistent with classical theories of governance, asserting that the term for statecraft, *jing ji* 經濟, is a terse rendering of the phrase *jing shi ji min* 經世濟民 or, as Bray puts it, "managing the realm and aiding the people".[27] As I have argued elsewhere, these concerns greatly informed the Qing dynasty's patronage of agrarian labour imagery in the eighteenth century.[28]

These claims of humanistic concerns that were theoretically at the heart of economic policies in China were not wholly unknown in Europe.[29] Not only did Europe have its own traditions of tending to the welfare of the people, some Enlightenment intellectuals, such as François-Marie Voltaire (1694–1778), famously regarded Chinese culture and government as civilized and humane. François Quesnay (1694–1774) and other French physiocrats promoted economic and social structures that were inspired by knowledge of China, based to a large extent on du Halde's publications. This essay is not the place to review an enormous body of literature on the impact of Chinese culture in eighteenth-century Europe. As art historian Christopher M.S. Johns has summed up, China in the eighteenth century was initially understood as an ideal kingdom of "philosopher kings, able administrators, and producers of modern luxury marvels".[30] Du Halde's representations of Chinese weavers and their technology are consistent with Johns' assessment.

In my interpretation, imagery of Chinese textile technology informed Britain's Industrial Revolution which provided the finances for its imperial expansionism. In the mid-eighteenth century, technological accomplishments garnered praise. However, within twenty years, the machines were denigrated. Literary scholar Jennifer L. Hargrave has connected depictions of Chinese labour and Chinese technology with Adam Smith's (1723–1790) concept of "stadial theory", in which civilizations all undergo the same stages of development but at different times.[31] As Adam Smith puts it, China was unable to advance economically, because it did not engage in international trade and therefore could not "naturally learn the art of using and constructing, themselves, all the different machines made use of in other countries, as well as the other improvement of art and industry which are practiced in all the different parts of the world".[32] Smith, writing in 1776 on the wealth of nations, implies that Britain had learned from the machines of other countries, an innovative approach that Chinese did not and could not have. Chinese fabric and textile technology were frozen in a pre-modern plight. For Smith, China had passed through the ages of "Hunters" and "Shepherds" but had not progressed from the "Age of Agriculture" to the final "Age of Commerce". Smith's commentary recognizes the value of Chinese technology as, at the same time, it belittles it.

Conclusion: Textile technology of the Industrial Revolution in Britain and its afterlife

Adam Smith's dismissal of the vitality of Chinese technology articulates a rejection of the value of tools and technology that, to paraphrase du Halde, the Chinese employed perfectly in the production of the fine and beautiful textiles imported into Europe. After aspects of the technology were recreated in Britain, China was subjected to imperialist impulses. Four years before the first Opium War (1839–41), Edward Baines posited the technological advances of the Industrial Revolution as a product of British ingenuity. The author regarded his country as replete with inventive talent and natural conditions to foster the development of mill manufacturing.[33] Baines announces in his preface,

> Without the aid of science, the arts would be contemptible; without practical application, science would consist only of barren theories, which men would have no motive to pursue. These remarks apply with peculiar force to the arts by which

clothing is produced, and, above all, the Cotton Manufacture of England, which is the very creature of mechanical invention and chemical discovery, and which has, in its turn, rendered the most important service to science, as well as increased the wealth and power of the country.[34]

In this early valorization of Britain's commercial success, Baines argues that the country was fuelled by steam and other mechanical marvels, generating great "wealth and power" through its genius. As he puts it, "That this vast aggregate of important and inventions should, with scarcely an exception, have proceeded from English genius, must be a reflection highly satisfactory to every Englishman".[35]

This triumphalist narrative elides the contributions of Chinese technology to the Industrial Revolution. The representation of technology and labour involved in textiles shifted into a nationalist construction of Britain's superiority that was projected and relocated favourably within the discursive realm of an inferior China in the nineteenth century. For du Halde at least, China was once the source for inspiration in technology. However, as components of the machinery became domesticated, China was regarded as unable to engage with the modern innovative modes of production. My close reading of the imagery and the interest in, or disavowal of, Chinese technology in the eighteenth century offers a reconsideration of its role in the formation of the Industrial Revolution.

Furthermore, a reappraisal of the theoretical ideals that initiated the dissemination of technology in China that informed Xu Guangqi's *Complete Book of the Administration of Agriculture* may be well warranted in view of our present twenty-first-century environmental crises. The creation of the technological treatises was motivated in part by the idea that the living conditions of the people, defined as the farming families, could be ameliorated, and not dictated solely by economic gains or by market demands. As eminent historian of Chinese technology Dieter Kuhn has recently concluded, the ambitions of the Industrial Revolution to control or dominate other people through colonization would have been "incomprehensible" to the authors of the technological treatises written in medieval China.[36] Their ideological approach could not have promoted the extractivism we now endure with its ruthless exploitation of the environment and labour.

The representation of material culture of textile production that was initiated in China documents its technological contributions to the world. The knowledge of China's superior technology was disseminated in Europe through woodblock prints, inspiring recreations of the processes in Britain. The reproduction of imagery in publications by Edward Cave reconstruct a technological dialogue on textile production in which Chinese technology and its role in the Industrial Revolution may be reclaimed.

Notes

1. Research in this essay was presented at various conferences including the Association of Asian Studies in 2019. I thank Kathleen Wyma for her insightful comments. Kevin

McLoughlin kindly offered suggestions for improving an earlier version of the manuscript. I would like to thank Sandy Ng for her generous support and encouragement in revising the material. The Hsu Long-hsing fund at the University of Hong Kong helped with resources. Finally, I would also like to thank the Institute for Advanced Studies, Nantes, France when in 2022–23, I was a Marie Skłodowska-Curie Fellow. The Institut d'Études Avancées de Nantes provided a wonderful environment for me to reflect on the roles of technology and labour that are central to this essay.

2. Charles More, *Understanding the Industrial Revolution* (Routledge, 2002), 2.
3. For example, Michael Adas, *Machines as the Measure of Men: Science, Technology, and Ideologies of Western Dominance*, Cornell Studies in Comparative History (Cornell University Press, 1989) and Kenneth Pomeranz, *The Great Divergence: Europe, China, and the Making of the Modern World Economy*, The Princeton Economic History of the Western World (Princeton University Press, 2000).
4. For a history of the genre, see Roslyn Lee Hammers, *Pictures of Tilling and Weaving: Art, Labor, and Technology in Song and Yuan China* (Hong Kong University Press, 2011).
5. See Hammers, *Pictures of Tilling and Weaving* for the scenes and their sequence.
6. Jean-Batiste du Halde, *Description géographique, historique, chronologique, politique, et physique de l'empire de la Chine et de la Tartarie chinoise, enrichie des cartes générales et particulieres de ces pays, de la carte générale et des cartes particulieres du Thibet, & de la Corée; & ornée d'un grand nombre de figures & de vignettes gravées en tailledouce* (Chez P.G. Le Mercier, 1735), vol. 2, between 222 and 223.
7. Jean-Batiste du Halde, *Description of the Empire of China*, vol. 1, 363.
8. Isabelle Landry-Deron, *La preuve par la Chine: la "Description" de J.-B. Du Halde, Jésuite, 1735* (The Evidence on China: The "Description" of J.-B. Du Halde, Jesuit, 1735) (Editions de l'Ecole des hautes études en sciences sociales, 2002), 155, 194.
9. Du Halde, *Description of the Empire of China*, vol. 1, 355.
10. Landry-Deron, *The Evidence on China*, 155.
11. Du Halde, *Description of the Empire of China*, vol. 1, 359.
12. Adas, *Machines as the Measure of Men*, 86.
13. John R. Pannabecker, "Diderot, the Mechanical Arts, and the *Encyclopédie*: In Search of the Heritage of Technology Education", *Journal of Technology Education* 6, no. 1 (Fall 1994): 45–57 and Pannabecker, "Representing Mechanical Arts in Diderot's *Encyclopédie*", *Technology and Culture* 39, no. 1 (1998): 33–73.
14. Francesca Bray, *Agriculture*. Part 2 of *Biology and Biological Technology*, vol. 6 of *Science and Civilisation in China*, edited by Joseph Needham (Cambridge University Press, 1984), 337–38.
15. For a translation of the text that accompanied Wang Zhen's device, see Mark Elvin, *The Pattern of the Chinese Past* (Eyre Methuen, 1973), 195, 198.
16. The China Science and Technology Museum site under Shui zhuan da fang che – Hua xia zhi guang 2017 Xin – Zhongguo shu zi ke ji guan 水转大纺车--华夏之光2017新--中国数字科技馆 . . https://www.cdstm.cn/museum/zphc/cn/201704/t20170427_483803.html (accessed 13 January 2019).
17. Edward Baines, *History of the Cotton Manufacture in Great Britain: With a notice of its early history in the East, and in all the quarters of the globe* (H. Fisher, R. Fisher, and P. Jackson, 1835), 125–38.

18. The controversy over who is to be regarded as the rightful inventor is beyond the scope of this article.
19. Baines, *History of the Cotton Manufacture*, 151–54.
20. Baines, *History of the Cotton Manufacture*, 183–84.
21. Du Halde, *Description of the Empire of China*, vol. 1, 363.
22. Baines, *History of the Cotton Manufacture*, 126.
23. Sir Leslie Stephen (ed.), Entry on "Edward Cave", in *Dictionary of National Biography* (Smith, Elder, & Co., 1885), 338–40, here 340. See also John J. Brown, "Samuel Johnson and the First Roller-Spinning Machine", *Modern Language Review* 41, no. 1 (January 1946), 19.
24. I am indebted to Chao Kang's research on the spinning wheel technology in this section. Chao Kang (also at times Romanized as Zhao Gang), *The Development of Cotton Textile Production in China* (Harvard University Asia Center Publications Program, 1977), 56–70.
25. For more on government policies and practices designed to improve standards of living, see R. Bin Wong, "Chinese Traditions of Grain Storage", in Pierre-Étienne Will and R. Bin Wong (eds.), *Nourish the People: The State Civilian Granary System in China, 1650–1850* (Center for Chinese Studies, University of Michigan, 1991), 1–16.
26. Francesca Bray, "Agricultural Illustrations: Blueprint or Icon", in Francesca Bray, Vera Dorofeeva-Lichtmann and Georges Métailié (eds.), *Graphics and Text in the Production of Technical Knowledge in China: The Warp and the Weft*, Sinica Leidensia, vol. 79 (Brill, 2007), 521–67, here 522–23.
27. Francesca Bray, "Introduction: Science and Confucian Statecraft in East Asia", in Francesca Bray and Jongtae Lim (eds.), *Science and Confucian Statecraft in East Asia*, Science and Religion in East Asia, vol. 2 (Brill, 2019), 6.
28. Roslyn Lee Hammers, *The Imperial Patronage of Labor Genre Paintings in Eighteenth-Century China* (Routledge 2021).
29. Martin Powers, *China and England: The Preindustrial Struggle for Justice in Word and Image* (Routledge, 2019).
30. Christopher M.S. Johns, *China and the Church: Chinoiserie in Global Context* (University of California Press, 2016), 7.
31. Jennifer L. Hargrave, "Romanticizing the Chinese Landscape", *European Romantic Review* 27, no. 3 (2016), 420, fn. 5.
32. We might notice that Adam Smith is paraphrasing Diderot's earlier description of Chinese commerce. Adam Smith in "Book IV, Chapter IX Agricultural Systems", *The Wealth of Nations: An Inquiry into the Nature and Causes of the Wealth of Nations* (Harriman House, 2010 reprint of 1776), 440. See also Guido Abbattista, "Europe, China and the Family of Nations: Commercial Enlightenment in the Sattelzeit (1780–1840)", in María Dolores Elizalde and Wang Jianlang (eds.), *China's Development from a Global Perspective* (Cambridge Scholars Publishing, 2017), 122–92, here 133–36.
33. Baines, *History of the Cotton Manufacture*, 220–27, 231, *passim*.
34. Baines, *History of the Cotton Manufacture*, 5.
35. Baines, *History of the Cotton Manufacture*, 13–14, 244.
36. Dieter Kuhn, *An Epic of Technological Supremacy: Works and Words of Medieval Chinese Textile Technology* (Abegg-Stiftung, 2022), 410.

References

Abbattista, Guido. "Europe, China and the Family of Nations: Commercial Enlightenment in the Sattelzeit (1780–1840)", in María Dolores Elizalde and Wang Jianlang (eds.), *China's Development from a Global Perspective*, Cambridge Scholars Publishing, 2017, 122–92.

Adas, Michael. *Machines as the Measure of Men: Science, Technology, and Ideologies of Western Dominance* (Cornell Studies in Comparative History), Cornell University Press, 1989.

Baines, Edward. *History of the Cotton Manufacture in Great Britain: With a notice of its early history in the East, and in all the quarters of the globe*, H. Fisher, R. Fisher, and P. Jackson, 1835.

Bray, Francesca. *Agriculture*. Part 2 of *Biology and Biological Technology*, vol. 6 of *Science and Civilisation in China*, edited by Joseph Needham, Cambridge University Press, 1984.

Bray, Francesca. "Agricultural Illustrations: Blueprint or Icon?", in Francesca Bray, Vera Dorofeeva-Lichtmann and Georges Métailié (eds.), *Graphics and Text in the Production of Technical Knowledge in China: The Warp and the Weft* (Sinica Leidensia, vol. 79), Brill, 2007, 521–67.

Bray, Francesca. "Introduction: Science and Confucian Statecraft in East Asia", in Francesca Bray and Jongtae Lim (eds.), *Science and Confucian Statecraft in East Asia* (Science and Religion in East Asia, vol. 2), Brill, 2019, 1–28.

Brown, John J. "Samuel Johnson and the First Roller-Spinning Machine", *Modern Language Review* 41, no. 1 (January 1946): 16–23.

Cave, Edward. *A Description of the Empire of China and Chinese-Tartary: together with the kingdoms of Korea, and Tibet: Containing the geography and history (natural as well as civil) of those countries. Enrich'd with general and particular maps, and adorned with a great number of cuts*, T. Gardner, 1738.

Chao Kang. *The Development of Cotton Textile Production in China*, Harvard University Asia Center Publications Program, 1977.

Elvin, Mark. *The Pattern of the Chinese Past*, Eyre Methuen, 1973.

Halde, Jean-Batiste du. *Description géographique, historique, chronologique, politique, et physique de l'empire de la Chine et de la Tartarie chinoise, enrichie des cartes générales et particulieres de ces pays, de la carte générale et des cartes particulieres du Thibet, & de la Corée; & ornée d'un grand nombre de figures & de vignettes gravées en tailledouce*, Chez P.G. Le Mercier, 1735, 4 tomes.

Hammers, Roslyn Lee. *Pictures of Tilling and Weaving: Art, Labor, and Technology in Song and Yuan China*, Hong Kong University Press, 2011.

Hammers, Roslyn Lee. *The Imperial Patronage of Labor Genre Paintings in Eighteenth-Century China*, Routledge, 2021.

Hargrave, Jennifer L. "Romanticizing the Chinese Landscape", *European Romantic Review* 27, no. 3 (2016): 413–21.

Johns, Christopher M.S. *China and the Church: Chinoiserie in Global Context*, University of California Press, 2016.

Kuhn, Dieter. *An Epic of Technological Supremacy: Works and Words of Medieval Chinese Textile Technology*, Abegg-Stiftung, 2022.

Landry-Deron, Isabelle. *La preuve par la Chine: la "Description" de J.-B. Du Halde, Jésuite, 1735*, Editions de l'Ecole des hautes études en sciences sociales, 2002.

More, Charles. *Understanding the Industrial Revolution*, Routledge, 2002.

Pannabecker, John R. "Diderot, the Mechanical Arts, and the *Encyclopédie*: In Search of the Heritage of Technology Education", *Journal of Technology Education* 6, no. 1 (Fall 1994): 45–57.

Pannabecker, John R. "Representing Mechanical Arts in Diderot's *Encyclopédie*", *Technology and Culture* 39, no. 1 (1998): 33–73.

Pomeranz, Kenneth. *The Great Divergence: Europe, China, and the Making of the Modern World Economy* (The Princeton Economic History of the Western World), Princeton University Press, 2000.

Powers, Martin. *China and England: The Preindustrial Struggle for Justice in Word and Image*, Routledge, 2019.

Smith, Adam. *The Wealth of Nations: An Inquiry into the Nature and Causes of the Wealth of Nations*, Harriman House, 2010 reprint of 1776.

Stephen, Sir Leslie (ed.). *Dictionary of National Biography*, Smith, Elder, & Co., 1885.

Wong, R. Bin. "Chinese Traditions of Grain Storage", in Pierre-Étienne Will and R. Bin Wong (eds.), *Nourish the People: The State Civilian Granary System in China, 1650–1850*, Center for Chinese Studies, University of Michigan, 1991, 1–16.

CONTRIBUTORS

Anneke Coppoolse is Assistant Professor in the Visual Communication Design program of the College of Fine Arts at Hongik University in Seoul, South Korea. Her research is located at the crossroads of culture and design. It explores material histories and conditions of production, repair, and wasting, as well as the visual cultures of cities, streets, and public spaces. She collects stories attached to tools and objects, and to the spaces that envelop these objects—often photographically. More recently, she has begun exploring more-than-human entanglements, also in the context of cities. She is currently looking into the cultural meaning, world-making, and world-destroying capacities of what in Korean is called *ssuk* (mugwort). She did her PhD in the Department of Cultural Studies at Lingnan University in Hong Kong. Prior to her appointment at Hongik University, she was Assistant Professor in the School of Design of the Hong Kong Polytechnic University.

Valentina Gamberi is MSCA-CZ fellow at Palacký University (UPOL). Previously, she held positions as Adjunct Lecturer (University of Bologna, 2022–2023) and Research Fellow (Research Centre for Material Culture in Leiden, 2021–2022 and the Department of Ethnology of Academia Sinica, 2019–2020). Her main research fields are material culture studies, museum anthropology, critical heritage, and religious studies, with a specific focus on Asian religious artifacts. Her most recent publication is *Experiencing Materiality: Museum Perspectives* (2021), along with single and co-written journal articles and chapters in English and Italian. She co-edited *Haunting Ruins: Ethnographies of Ruination and Decay* (2025).

Anna Grasskamp is Professor of Art History and Visual Studies at the University of Oslo. Her publications include *Objects in Frames: Displaying Foreign Collectibles in Early Modern China and Europe* (2019; second edition 2022); *Art and Ocean Objects of Early Modern Eurasia: Shells, Bodies, and Materiality* was published in the Amsterdam University Press series *Connected Histories in the Early Modern World* in 2021. She has recently curated the exhibition "The Art of Upcycling. Contemporary Jewelry from Hong Kong" at GRASSI Museum of Applied Arts in Leipzig and currently leads the project "An Ecological History of Eurasian Art: Natural Resources, Aesthetic Practices, and Early Modern Globalization" (European Research Council Consolidator Grant, 2024-2029).

Roslyn Lee Hammers is Honorary Associate Professor of Art History at the University of Hong Kong. She conducts research on the history of Chinese art and art theory with a focus on the representations of labor and technologically-informed imagery. Her book *Pictures of Tilling and Weaving: Art, Labor and Technology in Song and Yuan China* (Hong

Kong University Press, 2011) investigates the formation of a new type of genre painting that situates the labor of farming families at the nexus of classical theories of governance, the Song court, and emerging ideas on the role of art in society. Her second book *The Imperial Patronage of Labor Genre Paintings in Eighteenth-Century China* (2021) explores later iterations of imagery related to the production of rice and silk. This volume delves into the revitalization of the *Pictures of Tilling and Weaving* in the Qing era and the motives for successive emperors to commission differing versions of it. She is presently finishing a book-length manuscript on the Qing-dynasty *Pictures of Cotton* with an anticipated publication date in 2025.

Hui-Ying Kerr is Senior Lecturer in the Nottingham School of Art and Design at Nottingham Trent University, UK. She completed her doctorate in History of Design at The Royal College of Art and the Victoria and Albert Museum in London in 2017, for which she conducted her fieldwork as a visiting researcher at the National Museum of Ethnology (Minpaku) in Osaka, Japan. Hui-Ying's PhD explored consumer cultures of the Japanese Bubble Economy of the 1980s through lifestyle and design magazines. More broadly, her research interests focus on transnational cultures of design, consumption, and work, decolonising design history, Japanese aesthetics, and the intersectionality of encounters of the local with the international. Hui-Ying has presented her work at several international conferences and chaired and convened panels for the British Academy, the UK Design History Society, and the Midlands Conference in Critical Thought. She has also submitted chapters for anthologies on design, modernity, material culture and social agency in Asia, on work and leisure in Japan, and on international dance music and club cultures. Hui-Ying is a keen contributor to the online media outlet, The Conversation, and most recently was a guest speaker for the research podcast, NTU Research Reimagined.

Kwok-wah Tung is a PhD candidate (History of Art) at the University of Edinburgh and engages in an interdisciplinary and interregional study on the religio-aesthetics of medieval Zen dry stone setting. Tung holds a PhD in Visual Studies (Lingnan University), and a Master of Arts in History of Art and Archaeology of East Asia (SOAS). Before his study at Edinburgh, he acted as the principal designer of Replaces Studio Ltd., and served as a visiting lecturer at the School of Design, The Hong Kong Polytechnic University, and as a part-time lecturer at the Department of Visual Studies, Lingnan University. His teaching covers the fields of design studio, philosophy of architecture, and East Asian art history and material culture. His interest in researching the aesthetics of architectural heritage in South China has resulted in his published article "Chikan's Arcade Buildings: The Hybrid and Civil Architecture of Lingnan" in *Architecture and Culture*, vol. 6, issue 2 (Dec. 2018), and his chapter in this Volume.

Sandy Ng is Assistant Professor of Culture & Theory in the School of Design of The Hong Kong Polytechnic University. She received her PhD from the School of Oriental and African Studies (University of London). Her published works include articles that examine hybrid modernism and the formation of female identity in painting as well as cultural metaphor and female mental health in design. She was a Visiting Research

Fellow at the Bard Graduate Center in the United States and is presently College Art Association's *caa.reviews* Field Editor for Design History. Her book entitled *Portrayals of Women in Early Twentieth-Century China: Redefining Female Identity through Modern Design and Lifestyle* is published by Amsterdam University Press. She is currently working on a new project that explores craftsmanship, female identity, and materiality. She is also working with a postdoctoral fellow on two research projects that examine the assimilation of poetic metaphors in product design and designing for women's mental health.

Stacey Pierson is Professor of the History of Chinese Ceramics at SOAS, University of London. In addition to teaching and supervising research students in the School of Arts, she is the former President of the Oriental Ceramic Society (London) and is series editor for the Routledge title *Histories of Material Culture and Collecting, 1550-1950*. Previously, from 1995 – 2007, she was Curator of the Percival David Foundation of Chinese art, also at the University of London, which housed the world-renowned David collection of Chinese ceramics. She has published widely on aspects of Chinese ceramics, Percival David, and the history of collecting and exhibitions, including *Collectors, Collections and Museums: the Field of Chinese Ceramics in Britain: 1560-1960* (2007), *Chinese Ceramics: a Design History* (2009), *From Object to Concept: Global Consumption and the Transformation of Ming Porcelain* (2013), *Private Collecting, Exhibitions and the Shaping of Art History in London: the Burlington Fine Arts Club, 1866-1950* (2017) and the edited volume *Visual, Material and Textual Cultures of Food and Drink in China, 200 BCE – 1900 CE*, Colloquies on Art and Archaeology in Asia, no. 25 (2022). Her most recent research project focused on Dr Johnson's Chinese teapot, which is on display in the British Museum.

Megha Rajguru is Principal Lecturer in History of Art and Design at the University of Brighton, UK. Her research is in South Asian design history, and material and visual culture. She is co-editor of *Design and Modernity in Asia* (Bloomsbury, 2022) and has published articles in the *Journal of Design History*, *Studies in the History of Gardens and Designed Landscapes*, *Journal of Museum Ethnography*, and the *Journal of Visual Arts Practice*. She has also acted as Co-Director of the Centre for Design History (2022–24), University of Brighton and Trustee of the Design History Society, UK (2017–21).

INDEX

Locators in *italics* refer to illustrations
7 V Rule 181–2

accessories 114–18
activism 37–41
adaptation 72
Adas, Michael 197
adornment 107
    impact of modernity on women in Republican China 108–9
    modern women and accessories 114–18
    ornamentation and female identity 118–21
    women's adornment and female identity 109–14
advertisements 86, 92, 95, 97, 107, 115–16
advice 89
aesthetics 113, 114
    see also religious aesthetics
agency 97, 99
    material 48–9
    see also object agency
Ahmed, S. 128, 140
aid, relief 60
Alberti, Leon Battista 154
Alchemist creations 48
Alper, Svetlana 58, 68
Amoy 130, 131
amplifiers 65
analogue moods 70–1
ancestors 132
Animism 138
anthropology 1, 131
Antony, Robert J. 150
Appadurai, Arjun 57–8, 67
appearance, personal 87, 96, 115, 119
    women's 108
Aranya Housing (Township) 171, 174, 175, 181, 184, 185
archaeology 18
architecture (architects) 18, 152, 154, 156, 161, 162
archivists 48
Arkwright, Sir Richard 201
Artclub Sewoon 64–5
artefacts 21, 35–6, 66–8, 109
    religious aesthetics 128, 130, 138, 140
Artists' Village 171, 174, 175, 180–1, 184, 185
Asahi Beer Co. 92
ashes, incense 133, 134

Asia 7–9
aspirations 115
austerity 172
authenticity 67
automobiles 116, 119
autonomy 113, 120

Bachelard, Gaston 35, 49
bagua 48
Baines, Edward 200, 202, 204, 205–6
balconies 172, 181, 185
bandits 150, 151, 154, 155
Basire, Isaac 194
Batavian Society of Arts and Sciences 130
beans 133
beauty 85
    food for 90–4
    products 88–90
behaviours 97, 114
Belapur Housing 171
    see also Artists' Village
Bennett, Jane 35, 49
bicycles 185–7
bodies, female 95, 96, 99, 121
bodies, liberated 97–101
Book of Changes 48
boundaries, social and cultural 99
boundaries, social (societal) 109
Bourdieu, Pierre 107, 114–15
boutiques 115
bracelets (bangles) 47–8
brands, commercial 46
brashness 86
Bray, Francesca 198, 200, 204
Brill 129, 131, 132, 137, 139
brokenness 28
Bubble Economy 83–5, 87, 89, 101
Buckminster Fuller, Richard 40

caizhi yishu 38
capitalism 40
career advancements 94
Casa do Fresco entrance detail *23*
Cave, Edward 194, 201, 202

Index

censorship 48
Central Seoul 58–61
ceramics 17
    see also sherds as material and medium
Chambers, Robert 173, 187
Chandigarh 181
Chang, Eileen 118
change, social and political 49
Chan, Po-fung 46–7, 49
Chan, Wing-sze Cissy 41, 49
Cheonggyecheon Gigyegonggu Sangga 60
Cheonggyecheon stream 57–8
Cheung, Kevin 48, 49
China see religious aesthetics; textiles, Chinese
China, modern women see adornment
Ching, Sze-yin Cicy 44, 46, 49
Chun Ka-pang, Adrian 44
cities 108, 174
City and Development Corporation (CIDCO) 175
City and Industrial Development Corporation of Maharashtra 177
    see also Artists' Village
Clark, I. 131
Clifford, James 58, 68
Clock Alley 69
clothing industries 60
cluster housing, Aranya Township 176
cocoons, silk 195–6
coffeehouses 20
collaborations 131, 135, 152
collectibles 37
collectives, housewives 100
collectors 135
colonialism 128, 130, 131, 138, 139, 152
colonnades 161
    cantilevered 156, 159
commodification 95
commodities 117, 120
communal watchtowers 151
community interactions 178
Complete Book of the Administration of Agriculture 196, 197, 206
completeness 28
concrete see watchtowers, concrete
conflicts 60
Confucianism 60, 108
connections 25
connectivity 35
consumers 83, 84, 89, 101, 115, 201
    female 95
consumption 89, 90, 94
    conspicuous 99
    global 19
contexts 1, 21, 72
    natural 164
cooperation 70

cooperatives 65
corpothetics, transcultural 128
Correa, Charles 171, 173, 175, 178
    material culture and heritage 180, 182, 184–5, 187
Cosmetic case, mirror stand, and screen *111*
cosmetic cases 109, 110, 112, 119, 120
Cosmetics chest with folding mirror stand *112*
costumes 86
cottage industries 184
cotton 195, 197, 200
courtyards 177, 185, 188
craftsmanship (craftsmen) 114, 119, 158, 161, 164, 165
creation 49
crime rates 150
cultural practices 180
culture 1
    maritime 41
    see also material culture, maintaining
cultures 68
cupola lanterns 161
Curzon, Nathaniel, Lord Scarsdale 201

Dantwala, M.L. 174
Daoism 48
Davis, Howard 158
Dead Nature 28
debris 44
Deconstructed Neolithic Machang Jar 28
defense 153–4
de Groot, Jan Jakob Maria see Groot, Jan Jakob Maria de
De Groot's annotation on the base of the god of water *136*
De Groot's water official *136*
department stores 100, 115
Description géographique, historique, chronologique, politique, et physique de l'empire de la Chine et de la Tartarie chinoise, enrichie des cartes générales et particulieres de ces pays, de la carte générale et des cartes particulieres du Thibet, & de la Corée & ornée d'un grand nombre de defigures & de vingettes gravée en tailledouce (Description géographique) 193, 195, 197
Description of the Empire of China 194, 195, 200, 201, 202
designers 111
Design for sociability 179
design history 2–7
design motifs 119
designs, European 111
desirability 98, 116
development, urban 60 see also homes and the street

deviations 137
Dewey, John 120
disabled people 48
disasters, natural 155
disempowerment 128
dispositions, gods' 134
dissemination 204, 206
dissemination, knowledge *see* textiles, Chinese
Do It Yourself (DIY) 37–41
domains, public 108
Dongdaemun Market 60
Dongen, Paul van 129
Dosekun, Simidele 100
Doshi, Balkrishna 171, 173, 175, 187
    Indore and Bombay 178–9
    material culture and heritage 180–1, 184–5
dowries 110
dressing tables 110, 111, 112, *113*
du Halde, Jean-Batiste 193–4, 196, 197, 204, 205, 206

earthquakes 83
eco art, DIY, and activism 37–41
ecology 38
Economic and Political Weekly 174
economic capital 115
ecosystems 150
education 114, 119, 120
    women's 110
electricity 177
electronics market 63
elites 95, 98, 110, 114
emancipation 92, 99, 101, 116
embrechados 22
employment 175
employment, lower-waged 94
empowerment 92, 93, 94, 99, 101, 186
energy drinks 91–2, 93
Engel, Friedrich 171
entrepreneurs 184
environments, natural 162
Equal Employment Opportunity Law (EEOL) 84, 99
equality 101
equity 180, 187
Escobar, Arturo 174
ethnography 1, 127, 129, 130, 131, 139
etiquette 96, 119
events, green 39
excavations 70
ex-commodities 67
expectations 96, 99, 128
expertise 70
exploitation 96
extensions, gods' 134
External features *182*

factories 60, 66
families 110, 113, 119
fantasies 116
Far Sea Ring 41, *42*
fashions 120
fears 128
features, magazine 97
femininity 91, 93, 96, 97–8, 101, 102
    Japanese 87
    modern 114
feminism 101
feng shui 60
festivals 137–8
fieldwork 137
fishing 184
flexibility 185
flowers and butterflies, motifs 113, 119
food for beauty 90–4
Ford, Norman 38
Forty, Adrian 163
found objects 35–6
    conclusion 48–9
    eco art, DIY, and activism 37–41
    extending the life of objects 41–8
    material hierarchies 36–7
Freedman, Maurice 129
freedoms 99, 109, 119
fun 87
functionality 113, 137, 154
furniture 110, 111, 112

Galison, Peter 163
galleries 46
Gandhi, Indira 173–4
garbage 37, 41, 48
Garibi Hatao 173
gatherings 178
gas attacks 83
Geertz, Clifford 1
gender 99, 108–9, 114, 120
geomancy 162
gifts 98, 99, 120
glocalization 150
gods 132, 135, 139
golf 94, 95
grains 133
Grand Tour 18
Great Britain 40
green events 39
Green Summer Festival 39
Groot, Jan Jakob Maria de 130–1
    brief biography of statuary 131–2
    Chinese pantheon and relationship to scholarship 131–2
grottoes 22
Guangzhou 36–7

Index

Guimet, Émile 131
Gutierrez, Laurent 38

Haldane, John 162
Hanako magazine 83–5, 101
Hargrave, Jennifer L. 205
Hargreaves, James 201, 202, 204
Hauddard, Jean-Baptiste 194
health 90
health booms 83
    beautiful things 88–90
    the Bubble, women, and *Hanako* magazine 83–5
    conclusion 101–2
    food for beauty 90–4
    Hanako women 85–8
    the liberated body 97–101
    women and sport 95–7
He, Dean 152
HEGA Corp. 65
hemp 195, *199*
heritage 72
    see also homes and the street
Hicks, D. 140
Hillenbrand, Margaret 38, 41
history *see* design history
History of the Cotton Manufacture 202
homes and the street 171–3
    conclusion 187–8
    historical context 173–5
    Indore and Bombay 175–9
    material culture and heritage 179–87
homes in close proximity to one another *176*
Hong Kong 35–6, 37, 40, 44, 46, 49
housewives 100
housing *see* homes and the street
Housing Question 171
Houze, Rebecca 173
Hsu, Jeanine 48
Huang, Yaoji 161
huanhun 48–9
Hung, Maureen 48
hybridization 150, 154–5, 159, 165

identities 46, 61, 102, 115–17
    female 109–14, 118–21
    India 175, 179, 185
imagery *see* textiles, Chinese
imagination 49
imitation 163
incense 134
incrementality 171, 172
independence 101
India 40, 41
    see also homes and the street
individuality 119
Industrial Revolution 191, 205, 206

inequality, gender 99, 101
infrastructure 61
initiatives 63
inlay, porcelain 22
instability 28
Integrated Rural Development Programme 174
interactions, gods' 134
International Council on Monuments and Sites (ICOMOS) 154
investment, privatized 95
Iumpium: Sewing History Museum 65–6, 72

jade 36
Jesuits 192, 196
jewellery 18, 35–6, 37, 49, 108
Jingdezhen 21
Jinjiang Tower 155, *156*
Johns, Christopher M.S. 205
Journal of Contemporary Chinese Art 38
journals 117

Kaiping culture 149–50
Kai-Yin, Lo 46
Kaiyuan temple 23
Kang, Chao 202
Karim, Farhan 172
Kay, John 201
Kemske, Bonnie 29
kintsugi 26, 28, 29
klauss, liina 39
knowledge 37, 89–90, 120, 154, 158, 204
    cultural 114
    repair 70–1
Kopytoff, Igor 57
Kuhn, Dieter 206

Lacoste porcelain polo shirt 17
lacquers 29
Landry-Deron, Isabelle 196–7
landscapes 114, 119, 162
large spinning wheel *199*, *200*
Le Corbusier 181
leisure 83, 84, 94, 95, 101
leisure, night-time 98
Les Fêtes 137
Leung, Michael 38
Lewis, Paul 202
liberation 96, 99, 100, 108, 116
lifestyle, Japanese 85
lifestyles 180
    China 107, 109, 113–14, 116–17
    Japanese 84, 89–90, 93–4, 101
    tranquil 164–5
Ling Long 117
Lingnan region 22
Lin, W.-P. 132, 133, 135

Index

Lipovitan D 91
literature 18
lives, daily 162
Living 42, 44
    details *43*
Li, Xiaofeng 17, 25–6
Lo, Jeannie 90
Lo Lai-lai, Natalie 38
Loos, Adolf 119
lota 186
Lowther Casket 24, *25*
luxury items (commodities) 24, 37, 89, 101, 115

Made in Hong Kong 44
    details *45*
Madipur Widows Housing colony 172
Maekawa Report 83–4
Maffei, Grace-Lees 173
magazines 115
    Hanako 83–5
Makercity Sewoon 63
make-up 96, 108
maki-e 29
Malindi 22
Manchurian windows 45
marginalization 97
MARG Magazine 181
markers of time 64
marketing 48
markets 83
    sherd 21
marriage 97
    see also matrimony
massacres 130
mastery 25
material agency 48–9
Material Art 38
material culture, maintaining 57–8
    Central Seoul 58–61
    mechanical pocket watch 69–71
    printed circuit boards 61–5
    scissors 65–8
    things, values, places 71–2
material cultures 2–7, 37
material hierarchies 36–7
materiality 19, 27
materials
    local 185
    precious 133
materia sacra 133
matrimony 89
    see also marriage
m-curve 84
meanings 1, 21, 27, 184
    political 41
    see also material culture, maintaining

mediation 133, 139
memories 49, 71
micro plastics 41
migration (migrants) 23, 60
    urban 172, 174–5
Miller, Laura 100
Mimar 171
minimalism 119
minimal living 171, 177, 187
miracles 132
mobility 119, 178, 186
    social 174
models 85
Modern Girls 107
modernity 107, 116
Modern Style 162, 163, 164
Modern Woman 108
Moore, O. 135
morality 100
mosaics 22
motifs, design 119
motorists, women 119
Murphy, Henry K. 152
Musée Guimet 132
museum effect 58, 68
Museum of Ethnology 131, 132
museums 20–1, 63–4, 67–8, 127–9, 135, 139
music industry 64
mystification 68

Nandaku 20
narratives 27
    oral 132
natural elements 163
natural environments 162–3
natural forms 164
naturalization 164, 165
nature 163
necessaires 114, *115*
    automobile 116, *117*, 119
necessity 115
networks 58, 180, 184
New Women 107
New Youth 108
nightclubs 97
niin 48
Nong Zheng Quan Shu 191
norms, cultural 97
Novus atlas Sinensis 192

object agency 2–7
    extending the life of objects 41–7
objectification 101
objects (things) 71–2
obligations, mutual 132
oceanic culture 36

219

Index

octagonal shapes 48
Office Ladies (OLs) 84, 85, 88, 94, 100, 101
Of Greater Dignity than Riches 172
Ogasawara, Yuko 90
OL Shinkaron 86-7
Opium War 111, 205
Ornament and Crime 119
ornamentation 119-20, 154-5, 158, 163, 165
outdoor spaces 172
    see also spaces, outdoor
Outdoor spaces for domestic activities 181

Pannabecker, John R. 197
parapet walls 161
participation 101, 116, 173, 180
Patel, Shirish 175
patrons 152, 201, 204
pearls 36, 41
Pedestrianized street, 2 images 183
photographs 107, 117, 137
Photo taken in a studio 118
Pictures of Tiling and Weaving 191, 193
Pinney, Christopher 128
places 71-2
plants 37
plunder 21
pocket watches, mechanical 69-71
policies, governmental 101
pollution 41
populations 60, 61
Porcelain House, The 23, *24*
porcelain inlay 22
Portefaix, Valérie 39
postcolonialism 171, 181, 184
post-feminism 99, 100, 101
poverty *see* homes and the street
power 90, 98, 99, 100, 127
practices, cultural 180, 185
presentation, personal 96
prestige 90
printed circuit boards 61-5
printing 60
privilege 94, 100
production, ceramic 21
professionalism 87
progress, symbols of 63
property rights 110
prosperity, economic 101
Prown, Jules 1
public domains 108
public schools 108
public spaces 102
    see also spaces, outdoor (public)
Pyounghwa Clothing Market 61, 66

Quesnay, François 205

ragpickers 41, 46
Rain Pavilion Villa 158
Rath, Nilakantha 174
reading 110, 120
real estate 90
rebellion (rebelliousness) 97, 100, 101
recipes 90
reconstructions 131
recycling 36, 39
refuse 20
regeneration 63, 66-7
reincarnation 48
relationships (relations) 47
    international 84
relics 69
relief aid 60
religious aesthetics 127-8
    brief biography of de Groot's statuary 131-2
    conclusion 139-40
    de Groot's Chinese pantheon and its
        relationship with his scholarship 135-9
    Jan Jakob Maria de Groot 130-1
    research methodology 129-30
    Taiwanese material religion 132-5
    transcultural corpothetics 128
Religious System of China, The 129, 130
remains 20
repairs (repairs services) 28, 29, 62
repurposing 36
residential watchtowers 151
respectability 100
restaurants 90
restoration 70-1
Reveal the Cracks 47
rituals 120, 128, 131, 139
River of Rubbish 39
Robertson, Roland 150
roles, traditional 120
romance 90, 94
Royer, Jean Theodore 138
rubbish 44
ruins 18, 70
Ruishi Tower *153*, 155-62, 163, 164
    colonnades of hall on sixth floor *160*
    fifth-floor cantilevered colonnade *158*
    living room on the fourth floor *157*
    main core *159*
Rural Development: Putting the Last First 173

sanitation systems 178
scavanging (scaveners) 41, 48
scholarly motifs 119
School of Everyday Life 38
schools, public 108
Schulze-Elberfeld, Otto 120
scissors 65-8

Index

Scruton, Roger 154, 158, 161
sculptors (sculpture) 133
sea glass 46
Second World War 40
self-actualization 101
self-awareness 114
self-building 177
self-presentation 114
self-sufficiency (sustainability) 184, 187
Seoul, Central 58–61
Serrurier, Lindor 131, 132
Seshradi, Chetput Venkatasubban 35, 40, 49
sewing industry 65, 67
Sewoon Electronics Museum 63
Sewoon Sangga 63
sexualization 101
Shengfeng Tower 155, *156*, 161, 163
    composite columns on the fourth floor of Shengfeng Tower *160*
sherds as material and medium 17–19
    archaeology 20–1
    architecture 21–4
    conclusion 30
    contemporary art and craft 24–8
    restoration 28–30
Shilpa, Vastu 177
shortages 40, 60
shrines 134, 135, 156
silk 192, 193, 195, 197
    see also textiles, Chinese
Sites and Services project 172, 175
skills, women's 96
Smith, Adam 205
Smith, Laurajane 184
social awareness 117
social change 114, 121
social connections (interactions) 47, 48–9
Social Life of Things, The 57
social mobility 174
social status 110, 114
soft power 100
    see also power
Sohl, Lee 38
solidarity 46, 93
Somehow Crystal 89
Song, Yingxing 36, 48
souvenirs 21
spaces 187
spaces, outdoor (public) 102, 172, 178, 180
spaces, void 162, 164, 165
specialists 114
spectacles 118
spinning 197
Spinning Jenny, The *203*
spinning machines 200–4
spinning wheel *199*

sports 92, 93, 95–7, 101, 117
stability 28
standardization 139, 155, 180
standards, aesthetic 175
statues 127, 132, 133, 137
status 21, 119
stereotypes 109
storytellers 40, 49
streets, pedestrianized 181
students, female 108, 109
studies, object-based 7–9
subversion 35, 37, 49
Suri Suri Coop 65
sustainability 38

Taiwanese material religion 132–5
Tang, Connie 48
Taoci guwan shichang 21
Taoism 162
taste 115
technologies 119
    see also material culture, maintaining; textiles, Chinese
textiles 60
temples 134, 135
textiles 26
textiles, Chinese 191–2
    Chinese weavers in Europe and Britain 192–7
    conclusion 205–6
    labour in mid-eighteenth-century Europe 197–200
    motivations for imagery 204–5
    spinning machines in Britain and Chinese technology 200–4
texts 110, 191
textures 24
threads, coloured 133
Three Palace Memorials 150
tiles 22
timepiece repairs industries 69
tool manufacturing 60
tools 67, 72
Torabāyu 97
tourists 21
town planning 177
trade 20, 46, 60, 89
    global 149
    maritime 36
traditions 22
tranculturation 37
transformation 94, 159
transitions, sociopolitical 46
trash 37, 44, 48
Trump, Donald 46
Tsang, Tak-ping 38
Twisting Mill, A 198

Index

UCC Works 93
uniforms 96, 98
United Nations 174
United Nations Educational, Scientific and Cultural Organization (UNESCO) 149, 151
United States of America (United States) 40, 60
University of Leiden 130
upcycling 17, 23, 25, 35
urban development 60
uses 36

values 36, 180
    see also material culture, maintaining
variants 137
Venice Biennale, 2007 38
verandas 172, 182, 185, 188
vernacular watchtowers 150–2
visitors 63
Vistara: The Architecture of India 185–6
visual validity 161
Visvanathan, Shiv 40
Volkenkundemuseum 129
Voltaire, François-Marie 204
Vries, Bouke de 27–8

wabi-sabi 29
Wang, Meiqin 38
Wang, Zhen 198
wash facilities 177–8
waste 38
Wat Arun 23
watch repairs 69
watchtowers, concrete 149
    analytic study of their aesthetics 152–5
    conclusion 164–5
    culture of Kaiping 149–50
    function and structure 150–2
    phenomenological understanding 162–4
    Ruishi Tower 155–62
water containers 185–7
water sports 95

water systems 178
wealth 193
    family 110
wealth gaps 40
weavers (weaving) 192, 196
wellbeing 93, 180
Werblowsky, Zwi 129, 131
White, Merry I 84
Will, Pierre-Étienne 204
Winding from the Clews to the Bobbin *203*
windows 46
W;nk Atelier 48
women 60, 83–5
    aesthetic preferences 113
    Chinese 120–1
    Hanako 85–8
    rights 108
    sport 95–7
    see also adornment
Wong, R. Bin 204
Work of Heaven and the Inception of Things, The 36
workshops 114
World Bank 174, 175, 177, 187
World Heritage sites 149, 151
worshippers 134, 135, 139

Xu, Dishan 109
Xu, Guangqi 196, 197, 198, 206

year, Chinese 138
Yeesookyung 26–7
Yeji-dong 69
Yeung, Trevor 38
yobitsugi 29
Yinglong Tower 150–1

Zhang, Guoxiong 152, 155, 164
Zheng, Bo 38
Zhou, Qiyou 164